6000 99378

KT-511-791

Multimedia Servers

Applications, Environments, and Design

The Morgan Kaufmann Series in Multimedia Information and Systems

Series Editor, Edward Fox

Multimedia Servers: Applications, Environments, and Design
Dinkar Sitaram and Asit Dan

Managing Gigabytes: Compressing and Indexing Documents and Images, Second Edition
Ian H. Witten, Alistair Moffat, and Timothy C. Bell

Digital Compression for Multimedia: Principles and Standards
Jerry D. Gibson, Toby Berger, Tom Lookabaugh, Dave Lindbergh, and Richard L. Baker

Practical Digital Libraries: Books, Bytes, and Bucks
Michael Lesk

Readings in Information Retrieval
Edited by Karen Sparck Jones and Peter Willett

Introduction to Data Compression
Khalid Sayood

Forthcoming

Introduction to Data Compression, Second Edition
Khalid Sayood

Readings in Multimedia Computing
Edited by Hong Jiang Zhang and Kevin Jeffay

Multimedia Servers

Applications, Environments, and Design

Dinkar Sitaram and Asit Dan

Morgan Kaufmann Publishers, San Francisco California

Senior Editor: Jennifer Mann
Director of Production and Manufacturing: Yonie Overton
Senior Production Editor: Robin Demers
Editorial Assistant: Karyn Johnson
Cover Design: Ross Carron Design
Text Design: Penna Design and Production
Copyeditor: Progressive Publishing Alternatives
Proofreader: Ken DellaPenta
Composition: Windfall Software
Indexer: Ty Koontz
Printer: Courier Corporation

Cover image credits: Windmill, Eddie Soloway/Tony Stone Images;
Dam, Gary Braasch/Tony Stone Images; Dam Interior, Russell Illig/PhotoDisc

Editorial and Sales Office:
Morgan Kaufmann Publishers
340 Pine Street, Sixth Floor
San Francisco, CA 94104-3205
USA
Telephone 415/392-2665
Facsimile 415/982-2665
Internet *mkp@mkp.com*
Web site *http://mkp.com*

99 00 01 02 03   5 4 3 2 1

Library of Congress Cataloging-in-Publication Data is available for this book.
ISBN 1-55860-430-8

Dedicated to our wives,
Swarna and Karen,
and to our children,
Tejas, Tanvi, and IndraNeil

Contents

Figures and Tables

Figures

Tables

Foreword

The current euphoria over the World Wide Web does not do full justice to the potential of the Internet; with the manifold increases in CPU processing power and network bandwidth, it is inevitable that the Internet will support distributed applications and services of greater complexity. These applications will differ from conventional distributed applications in at least one dimension: they will involve storing, transporting, and processing multiple heterogeneous data types, such as images, audio, video, and text, collectively referred to as *multimedia*.

Future multimedia services will evolve from the beneficial alliance of different enterprises: content and service providers—such as publishing houses, libraries, news distributors, entertainment houses, radio and television stations—who will offer a multitude of services and content using multimedia storage servers, and network providers, who will own high-speed networks and will deliver the content from the service providers to end users. Thus, multimedia servers are critical components of the infrastructure required to deploy multimedia services of the future. The design considerations for such scalable multimedia servers is the subject of this book.

A multimedia server digitally stores audio, video, and textual information on a large array of extremely high-capacity storage devices such as optical or magnetic disks. The design of a multimedia server differs fundamentally from conventional text servers (or file systems) because of (1) the significantly larger storage space requirement of audio and video data, and (2) the timeliness requirement imposed by the need for their continuous storage, retrieval, and playback.

This book clearly articulates the challenges in designing multimedia servers and is an excellent repository of the central ideas and concepts that underlie the techniques for meeting these challenges. It covers a wide range of issues, including multimedia server architecture, placement and retrieval techniques for video and audio, disk and request scheduling algorithms, and caching. The authors have done an outstanding job of distilling the set of fundamental principles and techniques from a plethora of published papers and reports on multimedia server design. Furthermore, the authors have built upon their own experiences in designing and deploying commercial multimedia servers. Thus, the book reflects not just theoretical issues in multimedia server design but also the factors that matter in practice. Overall, the book contains a clear and concise description of the principles and techniques for designing multimedia servers.

This book will be a valuable resource not only for researchers and developers in related areas—such as databases, operating systems, networking, and CHI—but also for designers and implementors of multimedia servers. It will help designers of multimedia servers and applications to understand better the trade-offs between various techniques for implementing multimedia servers, and thereby help them make informed design choices. It will help researchers to understand and identify the limitations of the state of the art, and students to learn the key concepts and ideas in designing multimedia servers. Finally, it will help application designers to understand how to interact with and best utilize multimedia server resources.

It is a timely book: it discusses techniques, such as request and disk scheduling algorithms, that are currently used by multimedia servers along with an overview of emerging methods, such as the caching algorithms for next-generation Web servers. The breadth of topics—ranging from management of storage hierarchies to request and disk scheduling to caching—covered in this book, and the depth of the coverage on each topic, make this book unique.

Preface and Acknowledgments

The explosive growth and popularity of the World Wide Web have greatly widened the user base of computers, making it nearly universal. It has also provided a glimpse of the computer systems and pervasive applications of the future. User interfaces have evolved from being purely factual and text-based to having a much richer image content. Image-based content (such as photographs in shopping catalogs, banners in Web advertising, and news clips on news sites) has become an integral part of the user interface. The quantum leap in user satisfaction from these applications is simply unfathomable. However, the use of multimedia (video and audio) in such applications is still in its infancy. In the future, multimedia applications will be pervasive, commonplace, and essential, spanning from e-commerce to distance learning.

This revolution in multimedia applications will, however, not become a reality unless the technological development keeps pace. Advances in computer, networking, and display technologies have to come together to make this possible. Multimedia applications, due to their real-time delivery requirements, are fundamentally different from traditional nonmultimedia applications. Consider an example of a large-scale multimedia application (for example, broadcast radio over the Web and distance learning), where multimedia objects will be retrieved from a digital library or multimedia database and delivered to a large number of clients over a geographically distributed network. First, multimedia objects are large: even a short 5-minute compressed (MPEG-2) video clip will require 150 MB or more of disk storage. Hence, a large-scale multimedia server that can store large numbers of clips and other multimedia data may be built using many (possibly heterogeneous) system components: disks, tapes, processing nodes, network adapters, and so on. Second, multimedia data has to be delivered to the display at its playback rate. To avoid glitches in video display, the data delivery rate has to be guaranteed by reserving appropriate resources (for example, network bandwidth).

Hence, transporting such massive amounts of data to a large number of clients, while satisfying real-time requirements, will strain the capabilities of the systems of the foreseeable future. System architecture (that is, the proper organization of these system components) plays an extremely important role in the performance of such systems. Exploiting economies of scale through optimization algorithms (for example, batching client requests, VCR control via setting aside contingency capacity, caching, etc.) can improve the cost-performance of such large-scale servers. Further, future multimedia applications will demand support for more complex user interactions than simple playback. Therefore, creation, large-scale deployment, and support of such interactive multimedia applications will introduce many challenges.

This book will be an essential guide for both practitioners and designers alike. It introduces the key issues in building and deploying large-scale multimedia servers and applications. It analyzes the requirements of complex applications. It provides an understanding of the capabilities and limitations of the environments in which the servers and applications will be deployed. Finally, it illustrates the important design principles for building a large-scale (and cost-effective) multimedia server and focuses in depth on these issues.

Audience

This book is intended for three sets of readers: (1) *application designers,* who need to understand the requirements and the capabilities of the underlying platforms, (2) *service/content providers* and *system integrators,* who must have a total end-to-end picture of multimedia server environments to integrate new multimedia servers into the existing delivery infrastructure, and to deploy new multimedia applications, and (3) *multimedia server designers,* whose focus is on the design principles and algorithms for making a large-scale multimedia server cost-effective. This book can also be used as a textbook for graduate and advanced undergraduate level courses in multimedia.

Approach

The book attempts to provide breadth in describing all the components of a complex multimedia application/server environment, and at the same time depth in selected areas, namely, multimedia server resource management issues. It first provides an introduction to various types of multimedia applications—ranging from simple video-on-demand applications to more complex distance learning applications—and their requirements. An application designer has to be aware of the capabilities and limitations in designing applications for different environments. Future multimedia applications with more complex requirements than those of the applications with simple playback of a single long video stream—interactivity; retrieval of precomposed multimedia objects from many short video and audio clips, animation, text, and images; online composition of part or all of the multimedia documents—will in turn impose complex requirements on the storage and bandwidth resources of the underlying platform.

The book also provides a broad coverage of the deployment environments (business and consumer) and their components, as well as their limitations and capabilities. The environments in which multimedia applications will run will not be monolithic. Various heterogeneous components of the underlying network, storage, and presentation subsystems will have to interoperate. The network environment may be based on cable, ISDN, satellite, or ATM. The bandwidth limitations, or the differences in upstream and downstream bandwidth capacities, of the underlying network will determine the types of applications that can be run in these environments. For example, in a cable or satellite broadcast environment, only a small number of data streams can be broadcast simultaneously. Hence, applications such as NVOD that rely on sharing the channels across many users are appropriate for such environments.

Finally, this book covers in depth the design principles, architecture, and algorithms for building large-scale multimedia servers from heterogeneous sets of components for various economies of scale. Basic resource management functions—admission control, session setup, disk and CPU scheduling—are required in all multimedia servers to guarantee bandwidth reservation and jitter-free delivery of multimedia data. In a large-scale distributed server, resource management issues go beyond admission control and basic resource management issues that ensure quality-of-service guarantees. It includes issues such as data placement over multiple storage devices/nodes, dynamic load balancing, cache management, batching of requests, affinity routing, and so on. For large-scale multimedia servers, optimization algorithms can make an order of magnitude difference in efficiency. For example, multiple users requesting a popular video within a short period can be batched together and served using a single video stream. Clearly, the reduction in the required server capacity will depend on the user base. Another example is hierarchical caching in a geographically dispersed network, where it may not be possible to serve all the requests for a given video from a central server. Hence, caching popular multimedia materials at the local nodes will ensure scalability of the server complex.

Organization

This book is organized into four parts. Part 1, consisting of Chapters 1–3, provides an overview of multimedia applications, the deployment environments, and the overall architecture of multimedia servers. Part 2 of the book, consisting of Chapters 4–6, focuses on real-time requirements of multimedia applications—issues of quality of service (QoS) and the scheduling of system resources to achieve glitch-free playback. Unlike other subsystems, management of the storage subsystem needs to consider both bandwidth and storage capacities. Part 3, consisting of Chapters 7–10, describes the management and design of the storage subsystem in a multimedia server. Finally, traditional caching policies do not work well for large document size and sequential access patterns in multimedia applications, which demand new techniques for managing this cache. Part 4, consisting of Chapters 11–13, addresses design issues in caching policies for multimedia applications to improve server capacity.

Content

Chapter 1 introduces various types of multimedia applications and multimedia server environments, both of which will be of interest to application designers and service providers as well as multimedia server designers. The multimedia server environment is the subject of Chapter 2. We first describe the various common types of client systems (e.g., set-top boxes)and then the networking environment in detail, including the different types of networks, and various important multimedia protocols such as ATM, RTSP, and multicast. A general-purpose multimedia server architecture should operate in the heterogeneous environments of Chapter 2 and should support the various types of multimedia applications of Chapter 1. The details of this architecture and its components are described in Chapter 3. First, we discuss the important hardware components (such as disks, CD-ROM, processors) and standards (such as SCSI) used in multimedia servers. Then we describe the general software architecture. Chapter 3 concludes with specific server topologies and their impact on performance and availability.

Multimedia applications are distinguished by the requirements of QoS guarantees, which are achieved by admission control and device (e.g., CPU, disk) scheduling. The necessary resources required for delivery of a stream are reserved during the setup of an application session. Support of VCR control operations poses additional challenges because resources need to be reclaimed during pause and reallocated upon resume for efficient resource utilizations. In Chapters 4 and 5, these issues and various scheduling policies are described in detail. Device scheduling and the management of the CPU subsystem are discussed in Chapter 6.

Chapter 7 provides an overview of the issues involved in storage management. In Chapters 8 and 9, we focus on the management of the secondary storage devices. Chapter 8 deals with the basic issues of the storage of multimedia data on a single device, together with retrieval so as to satisfy QoS requirements. In

Chapter 9, more advanced issues of data placement, load balancing, and the organization of the storage subsystem to ensure recovery from failure are discussed. Chapter 10 describes the management of the tertiary storage system.

Traditional caching policies, such as LRU, cannot be directly applied for multimedia applications because of the larger size of multimedia files and the mostly sequential access pattern within a multimedia object. Stream-dependent caching such as interval caching can be quite effective in improving server capacity even with a small buffer. An overview of caching issues in multimedia systems is provided in Chapter 11. Caching of multimedia data in memory is detailed in Chapter 12. In a widely dispersed network such as the Internet, distributed caching in the nodes of the network can be important in reducing strain on the network capacity. Various caching policies for such environments are described in Chapter 13.

Acknowledgments

A few years ago, the newspaper headlines were dominated by reports on large-scale multimedia servers and their effect on the corporations anticipating the merger of various types of information delivery services. We were fortunate to participate in building video servers since the exciting early days and in writing several papers addressing some of the key aspects of video server design. However, in our discussions with others, particularly with the new students entering into this field, we realized that there are no books that introduce a reader systematically to the broad aspects of the design of a multimedia server. And although there are numerous papers dealing with individual aspects of the design, there is no digest of these papers to enumerate key design principles, and to provide a comprehensive survey of these papers. Our first attempt to satisfy this need was to present tutorials at the key conferences (ACM Multimedia, SIGMETRICS), and eventually these tutorials expanded into a book. We are extremely grateful to Ed Fox, the editor of the *Multimedia Information and Systems* series, and Jennifer Mann, the editor of this book, for their constant encouragement, feedback, and more importantly patience to get this book completed. We would like to thank the staff of Morgan Kaufmann—Karyn Johnson, for her role in coordinating the reviewers, Robin Demers for her role in production, and Sheri Dean for her role in marketing. The book embodies a shared viewpoint on multimedia computing for which we would like to thank our research collaborators, Junehwa Song, Kevin Almeroth, Perwez Shahabuddin, Renu Tewari, Don Towsley, and Harrick Vin. We would also like to thank Harrick for his insightful comments on the content and organization of the book, and for writing a foreword for this book. We are grateful to S. Balachandar for his detailed review comments, and to Srivibhavan

Balaram, Ramesh Jain, Narasimha Rao, Taruna Venkatesh, and Percy Tzelnic for their reviews of individual chapters. We would also like to thank our managers at IBM and Novell—Dan Dias, Nagui Halim, Martin Kienzle, Vikram Shah, and William Tetzlaff—for providing support, as well our colleagues at IBM—Richard Ludwin and Brent Hailpern—for many discussions during the formative years of many of these ideas. Finally, we would like to thank our families—Swarna, Tejas, Tanvi, Karen, and IndraNeil—for their patience and support through many hours while we excused ourselves in writing this book.

Asit Dan
Dinkar Sitaram

PART 1

Multimedia Server
Applications and Environments

1

Introduction

Multimedia is the natural next step in the evolution of user interfaces. Video images together with audio open up much richer possibilities than purely graphics- or text-based applications. For example, video clips of news events (e.g., films of astronauts in space) can convey more information (e.g., about weightlessness) than a mere description. Moving images on a screen can also be used to attract attention to a particular area, to emphasize particular points, or to illustrate how something works. Audio tracks are very effective at creating an atmosphere (like background music or sounds in movies—e.g., the sounds of *Tyrannosaurus rex*'s footsteps in the movie *Jurassic Park*). They can also clarify points that are not clear from the image (e.g., a narration in an educational video).

Currently, multimedia applications have entered a phase of rapid growth. This growth is being driven by two forces. First, the rapidly dropping cost of computer and networking hardware has made multimedia applications accessible to an ever-increasing number of users. This can be seen by the growing sophistication and realism of computer games like Doom. Second, the growing size of the Internet has made it possible to publish multimedia content comparatively cheaply to an immense audience. For example, millions of viewers visit the Web sites of news organizations such as CNN to view news clips.

At least three activities are needed for the deployment of multimedia applications. The first activity—content creation—refers to the creation of the actual audio-video clips and images that will be viewed by the user. This activity is clearly crucial to the success of multimedia because the availability of attractive content is perhaps the most important factor in the success of multimedia applications. Content creation requires some technical advancements, such as the development of tools for creating special effects. Nonetheless, this activity is clearly the province of artists rather than computer scientists.

Audio and video clips have to be integrated into applications before being presented to the user. This activity can be referred to as application creation. Multimedia can be used to make the presentation of virtually any information more effective. Therefore, the range of multimedia applications is correspondingly very large and diverse. For example, an on-line help database can use video clips to demonstrate how to carry out complex tasks. A very different application is the delivery of movies to the home through a network. Successful design of multimedia applications is again partly an art. However, efficient design requires knowledge of the capabilities and design of multimedia systems. This book provides an understanding of these topics and serves as a reference for them.

But it is the third activity—designing and building the systems for deploying multimedia applications and delivering multimedia content—that is the focus of this book. Multimedia servers are distinguished from conventional application servers in many ways that impact every aspect of their design [16]. Capturing even a small amount of multimedia content requires a large amount of data. Typically, this data is stored in a server or storage system from which the data is streamed continuously to the client display device at a given playback rate. Therefore, delivery of multimedia data is time-sensitive; that is, clients will notice glitches if audio or video data is not delivered on time. This implies that management of every component of the multimedia system must consider the time criticality of the data [15, 2]. A second factor is that managing this large amount of data creates requirements different from those of conventional systems. Hence, both of these factors need to be taken into account in designing policies for managing system resources—CPU, storage hierarchy, caching, and so on.

Figure 1.1 illustrates the typical multimedia environment considered in this book. To understand the demands on multimedia servers in this environment, we consider in this chapter various typical multimedia applications. From a historical perspective, the first multimedia application to generate a lot of interest was the delivery of movies to homes from a central server [57]. However, this did not develop as rapidly as expected due to the high cost and networking bottlenecks. Simultaneously, the growth of the Internet led to a parallel growth in multimedia applications over the Internet [64]. The Internet applications, where multimedia was integrated with the user interface [20, 28], tended to be complex. Currently, much research interest is focused on the development of such applications.

The rest of Chapter 1 contains a brief discussion of various types of multimedia applications, their requirements, and basic compression methods. Chapter 2 provides a detailed survey of the multimedia environments where multimedia applications can be deployed, consisting of clients and the networks connecting them to multimedia servers. Networking issues are particularly significant because networking bottlenecks are a major inhibitor to the growth of multimedia applications. These bottlenecks can be alleviated by caching and prefetching multi-

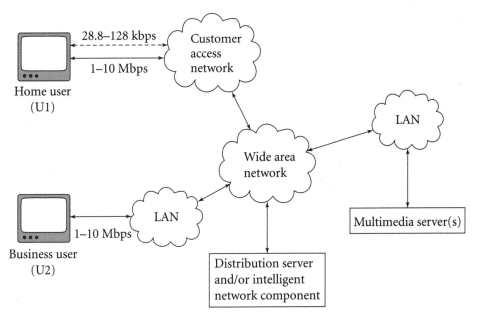

Figure 1.1   Multimedia system environment.

media data in the network [51, 59, 62]. In Chapter 3 we discuss at a high level the architecture of multimedia servers.

1.1   Multimedia Applications

Multimedia applications may be built either entirely anew or by enhancing user interfaces or delivery mechanisms of traditional applications. We describe in the following sections several examples of both types of applications. The example applications and their requirements are presented in an approximate order of increasing complexity and demonstrate that the characteristics of multimedia applications can be rather diverse. Designing a common platform for supporting diverse applications is indeed very challenging.

1.1.1   Broadcast Video

All multimedia servers must have the ability to store and play back a video. Therefore, the simplest type of application is one where a video server is used to play back a single stream. Such an application is used by the Middle Eastern subsidiary of MTV Europe, which uses video servers to store and play back the video that is broadcast [32]. In such an application, the video server is being used simply as a substitute for a bank of VCRs.

It is interesting that even in such a simple application, multimedia servers possess advantages over traditional tape-recording technology [32]. Tape players and robotic arms undergo increased wear and tear if a succession of short clips is played. With error correction (discussed later in this book), digital video servers can offer far greater reliability than tape players. This is particularly important for a broadcast, where failure can result in the loss of a very large number of users. Additionally, tape players have limitations in terms of the time needed to update spontaneously the list of clips to be played (i.e., from the time of update to playback). This reduces flexibility in making last-minute changes to the playlist. Finally, with a video server, it is easy for production staff to preview videos by requesting them from the video server. In contrast, with a tape system, it is necessary to circulate multiple copies of a new tape.

1.1.2   Video-on-Demand

Video-on-demand (VOD) is a slightly more complex application than broadcast video. In VOD, there may be a potentially large number of clients viewing video over a large, geographically dispersed area. However, as we will see, even this relatively simple application has hidden complexities. These include the necessity of nonsequential viewing and networking complexities (discussed later in this book). We describe two VOD applications, VOD to the home and educational VOD, that were deployed in actual trials that demonstrated different access patterns both within a video and across a set of videos.

VOD to the Home

The Bell Atlantic trial [6] is a typical VOD to the home application. In the trial, 1000 paying customers in Fairfax, VA, were connected to a multimedia server. The customers were able to order videos from a list of 700 choices each month. Interaction with the system was through a hand-held remote control that interfaced to a set-top box on the television set. To select a video, customers could either preview videos on-line or directly select the video from a monthly program guide magazine. The remote control could be used to pause, rewind, and fast-forward the videos. These operations are referred to as *VCR controls* because they are common controls on most VCRs. Interestingly, subscribers purchased on the average 3.6 videos per month. Additionally, new movies proved to be the most popular choice, accounting for 57% of the total. However, children's movies and specials were also popular.

Because new videos proved to be the most popular, it is logical to attempt to optimize the video server capacity by broadcasting new movies at periodic intervals. Viewers could then simply tune in to the video of their choice. This does away with the need to deliver an individual stream for each client. Such systems are referred to as *near-video-on-demand* (*NVOD*) systems. However, it is difficult to provide VCR controls in NVOD systems because a new delivery stream needs to be created for each individual user requiring such operations. A limited form of VCR control operations can be supported by switching the client to the nearest stream after a VCR control command (e.g., `pause`, `resume`, `jump`). (This issue will be addressed in further detail later in this book.) As the Bell Atlantic trial revealed, such systems are important for commercial customers. Later on, we will show that efficient support for VCR controls is a significant challenge in VOD systems as well.

Educational VOD

A VOD system was used by researchers at the University of Ottawa as part of an experimental study in enhancing a communications course [8]. The course was specifically designed to incorporate 40 titles (32 hours) of video materials from the National Film Board of Canada. As part of their assignments, students were required to watch one video per week to supplement the material taught in class. Students were also required to make two presentations using the video material. A number of interesting observations emerged from a survey of the students after the course.

The survey after the course was designed to assess the effectiveness of the VOD software and discover possible enhancements. A large majority of the students felt that the VOD material enhanced the course content both in supplementing course material and in aiding their own presentations. Consistent with the results from the Bell Atlantic trial, most of the students (69%) rated the VCR controls as being very important. Nearly an equal percentage (65%) reported making extensive use of these controls. Equally interesting was that a large number (58%) of students felt that a very useful enhancement would be increased user control over navigation through the video; for example, to search and retrieve a video segment. This can be achieved by hypermedia, an application described in the next section.

1.1.3 Hypermedia and Multimedia Databases

A VOD application allows a user limited navigational ability within a single video. Greater navigational facility can be provided by a system that presents multimedia documents with embedded links to other documents. Such a document, which may contain multiple images, videos, and graphics, is referred to as a *composite multimedia document* [58, 20]. The links in a multimedia document may be explicit or implicit. Explicit links are links between documents that are created by the author. Collections of multimedia documents with explicit links are referred to as *hypermedia.* In contrast, implicit links between documents are not created, but exist because the documents have common content. The contents of the documents can either be extracted by analysis of the document [35] or by human annotation [20]. A collection of multimedia documents with searchable content is commonly referred to as a *multimedia database.*

Composite multimedia documents may contain visible objects (e.g., buttons) that will cause the display of a related document when clicked. Alternatively, clicking on an object in the image may bring up information regarding that object. For example, in a swimming competition, clicking on a swimmer may bring up a video showing a close-up of the swimmer from a different angle. To allow viewing the competition from both angles, it may be desirable for the close-up to overlay part of the original video. Hence, the video server will need to transmit two videos to the client, leading to a sudden increase in the resource requirements at the server. Additionally, the two video streams need to be transmitted synchronistically. Note that the complexity due to synchronization may exist in complex VOD systems. An efficient method for storing multiple-language versions of a movie is to store a single video track and multiple audio tracks. In this case, the video and audio tracks have to be tightly synchronized. Support for such applications is thus more complex than the support for simple VOD applications.

Hypermedia documents on the Web can be specified using the Structured Multimedia Interchange Language (SMIL) of the World Wide Web Consortium (W3C) [58]. The components of the multimedia documents are specified using URLs. SMIL is media neutral; that is, just like HTML, it does not specify the type of documents that comprise the document. To support the requirements of hypermedia, SMIL contains tags to specify the order and synchronism among various media objects. Typical applications that can use SMIL are on-line shopping catalogs enhanced with video and audio.

1.1.4   Virtual Worlds: Collaborative Computing

In the applications we have discussed, the users of the multimedia system work in isolation without interacting with each other. However, multimedia allows the development of applications in which users can interact with each other in a simulated 2D or 3D world. A common example is videoconferencing, which allows businesses to substitute "virtual meetings" for physical meetings. This leads to a drastic reduction in travel costs and lost time while having very little impact on business efficiency.

An example of a typical collaborative videoconferencing system is Auditorium [47] from the PlaceWare Corporation. The system is written in Java and hence is portable across many environments. Auditorium is accessed via a Java-enabled Web browser with an audio plug-in. Users can access the virtual meeting either as presenters or as part of the audience. Audience members see an audience console that has a seating chart showing the other members of the audience (see Figure 1.2). The console also has text areas for writing comments to other audience members or the speaker, as well as a slide display area. The presenter console has presentation facilities as well as decision-making facilities. The presentation facilities include support for broadcasting speech to the audience, displaying slides, and drawing pictures. Decision-making support includes facilities for polling the audience as well as asking multiple-choice questions and tabulating the results on-line.

Auditorium is an example of a videoconferencing system where users access a video server that manages the conference. An alternative design can be based upon

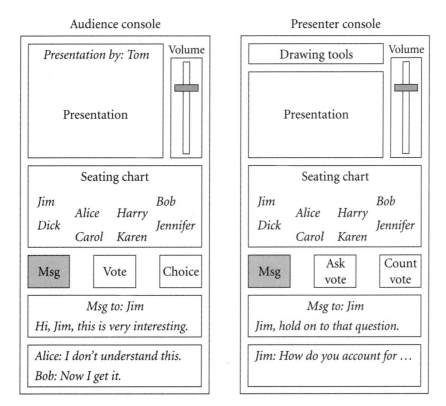

Figure 1.2 Typical collaborative application.

adapting peer-to-peer videoconferencing, where each participant broadcasts video to all other members of the conference and listens to all participants via different channels. However, the increased complexity of setting up multiple communication channels and the distributed management of the conference makes such systems less scalable than conferencing systems using a centralized video server [9]. A video server can also offer additional features, such as maintaining a log of the conference, that are difficult with purely peer-to-peer systems.

Unlike the applications described earlier, low latency is a significant additional requirement of videoconferencing applications. If the latency for the delivery of the video is high, different members of the audience may see the video at significantly different times, leading to confusion. Consider, for example, the case where user B receives the presentation significantly later than user A. During the presentation, user A may make a comment about the presentation to user B. If the delivery latency to user B is high, user B may see user A's comment before seeing the part of the presentation that the comment is about.

1.2   Multimedia Server Design Issues

To support the vast diversity of multimedia applications, multimedia servers need to satisfy many requirements. The requirements are imposed not only by an application but also by the business objectives for a specific deployment with specific workload and architectural configuration. Therefore, to compile a complete list of these requirements, we will consider the requirements from the points of view of multimedia application designers and businesses that operate multimedia servers as well as architectural configurations defined by multimedia server designers.

1.2.1   Application Requirements

The major characteristic of multimedia applications that distinguishes them from nonmultimedia applications is that multimedia data is time-sensitive. Successive frames of data have to be displayed according to the time relationships defined by the application designer (e.g., continuous streaming of a media segment, synchronized display of multiple media segments). To hide the complexities of the underlying system on which multimedia applications are deployed as well as to make applications portable, a second application requirement is to specify the information on time-sensitive display of data using standard interfaces. A third application requirement is specification of the capabilities of the underlying infrastructure (i.e., bandwidth, storage, and compute capabilities of the clients, networks, and servers) such that multimedia applications can be appropriately partitioned. For example, supporting complex multimedia applications may require simultaneous retrieval of multiple media segments (and, hence, supporting demand for variable and high-peak bandwidth) and dynamic composition capability at the client.

Time sensitivity. If delivery of multimedia data is not on time, users will notice interruptions. Multimedia files are generally too large to download completely. As a result, successive frames have to be delivered subject to time constraints. These constraints are referred to as the *quality of service (QoS) requirements* of the application. Satisfying QoS requirements entails setting policies for efficient scheduling of disks, memory buffers, and other system resources [66, 15, 2, 14]. Some applications may require the delivery of multiple video and audio streams, which means the delivery of the various streams must be synchronized [63]. Finally, collaborative applications may require low-latency delivery.

Open interfaces. As we have seen, the delivery time requirements of applications can vary widely. Hence, applications need interfaces for specifying their particular requirements. A number of characteristics are desirable in such interfaces. To facilitate portability and networking of applications, the interfaces should be open and standard. For ease of development, the interfaces should hide details of the structure of the multimedia server. For example, the fact that a particular video is replicated and can be played back from multiple servers is not relevant to most applications. It is important for multimedia servers to support common interfaces so that most precomposed applications can be deployed on them [55, 34].

Client, network, and server capabilities. For simple VOD applications, clients need to support continuous retrieval and display of video contents as well as support VCR control commands—for example, switching to a new stream or sending these commands to the multimedia servers. Networks connecting the clients to the servers need to support continuous streaming or back channels for carrying user commands. Multimedia servers support streaming of media content and possibly individualize the streams in response to the clients.

For more complex applications that require retrieval, composition, and display of composite or multiple media segments, desired client capabilities may include supporting complex user interfaces, computing capabilities for dynamic composition of presentation, and complex data retrieval protocols as well as attached local storage for dealing with variable bandwidth. Similarly, the networks need to support complex data retrieval protocols (i.e., dynamic bandwidth allocation) as well as command and data channels. The server capabilities include, in response to client requests, identification and retrieval of various media segments from the database on time, composition of presentation, and streaming of these media segments via one or multiple retrieval streams.

1.2.2 Business Deployment Requirements

In the real world, the load placed on a multimedia service may be unpredictable. Therefore, from the point of view of an operator of a multimedia service, the server should operate well under varying conditions. The service may serve a large or a relatively small number of users, and the demand for videos may be rapidly changing. For a large-scale service, interruptions may be expensive.

Scalability. The number of users supported by a multimedia server can be small (as in the MTV broadcast video application) or potentially very large (as in the VOD example). Hence, the multimedia server should be capable of operating efficiently over a large range of numbers of users. As will be shown later, various sophisticated optimization policies are feasible with a large number of users [1, 19]. Additionally, the number of users may grow with time. Therefore, the multimedia server should allow for easy incremental growth [15].

Reliability. In the VOD application, failure of the multimedia server can lead to large loss of revenue and goodwill. By using redundant components as backup, multimedia servers can offer very high reliability. Hence, video blocks or parity blocks may be replicated to provide protection against failure [30, 7, 56].

Dynamic adaptation to workload. In a multimedia system, the workload may change unpredictably. For example, the Bell Atlantic trial found that most of the demand was for new movies, which change periodically. As in the case of movies released in theaters, the actual demand may exceed or undershoot the predicted demand. It may also vary with time and have pronounced peaks and valleys. Policies that allow the multimedia server to adapt to varying loads may be required [17].

1.2.3 Architectural Requirements

Large-scale multimedia servers are built using preexisting system components (e.g., storage devices, processors, and so on). The characteristics of these already existing components (e.g., processing speed, space, connectivity) strongly influence the structure of multimedia servers and the optimization policies used to address cost performance.

Standard logical subcomponents. It is desirable to use standard utilities (e.g., backup programs) for managing multimedia servers. This can be achieved if the multimedia server is architected in terms of standard logical subcomponents. For example, if the storage component of the multimedia server is architected as a file system (i.e., it provides a file system interface), it can be backed up by standard backup programs [30].

Topology. The underlying design of the components used to build the multimedia server may dictate a particular topology (e.g, centralized, partitioned). As later chapters will show, the topology of the multimedia server has an important influence on its performance.

Cost performance. Particularly in large-scale multimedia servers, small increases in efficiency may lead to large reductions in multimedia server costs. For example, caching popular videos in memory may reduce disk storage costs [18, 14]. As mentioned earlier, with network bandwidth being a significant bottleneck, caching and prefetching in the network may be important [51, 59, 62].

1.3 Overview of Encoding and Data Compression Technologies

In this section, we provide an overview of video encoding and data compression technologies, a working knowledge of which is essential to all three communities—multimedia application developers, application deployers, and server designers.

In the physical world, video and audio data is continuous (analog) in nature. To be able to store this data in a computer, the audio and video data needs to be digitized. The first step in this process is to sample it at a sufficiently fine interval. For example, a still image may be divided into a large number of pixels. However, each sampled value is still analog in nature; in the previous example, the image parameters at each pixel (e.g., brightness) are analog. The final step in digitization is to quantize the sampled values; for example, by rounding off the sampled value to the nearest integer. The sampling and quantization ultimately determine the final quality of the resulting video. The greater the number of samples and the finer the quantization levels, the greater will be the resulting quality.

The digitized data obtained by this process is typically too large to be stored or delivered over a network. For example, consider a 1024×1024 monochrome display where the brightness at each pixel is represented by a single byte. Each pixel in such a display can have 256 brightness levels. Storage of a single picture will require 1 MB of storage, and delivery of a video will require 30 MB per second (MB/s). The resources required for storage and delivery can be reduced by taking into consideration the large degree of redundancy in the digitized data as well as the presence of fine and unnoticeable details. For example, successive lines of pixels in an image may be very similar. In the case of video data, successive frames in the video may also be very similar. By encoding only the differences between successive pixels or lines, the resource requirements of the video and audio data can be substantially reduced.

Because compression techniques exploit spatial and temporal redundencies in video, it follows that compression ratios could vary. For example, in a video segment with very little motion, there would be a very small difference between successive frames. Because the compression techniques encode the differences between successive frames, the compression ratio for this segment would be very high. Correspondingly, a segment with large amounts of motion could have a low compression ratio. Therefore, the bandwidth requirements of the compressed video could fluctuate. This is referred to as *variable bit rate (VBR)* encoding. VBR streams pose challenges in video storage, retrieval, and delivery. An alternative technique is to attempt to keep the bandwidth of the compressed stream constant and allow the resulting picture quality to fluctuate (imperceptibly one hopes). This technique is known as *constant bit rate (CBR)* encoding.

1.3.1   MPEG Standard

The Motion Pictures Expert Group (MPEG) has defined a set of standard audio and video compression algorithms based on the ideas above. The MPEG-1 standard defines a compression standard for audio and video data that has a bit-rate of around 1.5 Mbps [29]. MPEG-1 also defines the MPEG transport protocol, the format by which a set of concurrent audio and video streams (e.g., a movie and multiple soundtracks) can be interlaced and stored as a single stream. The interlaced stream has a header that describes the streams being combined, and this is followed by the interlaced blocks of the actual streams.

The MPEG-2 standard extends MPEG-1 to define a higher-quality compression standard that has a bit-rate of 4 Mbps to 9 Mbps [29]. MPEG-3 originally targeted high definition TV (HDTV) but is now defunct because it was discovered that MPEG-2 satisfies the HDTV requirements equally well. MPEG-4 is a standard currently under development for low bit-rate applications such as mobile communications and videophones [29]. Because MPEG-1 is widely used and is the basis for MPEG-2, we will describe it in more detail. Details of the other standards can be found in the references.

MPEG-1 video starts with an uncompressed 352×240 pixel frame. This frame is decomposed into one 352×240 luminance (brightness) channel and two color channels. Because lower resolution is needed for color, the resolution of the color channels is 176×120. The channels are further decomposed into macroblocks, which are the units on which encoding is actually done. Macroblocks are 16×16 in the luminance channel and 8×8 in the color channels. The data in each macroblock (or its difference from another macroblock) is encoded by applying discrete cosine transformation (DCT), which yields a sparse matrix. This matrix may be quantized into discrete levels for the purpose of reducing the storage space. The quantization may result in the zeroing of some terms. The matrix is then efficiently encoded.

MPEG-1 video compression exploits visual redundancies between frames as well as redundancies within a frame. An MPEG-1 video stream contains three types of frames, referred to as I, B, and P frames. The relationship among these different frame types is shown in Figure 1.3. I frames are independently encoded; that is, all the macroblocks of an I frame are encoded completely in terms of the information in this frame. The P and B frames attempt to exploit redundancies between successive frames of the video. The macroblocks of P and B frames are encoded in terms of the differences with other frames at the macroblock level. To extract the differences for P and B frames, each macroblock is compared with adjacent macroblocks in the preceding and/or following frames to find the closest match. The location of the closest match is recorded as a motion vector. The difference between the current macroblock and the matching macroblock is then extracted.

Note that not all macroblocks of P and B frames are encoded in terms of differences from corresponding macroblocks of other frames—that is, when no closest match can be found. Macroblocks in P frames are encoded in terms of the differences from the preceding I or P frame only. However, the macroblocks in B frames are encoded in terms of the differences from either the corresponding previous or the following I and/or P frames. The rationale behind using both preceding as well as succeeding frames in the case of B frames is as follows. Due to motion, the B frame may contain objects that are present in the following frame but not in the preceding one. Therefore, using both the preceding and following frames should lead to a more efficient encoding. Of course, it also leads to larger buffer sizes and greater complexity in the encoder. The number of frames of each type is not part of the standard and is specified in the video.

Audio data is compressed separately. MPEG-1 audio compression works by exploiting the characteristics of human perception. For example, frequencies where the sound is low can be masked by the presence of loud sounds at adjacent frequencies. Hence, these weak frequencies can be omitted. Details can be found in [29].

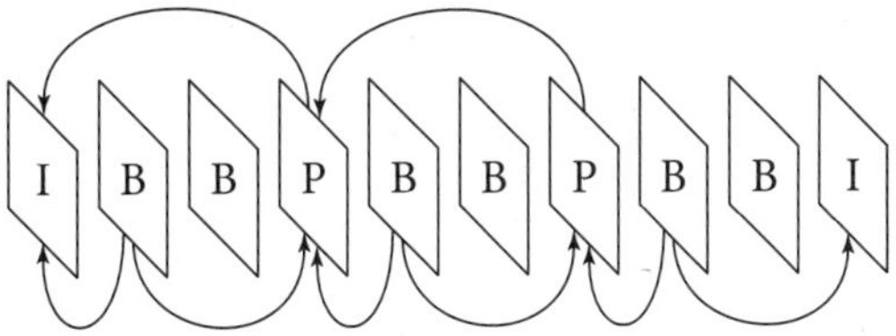

Figure 1.3 MPEG frame structure.

1.4   Summary

Multimedia can be used to enhance the user interface of almost any application. Therefore, the range of multimedia applications is very large. Typical examples of multimedia applications include video-on-demand, hypermedia, and videoconferencing. These applications have widely varying requirements, and efficient support of these requirements leads to a large number of design issues. Applications need to specify their requirements for time-critical delivery of video data, and various multimedia server components should cooperate to satisfy these requirements. Scalability and reliability are important issues from the point of view of the operator of the multimedia server. Finally, the topology of the multimedia server and architectural choices are important in terms of their impact on the efficiency of multimedia server design. The objective of this book is to address these issues systematically and at greater length.

2

Multimedia Server Environment

The deployment scenarios of multimedia applications surveyed in the previous chapter span many physical systems and may also span large geographical distances. Additionally, the multimedia applications have widely differing requirements due to their diversity. It is clearly impractical to create a special infrastructure tailored to each application and environment. Supporting such largely diverse applications on a common infrastructure is indeed a formidable challenge.

In spite of these complexities and widely different deployment scenarios, the multimedia server environment can be thought of as being built from just three components. These are illustrated in Figure 2.1. The clients represent the physical devices at which the users of the system view/play back the multimedia data. A communication network connects the clients and the multimedia server(s), and it is responsible for reliable and efficient transportation of data and control signals between the clients and the multimedia server. Finally, there is the multimedia server itself, which is the focus of the subsequent chapters of this book.

Rapid deployment of multimedia applications requires simultaneous advances in clients, the network, and multimedia servers. Due to the diversity of applications, as well as for historical reasons, there are a large number of different types of deployment environments—that is, clients and network types. The major application environments can be inferred by considering the applications described in Chapter 1 and categorized broadly into two major application environments: business and consumer. Business applications are typically deployed in the workplace, whereas consumer applications are normally intended to be used from home.

In this chapter, we first describe in detail the general requirements of multimedia applications on the underlying client systems and networks. Subsequently, we describe the two broad multimedia application deployment environments and their capabilities. We also discuss important limitations, such as the "last mile problem." Wherever possible, we also give actual examples of available products.

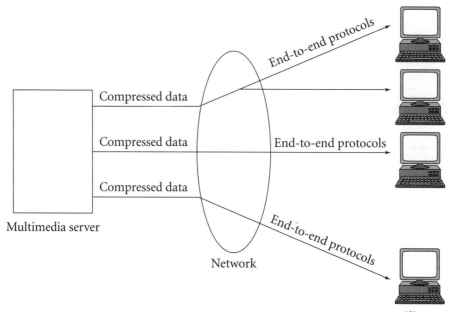

Figure 2.1   Multimedia server environment.

However, due to the rapid pace of change in the industry, these examples are intended to be illustrative and not exhaustive. You will need to consult the latest product catalogs for up-to-date specifications of the latest products. Finally, we provide a brief overview of the various protocols used by applications and networking infrastructure following the Open Systems Interconnection (OSI) and Asynchronous Transfer Mode (ATM) reference models.

2.1   Requirements of Multimedia Applications on the Underlying Environment

To support user interaction with the multimedia applications, the clients need to provide a user interface, retrieve the multimedia segments, and display the multimedia document. The networks need to support streaming of media segments from the servers to the clients in a timely manner as well as carrying back user commands to the servers. We discuss these functions in more detail in the following sections.

2.1.1   User Interface

User interface functions allow the user to select multimedia presentations of interest. To determine the interesting multimedia documents available (e.g., videos) or find multimedia documents that meet some criteria, the client needs to be able to formulate appropriate queries to the multimedia server. Displaying the choices available requires the ability to display nonmultimedia data such as menus. To allow users to make choices, it also needs methods for acquiring user inputs. Both the clients and the servers need to process user commands and retrieve different media contents in response. Finally, a back channel is required for carrying user commands to the server.

Providing these capabilities may not be a significant issue if the client system is a workstation modified for multimedia presentation. However, these issues may be important if, as described later, the client system is a special-purpose system (e.g., a special box attached to a TV set). Due to cost considerations or the necessity of providing a simplified user interface, such clients may have special-purpose user interfaces. Also, in a broadcast environment, it may be difficult to provide a back channel for individual users.

2.1.2   Multimedia Document Retrieval

After the user chooses a multimedia presentation using the user interface functions, the client system is responsible for retrieving the elements of the presentation. To retrieve the presentation, the client should work together with network and servers and, hence, support some standard video and composite multimedia document retrieval protocol. For a composite multimedia document, multiple videos or audios (or both) have to be retrieved in parallel and displayed (or played back) in synchronism. This can be achieved if the retrieval protocol supports time-stamping of video and audio frames—that is, retrieval of components in order. Retrieval protocols are described in a later section.

To retrieve the video and audio contents without glitches, the client system has to deal with the issues of bandwidth availability related to retrieval of continuous media. Sufficient bandwidth is needed in the network and multimedia servers for the retrieval of the multimedia contents at the required rate. Recall that the bandwidth requirements are variable, with high peaks for retrieval of even an individual video. For composite media documents this variability can be even greater. Therefore, sufficient bandwidth can be ensured by reserving the peak bandwidth.

This requires support of bandwidth reservation protocols (described later in this chapter). However, reserving the peak bandwidth may be very inefficient from the point of view of server and network utilization. Even if sufficient bandwidth is available, transient high network delays may result in a frame not being available at the required time. On the other hand, reserving less than the maximum bandwidth risks the possibility of the required bandwidth not being available when needed.

Both of these performance issues can be dealt with by buffering in the client. We describe these issues only briefly here because they are described in more detail in later chapters. If sufficient bandwidth is not available in the network, it is possible to prefetch some frames and buffer them in the client [59]. Effectively, the prefetching averages out the required bandwidth in the network. The remaining frames can then be retrieved at a slower rate.

2.1.3   Video and Audio Playback

Once the selected multimedia documents have been retrieved, the client subsystem needs to display the selected video presentation and/or play back the audio content to the user. Because the multimedia streams are transmitted in compressed form, they need to be decompressed for display. The decompression may be performed in the hardware, using a special-purpose adapter, or in the main processor, using software. Both approaches have their advantages and disadvantages. With a special-purpose adapter, the quality of the decoded picture (size and resolution) will generally be very high. For example, a card that produces a full-screen high-quality video on a workstation may cost only a few hundred dollars. However, advances in processor speed, together with special-purpose instructions for multimedia such as MMX (multimedia extensions), are tending to reduce the gap.

The main advantages of software decompression over hardware decompression are flexibility and cost. Players for popular compression formats (e.g., Real Player for Real Video and the MPEG Reference player) can be downloaded from the Web for free or at a nominal cost. Additionally, special-purpose adapters typically are not programmable once installed; that is, the decompression algorithm cannot be modified easily. Updating such adapters normally requires additional updates to the operating system or device drivers, which are difficult for nonexperts. With software decompression, multiple formats can be easily supported on the same client system. It is also possible to choose between multiple resolutions of the same format, depending on the capabilities of the client system [48]. The client system may have a library of procedures to decode the same compression format and choose a procedure based on the resources available. Consider the case where the multimedia server is transmitting color video, but the client system is not powerful enough to decode this in real time. It may be possible to select a decoding function that decodes and displays only the black-and-white components in real time.

2.2   Client Environment

In a multimedia environment, the client system is the component with which the user interacts directly. It provides the functions that will allow the user to effectively invoke and utilize multimedia applications. As we have stated, different clients have been developed for different application environments. This is evident from the fact that a client designed to allow users to view video at home is likely to be very different from one suitable for a distance learning course.

The exact implementation of the basic client functions depends on the application environment. As stated earlier, the two major application environments are the business and consumer environments. Typical applications in a business environment include distance learning or a multimedia database of news clips stored by a news agency. In a consumer environment, typical applications include catalog shopping and video-on-demand. The consumer environment is price sensitive; it is believed that users will not pay a great deal for a client system. Additionally, consumers may be confused by complex log-in procedures, system administration, and user interface of a typical workstation. Hence, the challenge is to develop special-purpose clients that are relatively inexpensive but simple and easy to use and maintain. In contrast, systems in industrial environments tend to be workstations or PCs equipped with whatever hardware is necessary for the multimedia application.

2.2.1   Consumer Environment

Client systems in consumer environments are also frequently referred to as *set-top boxes*. We will first present a simple line of argument that the cost of set-top boxes should be low, and then we will describe some popular, commercially available set-top boxes.

Consider a video-on-demand application for delivery of videos to the home. It can be argued that such a service should be comparable in price to the cost of cable rental in a typical city. In the United States, this price would currently be around $20 per month. Hence, a consumer may pay approximately $240 annually. Assume that the video-service operator would expect at least a return of 10% on its investment. It follows that the video-service operator can invest approximately $2400 per customer. Assume that this cost is split approximately evenly between content (e.g., movies), the video server, the networking infrastructure, and the set-top box. Thus, the cost of a set-top box cannot be much greater than $600.

An interesting consequence of this argument is that the cost distribution between the client system, server, and network depends upon the distribution of client load. Consider the scenario where during the peak-load period, only a fraction of clients are simultaneously active. The server and network capacity required is proportional only to the number of active clients, whereas the client capacity required is proportional to the total number of clients. Hence, it is preferable to shift as much functional capability as possible to the server and network. However, if all clients are active during peak load, lowering the client cost will require increasing the server and network cost by an equal amount.

Thus there are two approaches to reducing the cost of special-purpose systems for consumer environments. One approach is to build a special-purpose system that is similar to, but lower in cost than, a workstation or PC. Such a system may use standard protocols to communicate to the video network. An alternative approach is to attempt to shift as many of the client functions as possible to a server network. The client system then can have reduced cost, reducing the overall cost in some environments (as previously discussed). We will study both approaches.

Simplified workstation. A number of workstation manufacturers offer hardware components that can be used to build special-purpose systems based on their workstation lines. A typical example is IBM, which offers a set of ASICs based on PowerPC architecture for building set-top boxes. The system is based on the PowerPC 403 processor, which is a 32-bit RISC processor that is part of the IBM PowerPC line of workstations. It includes complementary MPEG-2 decoders as well as peripheral controllers for plugging in other peripherals. The manufacturers also typically provide special-purpose operating systems tailored to run on the special-purpose systems. This is because general-purpose workstation operating systems contain many features (e.g., e-mail support) that are not required in such systems. Also, some required features (e.g., support for real-time processing) are generally missing or inadequate. In the case of IBM, two operating systems—the pSOS real-time operating system from Integrated Systems, Inc. and the OS/9000 operating system from Microware—are offered.

Proprietary client. A contrasting approach is to build a special-purpose client system that does not resemble a conventional workstation. An example of this is the set-top box from WebTV. WebTV actually specifies the WebTV Reference Design, which is manufactured by licensees. It is based on the MIPS R640 64-bit RISC processor. The WebTV Reference Design is a specification for a client that is designed to connect to the WebTV network. The design pays attention to making the client system inexpensive as well as easy to use and maintain. To lower the cost of the client, much of the processing and storage of data that normally takes place on the client takes place in the WebTV network. For example, the WebTV network servers prefetch data as well as filter the data for objectionable content. To ease administration, the WebTV network also backs up user data, such as e-mail. User selection interaction is through the familiar remote control. The WebTV Reference Design also contains specifications for credit card readers, which allow magnetically encoded cards to be used for identification instead of requiring users to remember user IDs and passwords. They also simplify use of credit cards. Finally, WebTV has entered into alliances with a large number of service providers, such as banks, to ensure the acceptability of their design.

2.2.2 Business Environment

Customers in business environments may be willing to pay higher costs than customers in a consumer environment. Hence, the client system may be a workstation or PC equipped with multimedia adapters. Alternatively, the processor in the workstation may be specially designed for multimedia. We will discuss these two approaches in detail.

Multimedia adapters. Multimedia adapters consist of special hardware that is designed for the display of multimedia data. These adapters can be installed into a workstation to offload the processing of multimedia data from the main processor in the workstation. A typical example is the Mwave adapter, which is actually a digital signal processor (DSP) developed by the Mwave alliance consisting of IBM, Texas Instruments, and Intermetrics. It is a special-purpose processor that runs the Mwave real-time operating system developed specially for the card. Mwave adapters are available from many vendors. The Mwave card can be programmed to have multiple functionality; for example, it can simultaneously be used as a modem and an audio decompression card. It can also be reprogrammed to support newer multimedia algorithms.

Multimedia processors. An alternative to the adapter is to enhance the processors in conventional workstations with special instructions for multimedia display. These instructions allow the multimedia display software to process the multimedia data more efficiently. A typical example is the multimedia extensions (MMX) instructions for the Intel family of processors. MMX comprises extensions to the instruction set of the Intel x86 family as well as design changes specifically for enhancing multimedia applications. The MMX extensions include 57 new instructions that parallelize commonly performed operations on byte data types. Byte data types are emphasized because they are widely used in many multimedia algorithms. For example, 16-bit audio samples and 8-bit graphic pixels are common. The multiply-accumulate operation is an example of an operation that is commonly used in many compression algorithms (such as the DCT of MPEG-1). For parallelism, the MMX instruction set permits parallel operation on 64 bit quantities at a time (e.g., load eight graphic pixels into a register and change the values simultaneously). However, these parallel operations use the x86's floating point registers. Hence, mixing multimedia and floating-point operations is not recommended. Design changes include larger processor caches. It is reported that the speed of applications that use MMX technology can be increased by up to four times.

2.3   Network Environment

One of the major factors driving the increase in multimedia applications is the growing interconnection of all computer systems into a single unified network. This has given client systems access to a vast collection of data sources; in fact, the Internet can be considered the largest reference library to have ever existed. To allow clients access to the vast amounts of data stored on the Internet, networks have to satisfy at least two requirements. First, transport mechanisms are needed to deliver the requests and data. Second, the data has to be distributed with the required performance. These requirements are satisfied differently depending on the network; for example, the solutions for a geographically distributed network, dealing with many different interconnection nodes and configurations, and those for a high-speed local area network will be different. We first describe the main types of networks and then the impact of the requirements of multimedia applications on the network environment and how various protocols are used to support these requirements.

Before the emergence of multimedia, many different types of networks had evolved, each fulfilling a particular need. The three network types were computer networks, telephone networks, and cable networks. Because of the relatively low bandwidth and reliability of the underlying communication medium, each network was specialized for its applications. For example, the technique of retransmitting lost data was commonly used in computer networks but was unacceptable for telephone networks (due to real-time requirements). Furthermore, cable networks carried purely analog signals due to the expenses associated with digital applications and clients.

The situation changed dramatically with the advent of optical fiber, which has a virtually unlimited bandwidth and extremely high reliability. It has become possible to support these diverse applications (e.g., telephony and computer communication) on the same infrastructure. Additionally, digital clients are becoming less expensive. These forces are leading to the unification of these three previously distinct networks. This, in turn, is leading to an explosion in the number of servers that can be accessed by clients, making multimedia applications more attractive.

2.3.1   Computer Networks

In describing how the networking requirements of multimedia applications can be satisfied, we first consider computer networks because the evolution of computer networks has been very rapid, and they have contributed much of the technology that underlies networking. From the point of view of an application, a computer network may appear as a single entity that delivers messages. In reality, the network is made up of many layers, with each layer providing services to the layer above. The exact decomposition into layers may depend on the protocol. One layering scheme developed by the International Standards Organization (ISO) is known as the Open Systems Interconnection (OSI) reference model. This was intended to be a universal model into which different networking standards could be mapped. We discuss this model because it clearly separates networking functions into standard layers. However, networks directly built on the OSI model have not found acceptance due to the inefficiency of strict decomposition into multiple layers. Later in this chapter, after an overview of the OSI model, we discuss in more detail some of the important layers. We also provide an overview of the ATM model, which is an alternative to the OSI model and is the model underlying ATM networks.

2.3.2   Telephone Networks

Telephone networks are the oldest of the three network types. They are also the most widespread, connecting both the business as well as the consumer environments. Figure 2.2 shows the star topology of a typical telephone network. Subscribers in homes are connected to a central office using twisted-pair copper cables. Bundles of cables fan out from the central office, with each bundle splitting into smaller bundles as they come closer to the home. Because the central office may not be close to the home, *repeaters* are used to amplify the signal at intermediate points. The central office is connected to the rest of the telephone network using fiber-optic cable.

Because they carry voice, telephone networks have developed a circuit-switched architecture that guarantees steady delivery of voice data. When a subscriber dials a telephone number, switches in the central office and telephone network cooperate to establish a shared physical circuit between the two ends. Older systems established a dedicated physical circuit. This circuit is torn down when the conversation ends.

The development of modern fiber technology led to an increase in the capacity of the telephone network. Because the telephone network connected the business as well as the consumer environment, it was felt that the uses of the network could be expanded. Two important new high-bandwidth applications proposed were data communications between industries as well as consumer applications

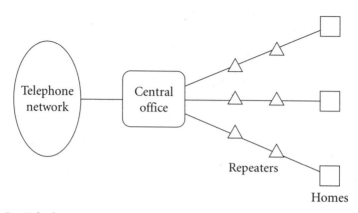

Figure 2.2   Telephone network topology.

such as video-on-demand to the home. However, these applications have very different characteristics. While voice transmission has relatively constant and low-bandwidth requirements, data communications has high but bursty bandwidth demands. The ATM technology (detailed later in this chapter) was developed with a view to efficiently supporting both types of requirements.

The ubiquity and age of the telephone network also led to a last-mile problem (bottlenecks occurring in the final part of the connection to the clients) in supporting high-bandwidth communications. As shown in the figure, subscribers are connected to the telephone network through twisted-pair copper lines. This is a relatively old technology with low bandwidth compared to fiber-optic cable. Due to the enormous number of subscribers, it would be prohibitively expensive to upgrade these lines to a higher-bandwidth connection. To solve this problem, telephone companies have developed the asymmetric digital subscriber line (ADSL) technology.

In summary, telephone networks faced two challenges in exploiting fiber-optic networks. These challenges were efficiently supporting traffic with varying requirements and delivering high-bandwidth data to consumer households over a low-bandwidth medium (the last-mile problem). The first problem is solved by ATM technology; ADSL technology is a solution to the second problem.

ADSL. Figure 2.3 illustrates the basic idea behind ADSL. ADSL divides the frequency range available over a telephone line into three channels. The lowest-frequency band is reserved for a telephone channel (plain old telephone service (POTS) channel). The POTS channel is created by POTS splitters that are directly connected to the telephone line. This allows the POTS channel to operate even if the ADSL modems fail. Advanced modulation techniques are used to provide a high-speed channel over the remaining frequency bands, which is possible due to the high quality of telephone lines over short distances.

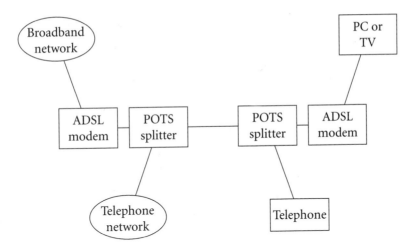

Figure 2.3 ADSL configuration.

The ADSL modems provide a medium-speed duplex channel and a high-speed unidirectional channel. The duplex channels can be used for control signals (e.g., play video and audio and responses), while the high-speed channel can be used for the actual multimedia data. The modems are available in various standard speed ranges, but the range available to a subscriber is limited by the maximum total bandwidth available on the wire. Due to the use of advanced modulation techniques, this is critically determined by the noise in the line. The noise is dependent upon many factors, such as the wire size, length of the wire connecting the telephone outlet to the telephone network, and cross-coupled interference. For example, with 0.4 mm wire, 2 Mbps is achievable with a wire length of 4.6 km, while 6 Mbps is achievable with a wire length of 2.7 km. The minimum configuration consists of a 16 Kbps duplex channel and a 1.5 Mbps high-speed channel.

2.3.3   Cable TV Networks

Cable TV networks form the third of the major network types. Because of their origin, they are most widespread in consumer environments. Figure 2.4 illustrates a typical cable TV network. From the figure, it can be seen that these networks contain a mixture of fiber-optic and coaxial cable links. Therefore, these networks are also referred to as *hybrid fiber coaxial (HFC)* networks. Cable networks have traditionally distributed analog television signals. However, by using cable modems, these networks can also be used to deliver digital signals. In the subscriber's home, the modems can be connected to a set-top box or to a PC. We will describe the topology of cable TV networks and then consider the bandwidth available.

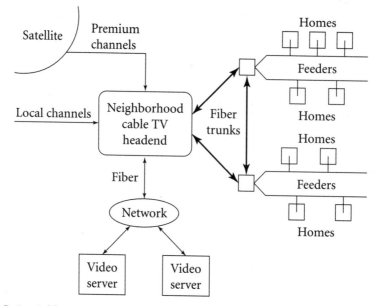

Figure 2.4 Cable TV network.

Cable TV network topology. At the hub of a typical HFC network is a cable TV headend (see Figure 2.4). Each headend distributes data over a wide geographical area (typically, a small town or suburb). The headend receives and combines signals from a variety of sources. These may include broadcast and premium channels received via satellite as well as local channels received directly. The headend may also be connected through high-speed links to computer networks. This allows the headend to connect subscribers to multimedia servers on a private computer network or the Internet.

The distribution network of a cable network follows a tree-and-branch topology. A number of fiber-optic trunks branch out from the headend. The trunks in turn distribute the cable TV signals to a number of feeders. Unlike the trunk lines, the feeder lines are made from coaxial cable. They pass physically close to the house of each subscriber. As they pass by each house, they are tapped to draw a signal to the house. Each feeder line typically serves between 500 and 2000 subscribers.

Cable feeder lines have a higher bandwidth than the twisted pair lines used in telephone networks. However, unlike telephone lines, which are dedicated to each subscriber, the feeder lines are shared among many subscribers. Therefore, each subscriber can receive only a fraction of the total bandwidth available. As we will see, this may not be a problem if the number of subscribers using digital service is small. As the number increases, it may be necessary to increase the number of feeder lines.

Cable TV network bandwidths. The total bandwidth available on feeder lines in HFC networks is typically around 750 MHz. This is divided into an upstream channel (from the subscriber to the headend) of 5 MHz to 42 MHz and a downstream channel of 54 MHz to 750 MHz. Each NTSC television channel requires a bandwidth of 6 MHz. Therefore, the downstream channel is divided into 116 TV channels. Many of these channels are currently unutilized. Using QAM technology, each 6 MHz channel can support an aggregate bandwidth of 30 Mbps. This is sufficient to support 7 MPEG-2 data streams of 4 Mbps or 20 MPEG-1 data streams of 1.5 Mbps. If half the channels are used to deliver analog TV signals and the other half are used for digital TV, each feeder line can support 406 MPEG-2 video streams or 1160 MPEG-1 video streams.

The upstream channel in HFC networks was originally intended to support pay-per-view access. Due to the fact that it is a noisy part of the RF spectrum, efficient modulation technologies such as QAM cannot be used. As a result, the aggregate bandwidth available on a single feeder line for upstream communication is only on the order of 2 Mbps. In contrast, the aggregate bandwidth available for downstream communication is 3480 Mbps, which is more than three orders of magnitude larger. The available upstream bandwidth has to be shared among all the subscribers on the feeder. While adequate for control signals, it is not sufficient for data transmission or applications like videoconferencing.

2.3.4   Other Network Types

We mention in passing some of the other network types that are no longer so popular. ISDN is a technology developed for telephone networks that offers speeds in the range of 56 Kbps to 128 Kbps. However, these speeds are lower than those offered by ADSL. Satellite systems typically offer bandwidths of around 400 Kbps. However, these systems are usable in the same environments as cable. The bandwidth available is lower than that available with cable modems; additionally, they require the installation of a dish antenna. Other wireless options, such as LMDS, are unlikely to become popular because of the increasing congestion in the radio frequency space.

2.3.5   Networking Transport and Distribution

The basic function of the network infrastructure is to connect the many different clients to the large number of available servers. This necessitates the development of networking protocols that allow any heterogeneous clients to retrieve data from any arbitrary servers. Different protocols have been developed for different network types; we describe these briefly in the next two sections.

After the basic requirement of connectivity is satisfied, clients must be able to retrieve the data from servers with satisfactory performance (i.e., QoS). One of the current well-known frustrations with using the World Wide Web is the slow response time during peak hours. In fact, as stated earlier, networking bottlenecks constitute one of the main inhibitors to the growth of multimedia applications. Without guaranteed bandwidth regardless of congestion in the network, video data may not be delivered on time, leading to glitches. Bandwidth availability is more challenging for multimedia applications because they require a comparatively high bandwidth. For example, as described in Chapter 1, a single MPEG-2 stream may require a bandwidth of 4 Mbps.

Networking bottlenecks can be classified into two categories: bottlenecks at the peripheral subnetworks and physical infrastructures that connect the large number of clients, and the bottleneck at the backbone network infrastructure that is responsible for distribution. The first type of bottleneck is referred to as the *last-mile problem* and is being overcome slowly due to the high cost of replacing the physical infrastructure connecting the large number of clients. The other type of bottleneck can be solved by upgrades because upgrading the distribution infrastructure is comparatively less expensive. In fact, a large fraction of the distribution network has already been upgraded in much of the world.

Bandwidth requirements in the distribution network can be reduced by the use of distribution or proxy servers [11, 62]. These are servers in the network that cache data. Because clients can be served directly from distribution servers, the bandwidth requirements on the network path from the actual server to the caching server are reduced. Proxy servers can also prefetch data, smoothing out bandwidth requirements of multimedia presentations with variable bandwidth [59, 20]. Bandwidth management methods in the network and video server are considered in greater detail in Chapter 4. Caching and prefetching of data are discussed more fully in Chapter 11.

2.4   OSI Model Overview

Figure 2.5 shows the layers of the OSI model. Their functions are briefly summarized here, with a more detailed discussion following later in the section. The physical-link layer is responsible for the actual transmission of data across a physical link, such as a telephone line. The data-link layer is responsible for the control of transmission over the (point-to-point) physical link. The network layer is responsible for routing of the message over multiple physical links on the network. The transport layer is responsible for end-to-end communication functions, such as

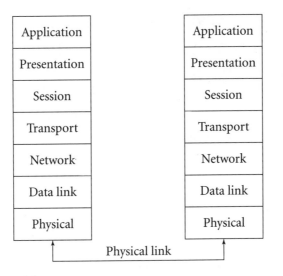

Figure 2.5 OSI model.

recovery from errors in transmission. The session layer is responsible for providing communication functions that span multiple user interactions. Finally, the presentation and application layers provide dialog functions such as control of video playback.

Under the OSI model, to deliver the message, each layer in the source node uses a predefined protocol to communicate with its peer in the destination node. The communication occurs as follows. Messages are delivered by the application at the source node to the highest layer. The message then travels down the different layers. Each layer in the source adds a header containing information for its peer in the destination. At the destination node, the message is received by the lowest layer. The message then travels up the layers, with each layer processing and stripping off the header added by its peer at the source.

A fundamental feature of the OSI model is the way in which it can accommodate heterogeneity in networks. For example, the same higher-level protocols can be supported on different lower-level protocols by changing the lower layer. Hence, the same higher-level protocols can run on different physical networks. Similarly, the same lower layers can support multiple sets of higher-layer protocols. In other words, the OSI model allows different higher-level protocols to share the same physical network. A set of protocol layers in a computer system is referred to as a *protocol stack*. We describe some of the important protocols in the different layers of the model next.

2.4.1   Physical Layer

The physical layer of the OSI model specifies protocols for the actual transmission of the data across the link. It specifies details such as the voltage levels to be used to signal 0 and 1 and the size and shape of the connectors to be used. Examples of physical layer standards are parts of the IEEE 802.3 standards for Ethernet, and the CCITT synchronous digital hierarchy standard that governs transmission of data over optical fiber. We do not discuss the physical layer further, since it is not important for our purposes.

2.4.2   Data-Link Layer

The data-link layer controls the transmission of data over the physical links in the network. Most computers today are physically connected to a local area network (LAN), which is in turn part of the Internet. Hence, we briefly describe Ethernet and token ring, the two most popular types of LAN protocols today. Following a brief description of each protocol, we consider their suitability for multimedia.

Ethernet. Ethernet was one of the earliest LAN protocols to be developed and today remains one of the most popular. Figure 2.6(a) illustrates the basic principle behind Ethernet. The figure shows five computers (also called stations) physically interconnected by a cable. Most computers are interconnected today using a coaxial cable–based standard that allows a maximum bandwidth of 10 Mbps. However, a fast Ethernet standard with a maximum bandwidth of 100 Mbps exists. Work is also progressing on a gigabit Ethernet standard with a bandwidth of 1 Gbps. Therefore, Ethernet bandwidths are increasing very rapidly.

The operation of Ethernet is as follows. When a computer wants to transmit a message, it first listens on the LAN to see if the LAN is free. When the LAN is free,

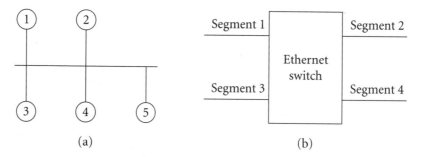

(a)   (b)

Figure 2.6 Ethernet protocol showing its basic principle (a) and the variant, switched Ethernet (b).

it begins to transmit the message. While transmitting, it needs to check if some other computer had simultaneously decided to begin transmission. This is referred to as a *collision*. To detect collisions, the transmitting computer listens to the message received on the LAN while transmitting. If a collision has occurred, the received message will not be identical to the transmitted message. Because of transmission delays on the cable, collisions may be detected only some time after transmission has started. When a collision occurs, all transmitters suspend transmission for a random period of time. Because of the random interval, one of the transmitters will succeed after a while. If repeated attempts at transmission fail, the average suspension time is increased exponentially. This is called *exponential backoff*. Due to the reliance on collisions for regulating access, the maximum achievable utilization for Ethernet is on the order of 25%.

Token ring. Figure 2.7 illustrates the other common LAN protocol, known as the *token ring* protocol. Its operation is defined by the IEEE 802.5 standard and is as follows. In a token ring, the processors are connected together into a logical ring by connecting each processor to its neighbors. A token circulates among the processors in the ring. The token is actually a small message consisting entirely of a message header in a predefined format. When a processor receives the token, it can transmit a message on the token ring to its neighboring node. After transmitting waiting messages, it retransmits the token. To prevent a processor from monopolizing the ring, there is a limit to the amount of data that can be transmitted in one turn. A processor that has no data to transmit simply retransmits the token.

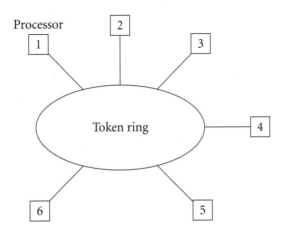

Figure 2.7   Token ring protocol.

Processors in the ring relay all messages to their neighbors. This relaying is done entirely in the token ring adapter without any involvement of the rest of the system. Thus, the token, together with messages, circulates around the ring. When a processor sees a message destined for itself, it first copies the message. Then, to signal the sender that the message was received, it retransmits the message after turning on a flag bit in the header. The message continues to circulate around the ring until it reaches the source node. The source node examines the flag bit to check if the message was received. It then deletes the message from the ring by not relaying it. If a node does not receive a message that it originated within a predetermined time, it assumes the message was lost.

Conventional token rings operate at 4 Mbps and 16 Mbps. Unlike Ethernet, very high utilizations (on the order of 75%) are achievable. A variant of token ring, called fiber distributed data interface (FDDI), operates over optical fiber at speeds of up to 100 Mbps. FDDI networks are common in campus environments and office buildings for interconnecting LANs.

Multimedia support. We now consider the suitability of Ethernet and token ring networks for multimedia. Recall that the main networking requirements for multimedia are its high bandwidth and the need for bandwidth reservation for streams. Ethernet bandwidths are increasing very rapidly, which allows support of high-quality video and audio. However, from our discussion it can also be seen that supporting bandwidth reservation for video and audio streams on the Ethernet is difficult. This is because there is no mechanism for preventing interference between a video stream with a reserved bandwidth and a nonmultimedia stream (such as a large file transfer) with no reserved bandwidth. In the case of a collision, both streams will suspend transmission and either transmission may succeed. Even if priority is added to give streams with reserved bandwidth a higher chance of success, there is the problem that the delay for access to the Ethernet is not bounded. A video stream attempting transmission may repeatedly collide with other video streams, leading to an unbounded delay.

Token ring protocol, on the other hand, prevents monopolization of the token ring by any node and shares the token ring bandwidth. Additionally, it has a priority messaging facility that can be used to provide preferential service to real-time streams. Hence, it is easier to implement quality of service on token rings. However, the token ring protocol is more complex; it requires mechanisms other than the basic mechanism we have described. These include, for example, error recovery mechanisms for regenerating the token if it is lost. As a result, the cost of token ring installations is typically higher than that of Ethernet installations. Hence, the token ring protocol is not as widely used as Ethernet.

The effective bandwidth of Ethernet can be enhanced by a variant known as switched Ethernet, shown in Figure 2.6(b). In switched Ethernet, the Ethernet

LAN is divided into a number of segments, and the segments are connected to the Ethernet switch. When the switch detects a message from a computer on one segment to a computer on another segment, it connects the two segments. Assuming that the bandwidth of each segment is 10 Mbps, multiple 10 Mbps transmissions can be in progress at the same time. Hence, the effective bandwidth of the LAN can be increased with only a small number of stations per segment.

2.4.3 Network Layer

Computer networks are geographically distributed and may include many data links. Messages will typically have to traverse many data links to reach their destination. Routing the data over the various data links is the function of the network layer. Hence, the network layer must include functions for uniquely naming the source and destination of every message and for selecting a route between the source and destination. In nonmultimedia networks, routes are selected so as to minimize the latency for message delivery. The route selected is not necessarily the shortest route because the links on the shortest route may be heavily loaded. Additionally, since the loads may also fluctuate with time, route selection in nonmultimedia networks is a complex problem. Route selection in multimedia networks is even more complex because bandwidth availability on the various links also has to be considered.

Due to the popularity of the Internet, the TCP/IP protocol has become by far the most widely used communication protocol. Consequently, we focus on the network layer of this protocol, known as the *Internet Protocol (IP)*. The IP protocol is a packet-switched, connectionless protocol. Packet-switched networks are networks where messages are transmitted over the network in fragments known as *packets*. Additionally, the packets are routed independently through the network by *routers* (described in detail below). Each IP router in the network has a maximum packet size that it supports; 4 KB is supported by almost all routers. Reassembly of messages from packets happens at the destination node. The IP protocol is also a connectionless protocol because it does not require any setup between source and destinations before packets are transmitted. However, multimedia applications need functions such as bandwidth reservation that are performed during connection setup. In an IP network, these functions have also to be provided by higher layers.

We will provide a brief overview of the IP protocol. The current version of IP is known as IPv4 [13, 49, 44, 42, 43], and the newer version is known as IPv6 [23]. Here, we focus mainly on IPv4. We first provide a brief overview of naming and routing in IP networks and then discuss IP multicast routing, an important feature of the IP protocol for multimedia.

Naming. Each node in an IP network has associated with it a unique IP address. This is a 32-bit integer, normally represented as four 8-bit integers separated by dots (e.g., 193.07.25.12). This address can be decomposed into a network id, and a host id within the network. In the original IP addressing scheme, the size of the network id was 8, 16, or 24 bits, with the rest of the bits representing nodes in the network. The size of the network id was determined by examining the first few bits of the IP address. However, the static partitioning of IP addresses into various classes led to a shortage of IP addresses of some types. As a result, IPv6 addresses are larger and use a different scheme. The current IPv4 addressing scheme (the Classless Interdomain Routing (CIDR) scheme) allows the network and host id sizes to be completely variable. The size of the network id field is indicated by a separate field.

For convenience, each node in the IP network also has a name. By convention, the name has a hierarchical structure with the components separated by periods. Names are translated into IP addresses by domain name servers (DNS).

Routing. Routing in an IP network is performed by routers. Typically, routers work under stringent performance requirements for routing large numbers of packets and handling large numbers of connections. Hence, routers tend to be special-purpose processors running customized software [12].

Routers maintain information about the state of the network in routing tables. This information is used to compute an optimum route. A commonly used algorithm is Dijkstra's shortest-path algorithm [13]. To take varying link loads and capacities into account, the weighted lengths of the paths can be used. Routers also need to exchange information about changes in network topology and state. The earliest such protocols were distance vector protocols (e.g., RIP [41]) that periodically exchanged routing tables. However, such protocols were found to be inefficient because they exchanged information even when there was no change. The more recent link-state protocols (e.g., OSPF [45]) exchange information only when changes in link state occur.

Other major components of the IP are the Address Resolution Protocol (ARP) for binding IP addresses to physical network addresses as well as protocols for signaling errors in transmission. Details can be found in [13].

IP multicast and MBone. Many multimedia applications, such as videoconferencing and video-on-demand, require transmission of the same material to multiple clients. In a conventional network, the sender would have to repeatedly transmit the data block to each client. Significant improvements in efficiency can be achieved by allowing the sender to specify multiple recipients for each data block. The network would then be responsible for duplicating the data block as required for delivery to the multiple clients. This is referred to as *multicast*. Multicast is also important for some non-real-time applications that have the same characteristics.

An example is software distribution, where large files have to be transmitted to many clients.

IP multicast is implemented in the Internet by multicast routers, which are routers that also support multicast. The basic idea is illustrated in Figure 2.8. The figure shows a single sender transmitting a multicast stream to multiple receivers. Multicast transmissions are recognized by examining the first few bits of the destination IP address, which will be 1110. The figure shows that the routers attached to the senders and the receivers have configured themselves into a multicast tree which allows efficient data transmission. Each router transmits the received data to the receivers in its domain as well as to its descendants in the multicast tree. Note that the network between two multicast routers need not be a network that supports multicast. For routing across nonmulticast networks, each router in the tree encapsulates the message into a unicast message addressed to the next multicast router.

The formation of multicast groups, and membership and exit from multicast groups, is not part of the IP protocol. This function is handled by higher-level protocols such as IGMP [22, 26], RTSP [55], and H.323 [34].

The MBone [40, 25] is a set of multicast routers that provide a "multicast backbone" for the Internet. The MBone started in 1992, when a group of researchers decided to hold a videoconference over the Internet. By 1994, the MBone had grown to cover 1700 subnetworks spread over 20 countries. The MBone has been used for a variety of purposes, including holding IETF meetings and

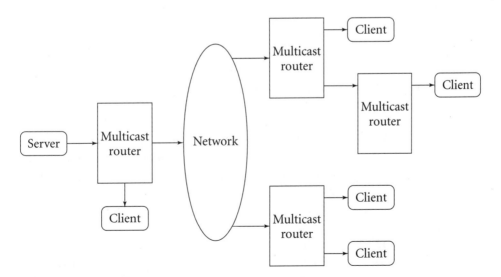

Figure 2.8 IP multicast.

broadcasting rock concerts. The success of these transmissions has proved the viability of IP multicast.

2.4.4 Transport Layer

The network layer is responsible for delivery of single messages over multiple data links in a network; however, it does not provide any reliability guarantees. The transport layer provides the additional functions necessary. Flow control may be required to ensure that the sender does not cause overload either in the receiver or intermediate nodes. If the network layer can deliver packets out of order, the transport layer has to guarantee in-order delivery. Finally, the transport layer has to provide error recovery.

Two transport-layer protocols are commonly found on the Internet layered on top of IP. These are the Transmission Control Protocol (TCP) and the User Datagram Protocol (UDP). TCP is a connection-oriented protocol in which the sender and receiver establish a connection before transmission of messages. For regulating the rate of transmission, TCP provides two mechanisms. Flow control ensures matching of transmission rates between fast senders and slow receivers and vice versa. Congestion control based upon estimated network congestion is also provided. If congestion is detected in the network, TCP congestion control will delay message transmissions. The motivation behind this is to reduce the congestion by slowing down all the senders. TCP also provides reliable delivery via retransmission of lost messages. In contrast, UDP provides only minimal functionality in addition to IP.

Multimedia support. For multimedia applications, UDP may be the appropriate protocol for transmission of data and TCP the appropriate protocol for transmission of control messages between clients and multimedia servers. TCP flow control, congestion control, and error recovery may not be appropriate for transmission of multimedia data. As we will see later, multimedia protocols already ensure that senders and receivers negotiate a transmission rate. By delaying real-time packets when network load is high, TCP flow control may cause glitches in the client display. Instead, multimedia applications may prefer to be notified of the congestion so that they can switch to a lower-quality video with a lower transmission rate. TCP error recovery is not suitable for video data because video data has a high redundancy and can tolerate occasional loss. For audio data, the latency involved in retransmission may be unacceptably high. Hence, TCP error recovery simply puts an additional burden on the network. However, the flow control and error recovery may be appropriate for control messages, which are less sensitive to delay and must be delivered reliably. For transmission of multimedia data, applications may prefer to use UDP together with higher-level multimedia protocols that provide flow control and error recovery.

TCP and UDP are general Internet transport protocols; the Real-time Transport Protocol (RTP) is a transport protocol tailored to the delivery of multimedia data [54]. RTP provides functionality important for multimedia applications, such as timestamping and sequence numbering of messages. The RTP header also identifies the type of data carried in the packet. This allows packets of different types to be treated differently in the network. For example, routers in intermediate nodes could choose to ignore transmission errors in video data while trying to recover from transmission errors in audio data.

2.4.5   Session, Presentation, and Application Layers

The session, presentation, and application layers are responsible for maintaining user sessions across multiple interactions as well as user dialog functions. For multimedia applications, this includes maintaining the state of the user session, controlling the display of multimedia data, and reserving the required bandwidth. We describe three important multimedia protocols. The Real-Time Streaming Protocol (RTSP) is an important protocol for controlling video-on-demand applications over the Internet. The Reservation Protocol (RSVP) is used for reserving bandwidth on the Internet, and the H.323 standard proposed by the International Telecommunications Union is rapidly becoming a standard for videoconferencing.

RTSP. The RTSP protocol is intended to be used by clients to request playback of video presentations or video clips from multimedia servers. The protocol contains commands for opening and closing sessions with a multimedia server as well as playback control commands. RTSP can run on top of any of the three transport protocols (TCP, UDP, RTP), and it supports multicast as well as unicast. Clients can also simultaneously request multiple audio-video streams as part of the same presentation.

The operation of the protocol is illustrated in Figure 2.9. Initially, the client and server establish a TCP connection. The client then sends a `Setup` command to the server specifying the desired video presentation (typically specified as a URL). The server makes any resource allocations needed (such as reserving memory buffers) and returns an acknowledgment. Next, the client sends a `Describe` command requesting a description of the presentation. The `Describe` command also contains a description of the protocols the client is willing to use for data transmission (typically RTP/UDP). In return, the server returns a description of the streams in the presentation and other information, such as the ports on which each stream will be available. The client can then request playback. The client may either send a `Play` command specifying the presentation or multiple `Play`

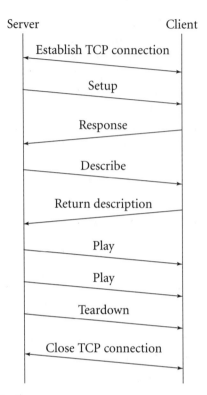

Figure 2.9 RTSP illustration.

commands specifying individual streams. In the first case, the server starts transmission of the entire presentation; in the second case, the server transmits each individual stream upon receipt of the corresponding command. Synchronization of the various streams is the responsibility of the client. Finally, the client sends a Teardown command to end the session and then terminates the TCP connection.

RSVP. The Reservation Protocol (RSVP) can be used by applications to reserve bandwidth in the network for the delivery of multimedia streams. It is designed to work in both unicast and multicast environments, the only difference being that in multicast environments, an application issues RSVP commands to reserve bandwidth after it has joined a multicast group. As stated earlier, this can be done using one of the group membership protocols (such as IGMP). We describe the operation of RSVP in the general case of multicast. The operation in a unicast environment can be inferred as a special case.

Figure 2.10 illustrates the operation of RSVP. The figure shows a multicast transmission in progress involving five routers (Router 1–Router 5) and five

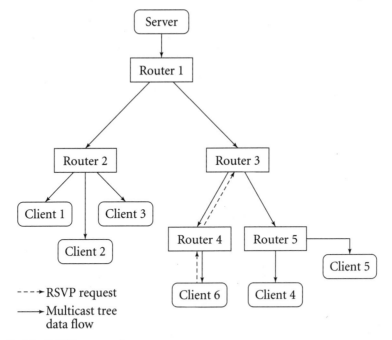

Figure 2.10 RSVP protocol.

clients (Client 1–Client 5). A new client trying to reserve bandwidth (such as Client 6) invokes RSVP after joining the multicast group. It does this by sending an RSVP request to the server on the proposed delivery path to the server. This request is processed by all the routers on the path. Hence, to reserve the bandwidth, it is necessary that all the routers support RSVP.

When a router receives an RSVP request, it takes two actions. First, it attempts to make the required reservation on the downstream path to the client. If the reservation cannot be made, an error is propagated back to the client. In this case, the client may try an alternative path. If the reservation is successful, the router forwards the request to the next upstream router. This may not be required in a multicast environment if the router is already receiving the requested stream. In this situation (illustrated at Router 3 in the figure), the router need not forward the request as upstream reservations have already been made for the existing multicast. After a successful reservation, the client receives a message specifying the path through the network on which the reservations have been made.

H.323. H.323 is actually a set of related standards for videoconferencing over the Internet. It includes standards such as T.120 for collaborative computing, the

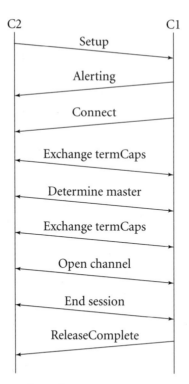

Figure 2.11   H.323 videoconferencing setup.

H.261 video compression standard, and the H.235 security standard. We describe typical H.245 and Q.931 signaling used to establish a videoconferencing session.

Figure 2.11 shows the typical exchange of messages between two clients (called *terminals* in H.323 terminology), C1 and C2, that want to establish a session. We describe the extensions needed to set up a multipoint conference among more than two clients later. One of the clients, C1, sends a `Setup` message to C2 requesting a session. C2 responds with `Alerting` and `Connect` messages that establish a connection between the clients. Next, the clients determine the type of data each client can receive and select a master for the session. To determine the type of data that can be sent, the clients exchange (`termCapSet`, `termCapAck`) message pairs. The `termCapSet` message specifies the capabilities (e.g., compression standards, bit-rates) supported by the client, and the `termCapAck` message is an acknowledgment. Master selection is accomplished by exchanging messages containing a random number.

The clients can then set up one or more simplex logical channels for transmission of multimedia data. The client wanting to create the channel sends an openReq requesting a channel. The other client then sends an openAck confirming the channel. Videoconferencing continues until one of the clients sends an endSession request. The other client then confirms the end by sending a endSession request. Finally, the first client sends a ReleaseComplete message.

Two types of multipoint videoconferences are supported by H.323. The first kind of videoconference is a peer-to-peer conference set up directly between the participants. In the second type, an entity called a *master control unit (MCU)* is responsible for setting up and managing the conference. As discussed in Chapter 1, it is advantageous to have an MCU because it reduces the complexity required in the clients. Additionally, data traffic is reduced because all of the clients can transmit data to the MCU, which can combine the data and retransmit to all of the clients. Finally, during retransmission, the MCU can also tailor the data to the client. For example, if one of the clients can receive only low bit-rate data, the MCU may send only one of the streams. The procedures used to set up these two different types of multipoint videoconferences differ slightly. To set up a peer-to-peer multipoint conference, each pair of clients exchanges the setup messages described earlier. In conferences where there is an MCU, each client simply establishes a session with the MCU, which is then responsible for managing the videoconference.

2.5   ATM Model

ATM networks are built upon a layered architecture similar to the OSI reference model discussed earlier. This architecture, called the *ATM reference model,* is shown in Figure 2.12(a). The physical layer of the ATM reference architecture corresponds to the physical layer of the OSI model. The physical layer is responsible for the transmission of data, which is transmitted in the form of ATM cells. The ATM layer is responsible for the routing of ATM cells over the network. Finally, the adaptation layer is responsible for interfacing to higher-level protocols. This includes disassembly and reassembly of messages into ATM cells. These layers are described in more detail in the following sections. More detailed descriptions can be found in [39].

2.5.1   ATM Layer

The operation of the ATM layer has been designed for maximum efficiency; thus it is very simple. An ATM network consists of a number of interconnected ATM switches. Before sending data, the sender establishes a connection path to the receiver. As part of the setup, each switch on the path stores routing information regarding the connection in switching tables. This information is used to efficiently switch incoming ATM cells to their destination. Any bandwidth reservation or

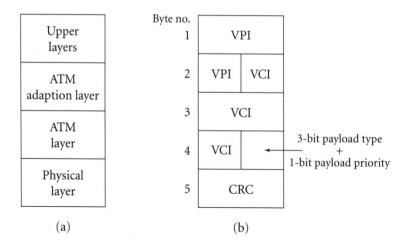

Figure 2.12 ATM reference model showing the layered architecture (a) and the header format (b).

latency required is specified during connection setup as well. The switches on the path perform any resource reservations required to satisfy these requirements.

2.5.2   ATM Cells

Figure 2.12(b) shows the format of ATM cells. The cell consists of a 5-byte header followed by 48 bytes of data. The fixed, small size of the cells facilitates efficient utilization of the network. The 16-bit virtual circuit identifier (VCI) field identifies the connection. It is used to index into the switching tables to retrieve the identifier of the next switch on the path. Groups of connections to the same endpoint can be bundled into virtual paths. These are identified by the 12-bit virtual path identifier (VPI) field. The notion of virtual paths facilitates some forms of error recovery. For example, if a particular switch on a virtual path fails, the VPI makes it easier to find all connections using the failed path. The VPI and VCI are local to each switch and are replaced by each switch on the path before transmission to the next switch. Finally, there is a 3-bit payload type field and an 8-bit CRC for the header.

2.5.3   ATM Adaptation Layer

ATM networks were intended to carry many different types of messages with different characteristics, ranging from voice to high-speed file transfer. These different types of messages may also have different requirements. The ATM adaptation layers define the mapping of these different message types into ATM cells.

Five ATM adaptation layers—AAL1 through AAL5—were originally defined for different types of applications. Of these, AAL3 and AAL4 were found to be very similar and were merged into a common standard called AAL3/4. AAL5 is the layer commonly used for computer applications. The current ATM adaptation layers are

- **AAL1**   Constant bit-rate streams

- **AAL2**   Variable bit-rate streams

- **AAL3/4** Connection-oriented and connectionless data streams

- **AAL5**   A simplified adaptation layer for data streams with less functionality than AAL3/4

2.6   Summary

The multimedia server environment can be considered to consist of clients and networks. Clients are responsible for interacting with the user, retrieving the multimedia data, and displaying it. Before display, the multimedia data needs to be decompressed. Decompression can be performed either in hardware or by software. There are many different client types depending on the application environment. In the business environment, clients tend to be modified workstations. In the consumer environment, where price and ease of use are important, clients tend to be special-purpose systems.

Networking bottlenecks constitute a major inhibitor to the growth of multimedia applications. Bottlenecks in distribution can be reduced by the use of prefetching and caching proxy servers. There are three major types of networks that may be important for multimedia applications. These are computer, telephone, and cable networks. Due to the evolution of networking technology, these three networks are tending to converge into a common network. The common network may support flexible and highly functional protocols (e.g., TCP/IP, RTSP) derived from computer networks. The basic infrastructure may consist of a high-speed fabric such as ATM. For solving the last-mile problem, ADSL or cable modems may be used.

Further Reading

The TCP/IP protocol is basic to the Internet; a detailed description of the protocol and its implementation can be found in [13]. The IPv6 protocol is described in [23], and ATM is covered in [39]. RTSP is described in [55] and H.323 in [34]. The RSVP protocol for end-to-end resource reservation is described in [10].

3

Multimedia Server Architecture and Components

3.1 Introduction

In the previous two chapters, we discussed the various types of multimedia applications that may be important in the future and the environment in which these applications may be deployed. We now describe a general multimedia server architecture and the hardware and software components that support such applications and environments. The software components of this architecture (e.g., scheduling, storage management, caching) are explored in further detail in subsequent chapters.

3.1.1 Simple Multimedia Server Architecture

Figure 3.1 illustrates a typical architecture for a multimedia server. The storage subsystem stores the multimedia data. It may contain devices of different types (e.g, disks, CDs) with different characteristics. An efficient and cost-effective server design exploits the differences in device characteristics as well as in costs. Similarly, the design process considers alternative network subsystems that can be used for the transmission of multimedia data to the clients.

The software processes executing in the processor subsystem are responsible for the management and operation of the multimedia server [21]. The application server receives application commands from the client. As discussed in Chapter 1, multimedia applications can be quite diverse. They may range from interactive applications that retrieve many small multimedia objects (e.g., shopping or medical applications) to videoconferencing applications involving many geographically distributed users [27, 50, 38]. Generally, there will be one application server

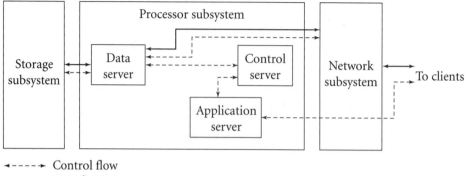

◄----► Control flow
◄----► Data flow

Figure 3.1 Architecture of a simple multimedia server.

per application (e.g., a videoconference manager for videoconferencing). Therefore, application commands are likely to be application specific (e.g., `join videoconference`). The application server converts these application commands into multimedia server commands for displaying specific images or video files.

The multimedia server commands are next received by the control server. The control server has three major functions. First, there are many control decisions that need to be made before the multimedia data can flow. For example, sufficient system and network resources need to be reserved for this request to be served [15]. If the resources are not reserved already for this application instance, or if enough resources are not available at present, the current request has to wait. This is referred to as *admission control* policy. During the process of reserving these resources, it may be necessary to decide which of several network adapters to use for delivering the data to the client. Or it may be necessary to decide whether to deliver the data from cache or disk. Because these control decisions are all interrelated, it is preferable to make them in a unified framework. As will be seen in later chapters, many of these decisions are actually optimizations that have an important impact on the overall efficiency of the multimedia server. For example, before delivering the data from cache, it is necessary to decide which videos to cache. Therefore, the second function of the control server is to perform various optimizations that increase overall server efficiency. The third function of the control server, in more complex configurations, is to hide the complexity of the configuration from the application server [15]. For example, there may be multiple data servers, each with a specific set of videos. In this case, after receiving the multimedia server command, the control server picks an appropriate data server. This relieves the application server of the burden of keeping track of the data servers and which video is on which data server.

Finally, the data server is responsible for the actual retrieval and delivery of the multimedia data. Recall from Chapter 1 that a major distinguishing characteristic of multimedia applications is their QoS requirements. These may include delivery bandwidth guarantees as well as bounds on delay. Providing data delivery while satisfying the QoS requirements is perhaps the most important function of the data server.

3.1.2   Distributed Multimedia Server Architecture

The simple multimedia server in Figure 3.1 is limited by the capacity available through a single system. For example, the amount of storage available is determined by the number of disks that can be attached to a single system. For larger systems, it is necessary to build a distributed multimedia server from simple servers.

Distributed multimedia servers will have the same hardware and software components as simple servers (e.g., storage subsystem, processor subsystem with application, control, and data servers). However, the various subcomponents, which can be arranged in many different ways (i.e., via hardware topologies and software algorithms), need to be orchestrated in order to make them act as a single, efficient large server. Each arrangement of components may result in different sets of advantages and disadvantages. Consider, for example, the distributed multimedia server illustrated in Figure 3.2. It consists of a number of independent simple multimedia servers connected to a network. Although this server has a larger capacity than that of the constituent servers, it may suffer from load imbalance among the individual servers. As a result, the capacity of the lightly loaded servers may be wasted.

One solution to this problem is to implement a load-balancing policy among the individual servers. This may, however, require additional hardware in the form of a data path among the constituent servers for copying video files. Furthermore, a distributed control server that spans the individual servers and implements the load-balancing policy may also be required. Hence, it is possible to achieve greater efficiency but at the cost of additional hardware as well as additional complexity in software. In designing a distributed multimedia server, it is important to consider these trade-offs.

Large-scale servers constructed out of smaller components do enjoy as well some benefits from economies of scale [15]. For example, multiple client requests for the same media component can be batched together and served with a single retrieval stream [19]. In the event the client requests for the same continuous media segment cannot be batched, a small running buffer can be used to cache the data retrieved by a preceding client data stream for serving the following client

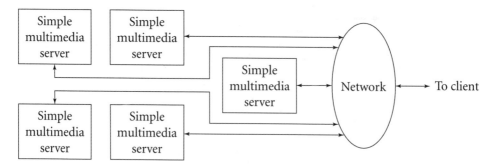

Figure 3.2   Architecture of a distributed multimedia server.

stream. This is referred to as *interval caching* [18]. Many other such optimizations are possible when a large number of clients are served by a single logical multimedia server. These algorithms will be addressed in greater detail in subsequent chapters as we cover the various software functions—scheduling, storage management, caching.

The design of a large-scale server also needs to address the issue of nonhomogeneity of the components. For example, it is difficult to achieve good utilization of both bandwidth and storage capacities of heterogeneous devices via well-known techniques—striping, for example, where the successive blocks of a single file are placed uniformly across the devices. The aspects of the design that handle such complex issues distinguish large-scale multimedia servers from simple video servers and are the main focus of this book.

In the rest of this chapter, we describe the hardware components of a multimedia server, such as the storage subsystem and the processor subsystem, focusing on understanding the impact of component characteristics on the server design. We then discuss in more detail the software components, such as the control and data servers. Because QoS support is an important function of the software components, the discussion includes issues relating to specifying QoS requirements and QoS support. Finally, we discuss common distributed server topologies and the resulting benefits and disadvantages.

3.2   Multimedia Server Hardware

In this section, we describe the hardware components of multimedia servers and their characteristics. As stated earlier, only the characteristics that may have an impact on server design are considered. The structure of disks, for example, strongly influences the policies for disk management. We focus on the components in the storage and processor subsystems. A detailed discussion of networking components is intimately connected with broad networking issues and is beyond the scope of this book. A brief overview of the networking components, however, has already been provided in Chapter 2.

Figure 3.3 shows the typical hardware components of a simple multimedia server. Multimedia data is stored on the various storage devices, which are connected to the processor through device interfaces or controllers. Device interfaces provide two important functions. First, the storage device may contain mechanical components, and therefore may be much slower than the processor. The storage interfaces buffer the data and provide matching of speed required for data transfer. Second, as we will see later, a sequence of commands may be needed to retrieve a single block from a storage device. The controller allows the processor to send the sequence of commands to the controller, relieving the processor of this burden. Because multimedia data travels through the controllers, the performance of the I/O subsystem is heavily influenced by the performance of the controllers, not just the storage devices.

The controllers are connected, in turn, to the processor. The internal architecture of the processor determines the precise manner in which the controllers are connected. Therefore, the processor architecture also has a strong impact on the performance of the I/O subsystem. We discuss some common processor architectures later in this chapter.

In discussing the characteristics of the various hardware devices, we concentrate on three primary measures. The first two measures, storage capacity and access time, apply only to storage devices. The storage capacity of the device is

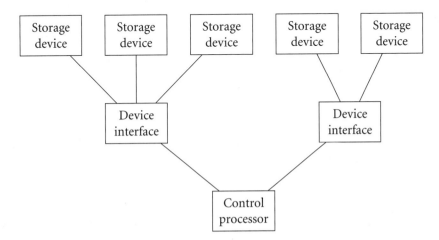

Figure 3.3 Multimedia server hardware.

important because multimedia files are large. The access time, the delay between the time the device receives the command to read or store multimedia data and the time the device actually begins to read or store the data, is important for two reasons. First, devices with large access times may not be suitable for interactive applications where quick response time is needed. Second, large access times also reduce effective data transfer rates. Consider the retrieval of successive blocks from the same device. Because no data is transferred during the access time, the larger the access time, the smaller the effective data retrieval rate. The third measure we consider is the bandwidth (i.e., data transfer rate) of the device—the maximum data rate that the device can deliver. The bandwidth has an important influence on QoS support. For example, if a device has a bandwidth of 10 MB/s and an application requires a bandwidth of 0.5 MB/s, the device will not be able to support more than 20 instances of the application.

3.2.1   Disks

Disks are currently the most common storage device in multimedia servers. This is due to the combination of their relatively high storage capacities and performance with relatively low cost. The performance characteristics of disk devices are dictated by their physical construction. We will describe the internal construction of a typical disk and show how the physical features determine the disk performance characteristics.

Disk Construction

Figure 3.4 shows the structure of a typical disk [5]. Data is stored on a number of stacked, magnetically coated aluminum platters mounted on a common spindle. Currently, it is common for platters to be 2.5 inches or 3.5 inches in diameter. During operation, these platters rotate at high speed (typically, 3600 or 7200 RPM), and data is read or written by a set of read/write heads. These heads do not touch the disk surface, but actually float on the cushion of air produced by the rotating disk platters. Amazingly, the height at which the heads float is around 2 to 7 millionths of an inch. In comparison, the width of a human hair is around 3 thousandths of an inch.

Data is recorded magnetically on both surfaces of each platter in concentric circles known as *tracks*. Each surface has its own read/write head, which moves in synchronism over the stacked platters. Therefore, at any given position, the heads can access two tracks on each platter. This set of tracks is referred to as a *cylinder*. The cylinders are numbered sequentially, with the outermost cylinder normally

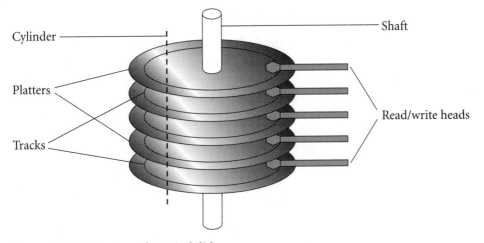

Figure 3.4   Structure of a typical disk.

being cylinder 0. The tracks are broken down into blocks for data storage and addressing information. Each block, together with the addressing information, is referred to as a *sector*. The addressing information allows the disk electronics to quickly locate any given sector. Most disks have sectors that are capable of holding 512 bytes. Sectors are also numbered sequentially. Therefore, each sector on the disk can be uniquely identified by a cylinder number and a sector number; these constitute the address of the sector.

Because the outer cylinders of a disk have a larger circumference than the inner cylinders, they can store more data. In spite of this, for simplicity, earlier disks used to store the same amount of data in each cylinder. More recent disks store different amounts of data in each cylinder and are referred to as *multizone* disks. Because the velocity of the disk increases as the heads travel to the outer cylinders, the data transfer rate (or the disk bandwidth) at the outer cylinders is greater than that at the inner cylinders.

The operation of a typical disk is as follows. Assume that a particular block of data from a multimedia file is to be read. The server software converts this into a list of blocks to be read and then commands the disk head to position itself at the cylinder number of the first sector to be read. The operation of positioning is referred to as a *seek*. After the seek to the required cylinder, it is necessary to wait for the platters to rotate until the desired sector passes under one of the read/write heads. The time it takes for the disk to rotate is called the *rotation latency*. Once the starting position is reached, the data can then be read or written.

Disk Storage Capacities and Bandwidths

The storage capacities and bandwidths of some typical disks are shown in Table 3.1. In comparison, the bandwidth required by a typical MPEG-2 video is 0.5 MB/s. From this, we can calculate that the storage space required by a typical 90-minute movie is around 3 GB. Thus, disks are able to easily store multiple MPEG-2 videos and deliver many MPEG-2 streams. (MPEG-2 is a high-bandwidth, high-quality video.) Hence, we can conclude that disk capacities and bandwidths are more than adequate to store and deliver the popular lower-bandwidth video formats.

Disk Access Times

The preceding description of how disks operate shows that there are two delay overheads before a sector of data on a disk can be accessed. The first delay, which occurs while the disk is seeking to the required cylinder, is called the *seek time*. Currently, the average and maximum seek time for typical disks is around 7 ms and 15 ms, respectively. In most cases, it may be reasonable to assume that, on average, one will have to wait for half a revolution of the disk. Hence, the average rotational latency will normally be half the maximum rotational latency. For a 7200 RPM disk, these will be 4.2 ms and 8.3 ms, respectively. The total access time for a disk is therefore around 11 ms, which is imperceptible, and so disks are very well suited for the storage of multimedia data that is to be accessed interactively.

   We next consider the implications of the access time for disk management. The seek time is the time it takes for the head to move from the current cylinder to the cylinder of the desired sector. Clearly, the time taken for the seek depends upon the relative positions of the starting and ending cylinders. If the next sector is in the same cylinder as the first sector, it can be read with no additional seek time overhead. In this case, only a rotational latency may be incurred. If the next sector sequentially follows the previous sector on the disk, there is, as well, no additional rotational latency.

Table 3.1 Typical disk storage capacities and bandwidths.

Disk	Storage capacity (GB)	Bandwidth (MB/s)
IBM Ultrastar 18LZX	18.2	17.5–23.5
Quantum Viking II	9.1	14
Seagate Barracuda 9LP	4.55	10.8–17.0

Two conclusions can be drawn from the preceding discussion. First, the overhead incurred (i.e., seek time and rotational latency) depends upon the order in which the disk sectors are accessed. Second, disks are extremely efficient at accessing contiguous data because there is no additional seek time or rotational latency overhead once the starting position is reached. Disk scheduling that addresses both of these factors is an important issue in multimedia server design.

Additional performance characteristics are relevant for multizone disks. Because the rotational time is identical for all cylinders but the outer cylinders store more data, the transfer rate from the outer cylinder is higher. More efficient retrieval can be accomplished if frequently used files are stored in the outer cylinders. For this, it is necessary to know the transfer rate of each cylinder. For simplicity, the disk may be divided into subregions, and a transfer rate associated with each subregion.

3.2.2   CDs and DVDs

Compact disks (CDs) were originally introduced in the audio consumer marketplace by Philips and Sony for the storage of digital music. Due to their success and their relatively large storage capacity, they were adapted for use in computer systems as well. Advances in CD technology led to the development of the digital versatile disk (DVD). Due to their similarity, we consider both CDs and DVDs together.

CD Storage and Performance Characteristics

Unlike magnetic disks, CDs are an optical storage medium. A CD consists of a platter of optically recordable material enclosed in scratch-resistant unbreakable plastic [46, 65]. Data is recorded onto the recording layer by a laser. There are actually a number of different CD types, which use different materials. CD read-only memories (CD-ROMs) are identical to the original audio CDs except that their recording format is modified for computer use. CD-interactive (CD-I) is a version of CD-ROM designed by Philips and Sony for multimedia home systems. Other types include CD write-once and CD magneto-optical. As in magnetic disks, data on CDs is stored in a series of concentric circles or tracks, which are subdivided into sectors of 2,352 bytes. This size was chosen because it is the size required to store 1/75 second of digital music, and the original CD audio standard called for the playback of 75 sectors per second. The sector format depends upon the CD type.

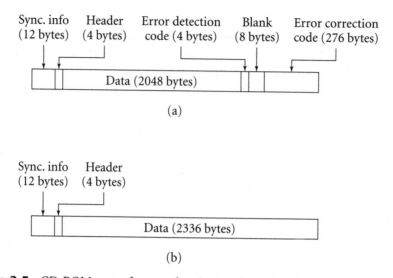

Figure 3.5 CD-ROM sector formats showing Mode 1 (a) and Mode 2 (b) formats.

We will describe the formats of CD-ROM and CD-I, as they are the most common types of CD used for multimedia. They share a common format, which is shown in Figure 3.5. Data can be recorded in one of two modes. Mode 1 is used for control information, such as the names of files, in which errors cannot be tolerated. Mode 2 is used for data, such as compressed images or video, in which occasional errors are normally permissible. In both modes, the first 12 bytes contain a synchronization code to mark the beginning of a sector. When a bad sector is detected, this is used to locate the start of the next sector. Following this is a header containing the sector number and a flag to indicate the mode of the sector. In Mode 2 sectors, the rest of the sector contains data. In Mode 1 sectors, the last part of the sector contains an error detection code as well as an error correction code. These are used to detect and correct errors found when reading the data. Because of the codes, the data length is smaller, and Mode 1 sectors are less efficient for data storage than Mode 2 sectors.

Table 3.2 Typical CD-ROM performance characteristics.

CD	Storage capacity (MB)	Bandwidth (MB/s)	Access time (ms)
Philips PCA36XCD	600	5.3	145
Sony CDU701	600	2.1–4.8	90

Table 3.3 Typical DVD-ROM performance characteristics.

DVD	Storage capacity (GB)	Bandwidth (MB/s)	Access time (ms)
Philips PCA532DK	8.5	6.5	135
Sony DDU220E	8.5	6.6	110

Typical CD-ROM performance characteristics are shown in Table 3.2. The CD-ROM storage and bandwidth capacities are not sufficient for storing high-quality MPEG-2 videos. However, they may be sufficient for the storage of lower-quality material. Additionally, the access times for the CD-ROMs are almost an order of magnitude higher than the average access times for disks. As discussed in later chapters, this degrades server performance significantly.

DVD Storage and Performance Characteristics

DVDs represent the next generation of CD technology [60]. They are the same size as a CD, but, due to advances in the manufacturing technology, their capacity is many times larger. Because CDs and DVDs are the same size, DVD players can be designed to read CDs as well. As with CDs, there are many types of DVDs. DVD-read-only memory (DVD-ROM) is targeted for use in multimedia computer applications. Unlike CDs, DVDs may be two-sided, doubling their storage capacity.

Table 3.3 shows the performance characteristics of some typical DVD-ROM players. Both of the systems shown are for single-sided DVDs. The storage capacity of DVDs is sufficient to store MPEG-2 movies and is much higher than that of CDs. However, in comparison to disks, the access times are still an order of magnitude higher while the bandwidth is lower. Additionally, unlike disks, DVD-ROM provides read-only capability.

3.2.3 Tape Devices

Magnetic tape devices store data on removable cartridges of tape. The cartridge is loaded into a tape drive connected to the processor. Tape cartridges come in many sizes, and even cartridges of the same size written on the drive of one manufacturer may not be readable by the drives of another manufacturer.

We describe two tape formats that are suitable for storage of large multimedia files. The helical scan system, shown in Figure 3.6, is of two different types (i.e., 4 mm and 8 mm systems), depending on the width of tape used. The system

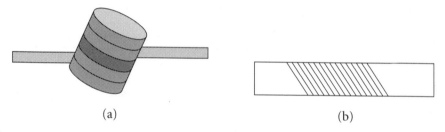

(a)   (b)

Figure 3.6 Helical scan systems showing the scan head (a) and the tape data tracks (b).

contains a rotating drum with read/write heads that is angled to the tape. The tape is itself moving and is partially wrapped around the drum. The angled, rotating drum increases the relative motion between the tape and the read/write heads. This helps increase the recording density. Due to the inclined heads, data is magnetically recorded in tracks that are angled to the tape (see Figure 3.6).

Figure 3.7 shows the digital linear tape (DLT) system. In DLT drives, the head is fixed and is not angled to the drive. As shown in Figure 3.7, data is recorded in a linear serpentine manner. After recording data from one end of the tape to the other, the head assembly moves up or down and starts recording data in the reverse direction. DLT drives do not need to be rewound before reading.

The performance characteristics of some tape drives are shown in Table 3.4. The Exabyte Mammoth is a helical-scan drive, while the others are DLT drives. It can be seen that the tape capacities are well above those needed for storing multimedia files. However, the access times are quite high (on the order of 100 seconds). Clearly, tapes are unsuitable for an on-line interactive system. However, their large storage capacity and cost per byte make them attractive for storing less frequently used multimedia material. When requested, this material can be retrieved from tape and played.

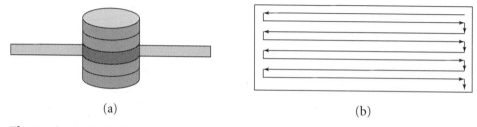

(a)   (b)

Figure 3.7 Digital linear tape systems showing head positioning (a) and tape data tracks (b).

Table 3.4 Typical magnetic tape performance characteristics.

Tape drive	Storage capacity (GB)	Bandwidth (MB/s)	Access time (s)
Exabyte Mammoth	20	3	57
Quantum DLT-4000	20	1.5	113
Quantum DLT-7000	35	5	100

3.2.4   Comparative Summary

The differing constructions and physical properties of the various devices result in different storage and access characteristics (see Figure 3.8). Disks provide much higher transfer rates (ranging from 10.8 to 23.5 MB/s) and, hence, are most suitable for serving multiple users concurrently. Their storage capacities (4.55–18.2 GB), while not as high as those of tapes (20–35 GB), are comparable to and even higher than those of DVDs (8.5 GB). Therefore, disks are an ideal storage device for frequently accessed files. Tapes provide large storage capacity but are not suitable for concurrent or interactive accesses (57–100 seconds). Therefore, less frequently accessed files can be archived on tapes and brought to disks for playback. Both DVDs and CDs are designed for single-stream delivery (due to their high access time). DVDs provide both higher bandwidth and storage capacity, making them suitable for video storage and playback, while CDs are better suited for audio storage and playback. DVDs and CDs are also suited for storage of infrequently used multimedia objects.

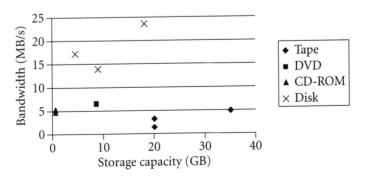

Figure 3.8 Bandwidth and storage capacity of storage devices.

3.2.5   Storage Interfaces

Following is an overview of the Small Computer System Interface (SCSI) standard. This is the most widely used standard for connecting all types of peripherals (e.g., storage devices) to processors. SCSI was invented by Shugart Associates as a protocol for connecting magnetic disks to processors and was standardized as SCSI-1 in 1986 [3]. SCSI-1 allowed the parallel transmission of 8 bits of data at 5 MHz. Therefore, the maximum transmission speed achievable was 5 MB/s. The next version of SCSI, SCSI-2 [4], doubled the transmission speed to up to 10 MHz and increased the amount of data that could be transferred in parallel to 16 and 32 bits. These are sometimes referred to as *fast SCSI* and *wide SCSI*, respectively. It can be seen that the theoretical limit of SCSI-2 speed is 40 MB/s. In addition, SCSI-2 generalized the SCSI standard beyond magnetic disks and tape to devices such as CD-ROM. Currently, SCSI-3 is currently under definition; it is actually being defined as a family of standards. To allow the SCSI protocol to run over a wide variety of physical links and adapters, the protocol has been decomposed into a number of layers (as in networking standards), with each layer having its own set of standards. For example, one of the standards defines how SCSI can run over high-speed fiber-optic cables.

The SCSI architecture is bus-based. A *bus* is a single (linear) data path that links a number of hardware components. The SCSI architecture links processors and I/O devices using SCSI busses [52, 53], each of which consists of a chain of up to eight devices (including processors). The devices on a single bus have an address between 0 and 7, which also assigns the priority of the device; normally, processors are at priority 7. A device can be on multiple busses; for example, a processor that wants to attach 12 disks can be on two SCSI busses (see Figure 3.9). This feature also allows two processors to share a chain of devices, which increases reliability. This is also illustrated in Figure 3.9, where processors 1 and 2 share the devices on SCSI bus 2. Devices on the SCSI bus may be initiators or targets. After obtaining control of the bus, initiators issue I/O commands to the targets, which

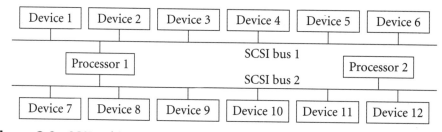

Figure 3.9 SCSI architecture.

may disconnect from the bus, execute the command, and reconnect for sending the reply. The set of permissible commands depends upon the device type. SCSI predefines eight device types (e.g., magnetic disk).

This description shows that, in addition to device performance, the configuration of the I/O subsystem has an important influence on I/O subsystem performance. For example, even if all six disks on SCSI bus 1 in Figure 3.9 have a bandwidth of 10 MB/s, the total bandwidth may not be greater than 40 MB/s (if the bus is a SCSI-2 bus). In practice, the achievable bandwidth will be less due to inefficiencies caused by contention for the bus. Therefore, a SCSI-2 bus is not likely to be able to effectively utilize more than three 10 MB/s disks.

3.2.6   Processor Architecture

In a multimedia server, the multimedia data has to traverse the server CPU in addition to traversing the server I/O subsystem. Typically, the data will be read from a storage device, buffered in memory, and then transmitted at an appropriate time to the network. The data has to traverse the internal CPU components while being written into or read from memory. Just as the actual configuration of the I/O subsystem determines the rate at which data can be read from disk, the actual I/O data paths through the processor determine the rate at which data can be pumped through the CPU.

We will describe the evolution of the I/O architecture of the Intel processors. Initially, the Intel processors used the Industry Standard Architecture (ISA) of the early IBM PCs. The I/O bandwidth of the ISA processors was comparatively low. As the demand for greater I/O bandwidth grew, Intel successively implemented the extended ISA, Video Electronics Standards Association (VESA) local bus, and the current Peripheral Component Interconnect (PCI) I/O architectures. All these architectures are bus-based; hence we discuss only the PCI architecture. However, with the PCI architecture, Intel became aware of the need for more sophisticated architectures, such as those found in IBM mainframes. This has led to a proposal for the Next Generation I/O (NGIO) architecture, described below. The I/O architecture of the IBM mainframes is described in detail in [31].

PCI Architecture

Figure 3.10 illustrates the PCI architecture. Because it is a bus-based architecture, there is a central bus (the PCI bus) that interconnects the various I/O adapters (e.g., SCSI adapters). The PCI bus is a 32-bit bus that can run at a maximum rate of 33 MHz. Therefore, the maximum data rate of the bus is 132 MB/s. The PCI bus is thus much slower than system memory and is therefore not connected to

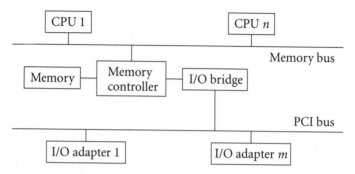

Figure 3.10   PCI architecture.

the memory directly. Instead, it is connected to the memory via a number of speed-matching and buffering components (the memory controller and I/O bridge). The memory, in turn, is connected to the CPUs via the memory bus.

Although a data rate of 132 MB/s is large by historical standards, it may not be large enough to support I/O devices in the future. For example, a single gigabit Ethernet card has a bandwidth of 128 MB/s. Clearly, a PCI architecture processor with a single gigabit Ethernet card would have no bandwidth available for supporting other I/O devices. A possible solution would be to speed up the PCI bus or connect multiple PCI busses to the processor [37]. However, the PCI architecture has other disadvantages [33]. First, because the PCI bus is designed to be internal to the system, there are limits to its physical size. This, in turn, limits the number of adapters that can be connected to the bus. Another limitation arises from the fact that if there are too many adapters on the bus, contention will reduce the throughput. Finally, the base system cost is high because the system must come with support (power, cooling) for the maximum number of adapters that it can use.

Next Generation I/O

The NGIO architecture was invented by Intel in order to solve the problems of the PCI architecture. As stated earlier, the NGIO architecture borrows ideas that have proved successful in mainframe architectures. The I/O subsystem is connected to a special-purpose processor called the *channel adapter* (see Figure 3.11). The channel adapter relieves much of the burden of I/O processing from the main processor. Furthermore, the I/O adapters are connected to the channel adapter via a high-speed switch. Switches can be designed so that the effect of contention is lower than that in busses, and so the bandwidth achievable in a switch-based architecture is much greater than that in a bus-based architecture. Furthermore,

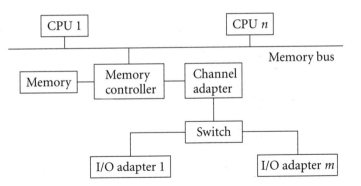

Figure 3.11 Next Generation I/O architecture.

the use of switches allows cables, such as optical cables, to be used, allowing I/O devices to be connected to the system externally and thus removing the restrictions on the number of devices that can be connected. Finally, none of the components of the I/O subsystem need be internal to the system. As a result, the base cost of the system can be reduced because only the necessary components need to be purchased.

3.3 Multimedia Server Software

As mentioned earlier in Section 3.1.1, there are three primary software components in a multimedia server: namely, the application server, the control server, and the data server. Collectively, a major function of these components in a multimedia server (not needed in nonmultimedia servers) is the continuous delivery of data in real time to the client. Since this is an important requirement, we first provide an overview of how it is achieved. We then discuss the other functions of the software components in more detail.

3.3.1 Continuous Delivery

Consider the process of transmission of multimedia data from the server to the viewer. Video and audio data has to be delivered in a continuous stream without any interruptions. For example, in a video, the frames have to be delivered at a rate of 30 per second. More complex presentations may require the synchronized delivery of multiple streams. This constant delivery rate has to be maintained for all streams even though the data blocks have to pass through a number of server and network devices. In a video-on-demand example, the video may have to be retrieved from disk, transmitted to a network adapter, and then transmitted over a number of network routers before finally being delivered to the viewer.

Because the data has to pass through many devices before reaching the client, overload on any device will cause irregularities in delivery. Two measures are necessary to ensure continuous delivery and to avoid irregularities. First, overloading any device must be avoided. This is done by reserving needed resources (e.g., buffer space) on all server and network devices required to deliver the continuous media. Because each device has a finite capacity, resource reservation has the effect of limiting the number of streams being delivered through a device. As a result, the congestion at each device is limited. This process is also referred to as *admission control*.

Continuous delivery may not always be achieved even if device overload is avoided by adequate resource reservation. For example, consider the case where many streams are being transmitted through a single device. Assume that the device operates by randomly picking a stream, transmitting data for that stream, and then repeating the process. It is possible that due to the random variations in access times, there may occur a large delay between transmission of successive blocks for a particular stream. Therefore, in addition to resource reservation, each stream must get a fair share of the device capacity, and the maximum delay in transferring successive blocks must be minimized. This is achieved by scheduling the devices appropriately to ensure continuous delivery of video data. Device scheduling ensures that no stream exceeds its reservation and that video data is delivered without interruptions.

A common misconception formed by many people when first encountering the concept of continuous delivery concerns the time required for data retrieval. Assume that at any particular instance the user is viewing a frame or data block i of the video and that this will be displayed for t seconds. It is mistakenly assumed that to ensure continuous delivery, the client, in parallel, needs to be able to retrieve the next frame in less than t seconds. This is a misconception because the video data blocks can be pipelined over the server and network components. Thus, while the presentation device is displaying the frame block i, block $i + 1$ may be buffered in the display, blocks $i + 2$ and $i + 3$ may be in transit over the network, block $i + 4$ may be in the process of transmission in the network adapter, and block $i + 5$ may be in the process of being retrieved from the disk. Because of the pipelined transmission, it is sufficient that each device in the pipeline not starve the next device; that is, that the delay in each device in the transmission pipeline is less than or equal to the transmission delay in the next device.

3.3.2 Overview of Software QoS Components

The software interactions required for guaranteeing continuous delivery are illustrated in Figure 3.12. The figure also shows how multiple multimedia applications

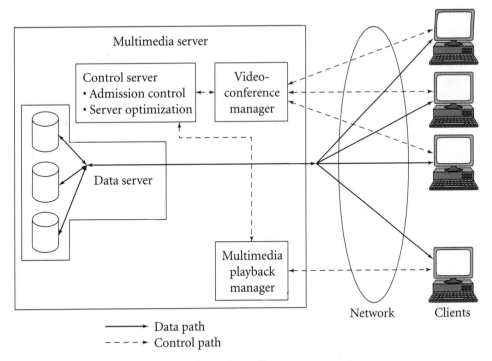

Figure 3.12 QoS architecture of a multimedia server.

can cooperate to share the same multimedia server. The multimedia server in the figure is supporting two multimedia applications—a videoconferencing application and a video-on-demand application. The videoconference manager handles videoconference requests (e.g., `join video conference`) from the videoconferencing clients. The video-on-demand manager, on the other hand, handles requests for stored videos (e.g., `play video`) from its clients. To obtain resource reservations, both application servers interact with the control server. Typically, the applications will specify their requirements in application-specific terms. For example, the videoconference manager may specify a particular bit-rate for the video or a maximum allowable transmission delay. The control server has to support a common set of requests that is general enough to allow most applications to specify their requirements.

After receiving an application request, the control server decides how to satisfy it. This involves interaction between the server optimization and admission control components. As discussed earlier, the server optimization component implements policies that attempt to satisfy the application's QoS requirements while maximizing server efficiency. These policies will depend upon values that are maintained by the admission control component. For example, consider a scenario in which there is a network adapter that can communicate with all three videoconferencing clients. One option in multicast networks (see Chapter 2) is to transmit a single stream through the adapter using multicast. However, this would require interaction with the admission control component to ensure that sufficient resources (e.g., bandwidth) are available in the adapter. We refer to these components together as the *resource manager* because they effectively manage the resources of the control server.

The control server next interacts with the data server to execute the application request. Note that though the figure shows only one data server, clearly there is no difficulty (conceptually) in having multiple data servers. There are two modes in which the control server can interact with the data server. In the first mode, the control server may be aware of the internal structure and capacities of the devices in the data server. For example, the control server may be able to explicitly select the specific devices to be used for satisfying an application request. Clearly, it is possible to implement sophisticated optimization policies that exploit knowledge of the internal structure of the data server. Alternatively, the control server may regard the data server as a sort of "black box" with a certain capacity. In this case, the optimizations possible will be less sophisticated. In either case, the data server will have internal scheduling components (such as the disk scheduler and network scheduler shown) that will ensure the data server devices are shared fairly between the streams.

3.3.3 Application Server

In the previous section, we considered software subcomponents that help to ensure quality-of-service for multimedia applications. We now describe the other subcomponents, starting with the application server.

Figure 3.13 shows the subcomponents of a typical application server. The user interface receives application commands from the user and sends back appropriate messages. For example, in a videoconference, the user interface may allow users to join the videoconference and request permission to speak. The contents database contains data about the multimedia data available. In a video-on-demand example, the contents database may contain information about the available videos and their prices. It may be searchable by actor, director, or other fields of interest to the viewer. The user database contains information that can identify the user to the application (e.g., a password) as well as other information, such as user profiles and preferences. The billing database contains information needed for charging clients for use of the application. Finally, the

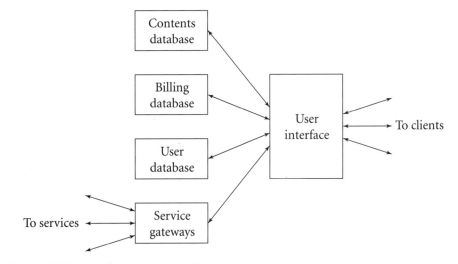

Figure 3.13 Application server subcomponents.

application server may contain service gateways for interacting with various services. For example, in a catalog shopping application, the application may need to interface with various legacy databases to place an order or find out whether a particular item is in stock.

3.3.4 Control Server

Figure 3.14 illustrates the typical structure of the control server. The administrator interface is used by the administrator of the multimedia server for management of the server. This includes server initialization and shutdown as well as modification of the server configuration. Server initialization requires initialization of both the hardware and the software, which may need to be done in a particular order. This information is stored in the configuration database. After initialization, the server initialization subcomponent updates the configuration database to reflect the current status of all the components (for example, marking off-line any devices that had errors during initialization). Additionally, the configuration database may store parameters that can be set by the administrator (e.g., assigning high priority to some application processes). The server shutdown subcomponent performs similar functions during shutdown.

The resource manager also uses the information in the configuration database to reserve server resources for each stream in order to prevent overload of any

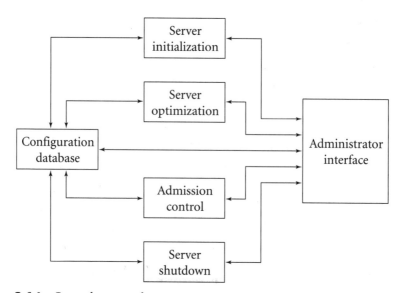

Figure 3.14   Control server subcomponents.

device. Resource reservation requires knowledge of device capacities and performance characteristics. As discussed in Section 3.2, the effective device capacities depend upon the actual device characteristics as well as the device interconnections. During startup, the resource manager copies this information from the configuration database. However, this information may dynamically change during run time (e.g., a data server can fail or an administrator can change a parameter). Therefore, a mechanism is required to update the configuration database as well as the internal tables of the resource manager.

3.3.5   Data Server

The data server is responsible for the actual delivery of the multimedia data to the client. Figure 3.15 shows the architecture of a typical data server. The file system stores and retrieves data from the main storage devices, generally magnetic disks. Because the multimedia data is never directly accessed by users, in reality the file system need not provide all the functionality of a full-fledged computer file system. For example, features such as the locking of specific byte ranges of the file that are supported by many file systems are unnecessary. In addition, functions not supported by conventional file systems, such as QoS, may be supported. However, we use the term *file system* to emphasize the fact that similar functional-

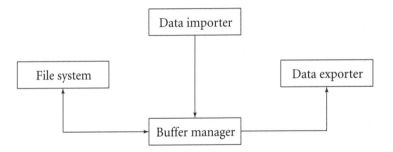

Figure 3.15 Data server.

ities are provided. Additionally, if this functionality is provided via standard file system calls, standard utility programs such as backup and file system repair utilities may be usable. These utilities need not be rewritten for the multimedia server.

The data importer is necessary for the management of devices from which multimedia data can be brought into the system. The device may have special interfaces and calling sequences that have to be invoked before use. An example of such a device is a video camera, which provides live multimedia data. Another example, which does not produce live multimedia data, is a tape device. As discussed in Section 3.2.3, tape devices are not suitable for direct playback to the user. Typically, the data importer will stage the multimedia data to disk, from which it will be played back. Similarly, the data exporter is responsible for transmission of data to the user.

The buffer manager is responsible for the management of memory in the data server. Generally, data read in from a device has to be buffered in the data server before being written out. Allocation and deallocation of buffers is performed by the buffer manager. In a system that caches frequently accessed data, the buffer manager is also responsible for the management of the cache.

3.4   Multimedia Server Topology

Distributed multimedia servers are constructed in order to provide a greater scalability and reliability than single servers. In the following section, we consider various server topologies that are distinguished by the interconnection of their components [36, 61]. For each topology, we discuss the complexity of the software required for management of the server. The efficiency of a server is estimated via a statistical analysis as follows. The required peak server capacity is estimated based on the assumptions of random traffic fluctuations and an average of 1000 active users at 0.1% rejection probability. The peak server capacity required will be greater than 1000 because the random fluctuations ensure that there will be times when more than 1000 users may be active. Comparison of the peak server capacities for various topologies is used to decide which topologies are more efficient. For example, if two topologies require peak capacities of 1500 and 1100, respectively, clearly the second topology is more efficient. Similar analysis is widely used in capacity planning for telephone networks. More details can be found in [36].

3.4.1   Partitioned Server

Figure 3.16 shows the configuration of a partitioned server, which is the simplest kind of distributed server. The users have been divided into (equal) groups, with each group being connected to their own server.

The peak capacity required in a partitioned configuration is shown in Table 3.5. The peak capacity required varies with the capacity of each individual server (measured in terms of the number of users it can support). Intuitively, if each individual server is small, the impact of statistical fluctuations is greater, and hence the overall peak capacity required is larger. As seen from the table, with typical server capacities of 50 and 100, 32 and 14 servers, respectively, are needed. This corresponds to systems capable of supporting 1600 and 1400 users, respectively. Therefore, the excess capacity required, respectively, is 60% and 40%.

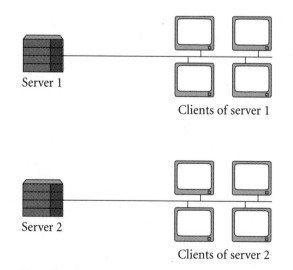

Figure 3.16   Partitioned multimedia server.

Table 3.5 Excess capacity required by partitioned server.

Server capacity	Required peak capacity	Number of servers	Excess capacity (%)
50	1562	32	60
100	1333	14	40

Additionally, each server will have a copy of each multimedia object to be served. Thus, large amounts of storage space are wasted as well.

3.4.2 Externally Switched Servers

A major inefficiency in the partitioned server we have described is the wasted server capacity that arises from load imbalance. Due to statistical fluctuations, it is possible that one server will be heavily loaded while another server is only lightly loaded. Users cannot be shifted from one server to another because each user is connected to only one server. A solution to this problem is to connect the clients and servers through a network. As shown in Figure 3.17, a control server directs requests to the appropriate (least-loaded) server. Note that though the control server is shown as a physically distinct server, it could just as well be implemented as a distributed process that runs over all the servers. Hence, a physically distinct server is not required.

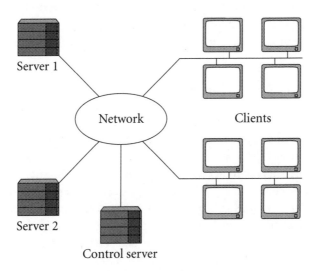

Figure 3.17 Externally switched multimedia server.

Table 3.6 Excess capacity required by externally switched server.

Server capacity	Required peak capacity	Number of servers	Excess capacity (%)
50	1081	22	10
100	1081	11	10

Table 3.6 shows the excess capacities required by an externally switched server. It can be seen that the externally switched server is very efficient in terms of the server capacity, with an overhead of only 10%. In fact, this is the minimum overhead required in order to deal with statistical fluctuations [36]. The externally switched server is efficient because the network effectively pools the capacities of all the individual servers. From the user's point of view, the request could go to any of the individual servers. Therefore, the set of servers appears as a single large server.

Although external switching reduces the wastage of server capacity, it does not reduce the wastage of storage space. Each server still has to have a copy of every multimedia object, otherwise it will not be possible to direct every request to any server. Replicating each multimedia object on only some servers limits the servers to which a request can be directed. In the extreme case, where each multimedia object is replicated on only one server, each request can be sent to only one server. As a result, the externally switched server effectively becomes a partitioned server, with high storage efficiency but large inefficiencies in server capacity. Replicating some multimedia objects will reduce the inefficiency in server capacity but increase the storage wasted. Therefore, by selectively replicating multimedia objects, either the storage or server capacity efficiency (but not both) can be increased.

3.4.3   Fully Switched Servers

The externally switched server achieves high efficiency in server capacity by using a network to pool the capacities of the individual servers. It is possible to reduce the inefficiency in storage by a similar method—that is, by the use of an I/O switch that allows all the servers to access all the storage devices. Such a fully switched server is shown in Figure 3.18. The resulting server has very high efficiencies both in server capacity as well as in storage. However, it requires additional hardware in terms of the external network connecting the users and the servers as well as the I/O switch. Whether such a configuration is cost-effective depends upon the relative costs of the components involved. This kind of configuration has been implemented by a large number of server designers [38, 24, 30, 33].

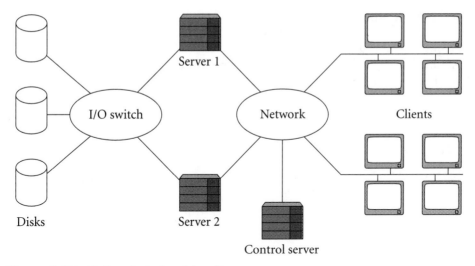

Figure 3.18 Fully switched multimedia server.

3.5   Summary

In this chapter, we described the hardware and software elements of a multimedia server. It is important to understand the characteristics of the hardware components and the constraints they pose. The various storage devices differ in terms of storage space, access time, and bandwidth (i.e., data transfer rate). As we will see later, these characteristics as well as their costs determine the types of devices to be used for satisfying a particular set of objectives (e.g., direct play, archiving, storage of frequently accessed media files, etc.).

The software architecture consists of three primary elements: the application server that interacts with a user and selects a specific media segment to be retrieved, the control server that performs admission control and resource reservation as well as resource optimization, and the data server that delivers the data to the network. Various software components also support QoS: avoiding overload in any system component and proper scheduling to avoid large delays in transferring successive data blocks.

Large-scale servers can be built using many small components. Topology and orchestration algorithms play an important role in determining how effective a server is. Although partitioned servers are relatively easier to build, they can also cause resources to be underutilized and the rejection of client requests. Large-scale servers built from small servers and components can also benefit from economies of scale.

Further Reading

The implementation of a video server in an IBM OS/390 mainframe platform is described in [15]. The impact of server topology on video servers is explored in [36]. The architecture of distributed video servers is explored in [61, 21].

Part 1 References

[1] K. Almeroth and M. Ammar. The use of multicast delivery to provide a scalable and interactive video-on-demand service. *IEEE Journal of Selected Areas in Communication*, 14(6):1110–1122, August 1996.

[2] D. P. Anderson. Metascheduling for continuous media. *ACM Transactions on Computer Systems*, 11(3):205–225, August 1993.

[3] ANSI. Small computer system interface. Technical Report X3.131-1986. ANSI, 1986.

[4] ANSI. Small computer system interface—2. Technical Report X3.131-1994. ANSI, 1994.

[5] K. Ashar. *Magnetic Disk Drive Technology: Heads, Media, Channel, Interfaces, and Integration*. IEEE, 1997.

[6] Bell Atlantic Corporation. Bell Atlantic video-on-demand effort begins commercial transition. *Bell Atlantic News Release*, October 1996.

[7] S. Berson, L. Golubchik, and R. Muntz. A fault tolerant design of a multimedia server. In *Proceedings of the ACM SIGMOD International Conference on Management of Data*. ACM, May 1995.

[8] Data courtesy of P. Boulanger, University of Ottawa, Ontario. Private communication.

[9] D. G. Boyer and M. E. Lukacs. The Personal Presence System: a wide-area network resource for the real-time composition of multipoint multimedia communications. *Multimedia Systems*, 4(3):122–131, June 1996.

[10] R. Braden, L. Zhang, S. Berson, S. Herzog, and S. Jamin. Resource ReSerVation Protocol (RSVP)—Version 1 functional specification, Technical Report RFC 2205. IETF, September 1997.

[11] A. Chankhunthod, P. Danzig, C. Neerdaels, M. F. Schwartz, and K. J. Worrell. A hierarchical internet object cache. In *Proceedings of the USENIX Conference*. Usenix, 1996.

[12] Cisco Corporation. High-end routers. In *http://www.cisco.com/warp/public/733*.

[13] D. E. Comer and D. L. Stevens. *Internetworking with TCP/IP*. Prentice-Hall, New York, 1993.

[14] A. Dan, D. Dias, R. Mukherjee, D. Sitaram, and R. Tewari. Buffering and caching in large scale video servers. In *Proceedings of IEEE CompCon*. IEEE, 1995.

[15] A. Dan, S. Dulin, S. Marcotte, and D. Sitaram. Multimedia resource management in OS/390 LAN server. *IBM Systems Journal*, 36(3):393–410, 1997.

[16] A. Dan, S. Feldman, and D. Serpanos. Evolution and challenges in multimedia. *IBM Journal of Research and Development*, 42(2):177–184, 1998.

[17] A. Dan, M. Kienzle, and D. Sitaram. Dynamic policy of segment replication for load-balancing in video-on-demand servers. *Multimedia Systems*, 3(3):93–103, July 1995.

[18] A. Dan and D. Sitaram. Multimedia caching strategies for heterogeneous application and server environments. *Multimedia Tools and Applications*, 4(3):279–312, May 1997.

[19] A. Dan, D. Sitaram, and P. Shahabuddin. Dynamic batching policies for an on-demand video server. *Multimedia Systems*, 4(3):112–121, June 1996.

[20] A. Dan, D. Sitaram, and J. Song. BRAHMA: Browsing and Retrieval Architecture for Hierarchical Multimedia Applications. *Multimedia Tools and Annotation*, 77(1/2):83–101, July 1998.

[21] DAVIC committee. Introduction to DAVIC. In *http://ftp.davic.org/intro.htm*, 1997.

[22] S. Deering. Host extensions for IP multicasting. Technical Report RFC 1112. IETF, 1989.

[23] S. Deering and R. Hinden. Internet Protocol v6 (IPv6) specification. Technical Report RFC 1883. IETF, December 1995.

[24] D. Deloddere, W. Verbiest, and H. Verhille. Interactive video-on-demand. *IEEE Communications Magazine*, 1994.

[25] H. Eriksson. MBone: the multicast backbone. *Communications of the ACM*, 37(8):54–60, August 1994.

[26] W. Fenner. Internet group management protocol version 2. Technical Report RFC 2236. IETF, November 1997.

[27] E. Fox. The coming revolution in interactive digital video. *Communications of the ACM*, 7(32):794–801, July 1989.

[28] E. Fox, R. Akscyn, R. Furuta, and J. Leggett. Digital libraries. *Communications of the ACM*, 38(4):23–28, 1995.

[29] B. Furht, S. W. Smoliar, and H. Zhang. *Video and Image Processing in Multimedia Systems.* Kluwer Academic Publishers, Norwell, MA, 1995.

[30] R. Haskin and F. Schmuck. The Tiger Shark file system. In *Proceedings of IEEE CompCon,* pp. 226–231. IEEE Press, Piscataway, NJ, 1996.

[31] J. Hennessy and D. Patterson. *Computer Architecture: A Quantative Approach.* Morgan Kaufmann, San Francisco, 1990.

[32] Hewlett-Packard Corporation. Broadcast video servers are part of MTV Europe's digital future. *HP Telecommunications News,* February 1997.

[33] Intel Corporation. Next generation I/O for today's servers. In *http://developer.intel.com/design/servers/future_server_io/documents/ngioapp.pdf.*

[34] International Telecommunications Union. H.323—Packet-based multimedia communication systems. Technical Report. International Telecommunications Union, 1997.

[35] R. Jain. Infoscopes: Multimedia information systems. In B. Furht, ed., *Multimedia Systems and Techniques.* Kluwer Academic Publishers, Dordrecht, Netherlands, 1996.

[36] M. Kienzle, A. Dan, D. Sitaram, and W. Tetzlaff. The effect of video server topology on contingency capacity requirement. In *Proceedings of Multimedia Computing and Networking.* SPIE, 1996.

[37] J. Laudon and D. Lenoski. System overview of the SGI Origin 200/2000 product line. In *http://www.sgi.com/origin/images/isca.pdf.*

[38] A. Laursen, J. Olkin, and M. Porter. Oracle media server: Providing consumer based interactive access to multimedia data. In *Proceedings of the ACM SIGMOD International Conference on Management of Data.* ACM, May 1994.

[39] J.-Y. Le Boudec. The asynchronous transfer mode: A tutorial. *Computer Networks and ISDN Systems,* 24:279–309, 1992.

[40] M. R. Macedonia and D. P. Brutzman. MBone provides audio and video across the Internet. *IEEE Computer,* 27(4):30–36, April 1994.

[41] G. Malkin. RIP version 2, carrying additional information. Technical Report RFC 1723. IETF, November 1994.

[42] J. Mogul. Broadcasting internet datagrams. Technical Report RFC 919. IETF, October 1984.

[43] J. Mogul. Broadcasting internet datagrams in the presence of subnets. Technical Report RFC 922. IETF, October 1984.

[44] J. Mogul and J. Postel. Internet standard subnetting procedure. Technical Report RFC 950. IETF, August 1985.

[45] J. Moy. Ospf version 2. Technical Report RFC 2178. IETF, July 1997.

[46] M. Nadeau. *The Byte Guide to CD-ROM.* Osborne/McGraw-Hill, Berkeley, CA, 1995.

[47] PlaceWare Corporation. The PlaceWare Auditorium 1.1. In *http:// www.placeware.com/products/productinfo.html.*

[48] E. Posniak, H. Vin, and R. Lavender. A presentation processing engine abstraction for multimedia applications. In *Multimedia Conferencing and Networking,* pp. 234–245. SPIE, March 1996.

[49] J. Postel. Internet protocol. Technical Report RFC 791. IETF, September 1981.

[50] P. Rangan, H. Vin, and S. Ramanathan. Designing an on-demand multi-media service. *IEEE Communications Magazine,* 30:56–65, July 1992.

[51] Real Networks. Inktomi and Real Networks team up to create the world's first cache for streaming media. In *http://www.real.com/company/pressroom/ pr/98/trafficserver.html.*

[52] B. Sawert. *Programmer's Guide to SCSI.* Addison Wesley, Reading, MA, 1998.

[53] F. Schmidt. *The SCSI bus and IDE interface.* Addison Wesley, Reading, MA, 1997.

[54] H. Schulzrinne, S. Casner, R. Frederick, and V. Jacobson. RTP: A transport protocol for real-time applications. Technical Report RFC 1889. IETF, January 1996.

[55] H. Schulzrinne, A. Rao, and R. Lanphier. Real time streaming protocol. Technical Report Internet-Draft. IETF, February 1998.

[56] P. Shenoy and H. Vin. Failure recovery algorithms for multi-disk multi-media servers. Technical Report 96-06. University of Texas at Austin, 1996.

[57] W. Sincoskie. System architecture for a large scale video on demand service. *Computer Networks and ISDN Systems,* 22:155–162, 1991.

[58] SMIL committee. Synchronized multimedia integration language. In *http:// www.w3.org/TR/WD-smil.* W3C, 1997.

[59] J. Song, A. Dan, and D. Sitaram. Efficient retrieval of composite multimedia objects in JINSIL distributed system. In *Proceedings of the ACM SIGMETRICS Conference.* ACM, 1997.

[60] J. Taylor. *DVD Demystified: The Guidebook for DVD-Video and DVD-ROM.* McGraw-Hill, New York, 1997.

[61] W. Tetzlaff and R. Flynn. Elements of scalable video servers. In *Proceedings of IEEE CompCon,* pp. 239–248. IEEE, 1995.

[62] R. Tewari, H. Vin, A. Dan, and D. Sitaram. Resource-based caching for web servers. In *Multimedia Conferencing and Networking,* pp. 191–204, SPIE, 1998.

[63] H. Vin and P. Rangan. Designing a multi-user HDTV storage server. *IEEE Journal of Selected Areas in Communication,* 11(1):153–164, January 1993.

[64] M. Willebeek-LeMair, K. Kumar, and E. Snible. Bamba—Audio and video streaming over the Internet. *Computer Networks and ISDN Systems,* 22:155–162, 1991.

[65] E. Williams. *The CD-ROM and Optical Disc Recording Systems.* Oxford, New York, 1996.

[66] P. Yu, M. Chen, and D. Kandlur. Grouped sweeping scheduling for DASD-based multimedia storage management. *Multimedia Systems,* 1:99–109, 1993.

PART 2

Scheduling

4

Client Session Scheduling

4.1 Introduction

In Part 1, we considered the diverse set of applications to be supported by a multimedia server and provided a broad overview of the system architecture. The applications may range from interactive applications that retrieve many small multimedia objects (e.g., shopping or medical applications) to videoconferencing applications involving many geographically distributed users [29, 41, 36]. As stated earlier, in spite of their diversity, all of these applications have in common the requirement of continuous delivery of video and audio data. For example, video representing a movie has to be delivered at 30 frames per second. Viewers will perceive glitches if the display does not receive video frames in time. In Part 2, we explore in detail the issue of QoS support—that is, resource reservation and scheduling of data delivery in each system component for supporting continuous delivery.

Consider a typical multimedia server environment, as shown in Figure 4.1. In Chapter 3, we summarized the interactions of the various system components (see Figure 3.1) for QoS support. Here, we provide details of these operations. To recapitulate, to understand how continuous delivery can be guaranteed by coordinating the operations of all system components, consider the process of transmission of the multimedia data from the server to the viewer. In a typical multimedia server environment, the multimedia data frames are generally stored as multimedia data blocks. Disassembly into frames is done only in the display. Before delivery to the viewer, these data blocks pass through a number of server and network components. In a video-on-demand example, the video may have to be retrieved from disk, transmitted to a network adapter, and then transmitted over a number of network routers before finally being delivered to the viewer. Irregularities in delivery can arise due to overload in any component. Hence, continuous delivery

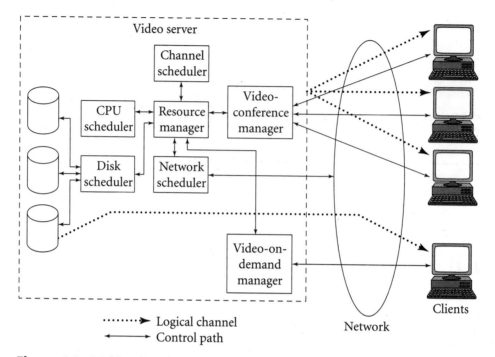

Figure 4.1   Multimedia server environment.

is guaranteed by (1) reservation of resources on all server and network components that are required to deliver the video and (2) appropriately scheduling data transfer operations in each component to ensure continuous delivery of video data. Because each component has a finite capacity, resource reservation limits the number of streams being delivered through a component. As a result, the congestion at each component is limited. Operational scheduling in each component during actual data retrieval furthermore ensures that no stream exceeds its reservation and also ensures delivery of the video data so as to avoid interruptions.

Also recall that continuous delivery does not require the total transmission delay from the server to the client of a multimedia data block to be less than the time for its display. A less stringent requirement that each component in the pipeline not starve the next component is sufficient; that is, the delay in each component in the transmission pipeline need only be less than or equal to the transmission delay in the next component. Hence, during actual data transmission, the multimedia data blocks are pipelined over the server components and the network such that while the display is displaying frames in block i, block $i + 1$ may be buffered in the display, blocks $i + 2$ and $i + 3$ may be in transit over the network, block $i + 4$ may be in the process of transmission in the network adapter, and block

$i + 5$ may be in the process of being retrieved from the disk. We refer to the set of resources (in a pipeline) that are reserved for guaranteeing continuous delivery of a multimedia stream (e.g., disk bandwidth, buffer, CPU, network bandwidth) as the *logical channel* [22]. As we will explore later in this chapter, setting up such a pipeline or channel is nontrivial in a complex environment with many different components. Before embarking on the details of QoS specification, the setting up of a channel, and the scheduling in each component, we first summarize the coordination of system components and broad issues affecting the scheduling in each component.

4.1.1 Software Server QoS Components

The software components required for guaranteeing continuous delivery are illustrated in Figure 4.1. The thin lines represent the interaction of the components and control flow prior to data flow, and the thick lines represent data flow during actual playback or retrieval and continuous delivery of data blocks. All multimedia applications will generally have a server component that is responsible for handling application requests. Two such components are shown in Figure 4.1 as examples of two different applications. The videoconference manager handles videoconference requests (e.g., `join video conference`) from the clients. The video-on-demand manager, on the other hand, handles requests for stored videos (e.g., `play video`) from its clients. For obtaining resource reservations, both applications interact with the resource manager. Typically, the applications will specify their requirements in application-specific terms. For example, the videoconference manager may request sufficient reservations to allow the three clients shown in the figure to conference. It may also specify application-specific characteristics (e.g., a particular bit-rate for the video or a maximum allowable transmission delay). The resource manager has to support a common set of requests that is general enough to allow most applications to specify their requirements.

After receiving an application request, the resource manager selects the components for which reservations are necessary and makes the required reservations. In the earlier example, reservations may be required for the CPU, buffer, and network. To make reservations, the resource manager interacts with the scheduler for the component (e.g., the CPU scheduler for the CPU). Note that each component may have its own units (e.g., the buffer may be specified in MB and the CPU in terms of MIPS). It is the function of either the resource manager or the component scheduler to translate the application requirement into the appropriate unit in each component. After the required reservations have been made, the logical channel is ready for use (as shown in Figure 4.1).

The resource manager interacts with the channel scheduler to allocate the logical channels in the multimedia server to the requests. A simple scheduler would allocate each logical channel to a single request. However, this may not always be desirable. For example, in video-on-demand systems, there may be many requests for the latest hit within a short period of time. The channel scheduler may combine these multiple requests and serve them using a single video stream. In Chapter 3, we outlined several optimization algorithms for exploiting the economies of scale [16]. Some of these algorithms will be described in detail in the relevant sections. In this chapter, we consider various policies for allocating logical channels among multiple waiting requests for different multimedia objects. The channel scheduler also has to deal with the problem of VCR control, where a viewer of a combined stream requests a pause in the video. When the viewer requests a resume, the channel scheduler has to guarantee that a channel is available. This problem also may arise in interactive applications, where many short video clips are displayed in response to user commands. Each successive request may require a different logical channel (e.g., because different videos on different disks are required). The channel scheduler has to guarantee that once the interactive session starts, successive requests are not denied access due to unavailability of logical channels (i.e., unavailability of resources).

4.1.2   Scheduling of Data Delivery

The scheduler for each component selects requests for a service so as to ensure continuous delivery to the next component in the logical channel. A secondary objective is to enforce the reservations made on the component by the resource manager to prevent the component from being overloaded. Real-time scheduling of operations is essential for avoiding jitters and providing glitch-free continuous delivery. This is in contrast to traditional scheduling policies—that is, best-effort scheduling. As we will see later, many component scheduling policies have a common approach. They assign a deadline or priority to each request. These deadlines or priorities are used to guide the selection of the order in which requests are serviced.

In the case of scheduling policies for some components (e.g., the storage subsystem and network adapters), additional component-specific constraints need to be considered. An important consideration in disk scheduling is the overhead for servicing the request. As we will show, this overhead is dependent on the sequence in which requests are serviced. Therefore, disk scheduling policies have to take into consideration the different overheads arising out of different retrieval sequences. Additional scheduling issues arise because the disks may be striped together into striping groups. The requests for disks in a striping group cannot be considered in isolation from one another. In case of the failure of a disk, the scheduling policies may be able to retrieve the data from other disks in the striping group. Finally, storage devices may be arranged into a storage hierarchy based upon their retrieval characteristics. Scheduling policies need to be able to move multimedia data between the various levels in the hierarchy. For network adapters, the additional complexity arises because of the distributed nature of communication networks. The scheduler for each network adapter has to interact with the scheduler in other adapters in the network to guarantee continuous delivery.

Because of the specialized nature of scheduling in each component, we discuss it in separate chapters. Selecting which among many waiting client requests for a new playback stream to serve next is referred to as *client request scheduling* and is discussed in detail in Chapter 5. CPU scheduling policies during actual data delivery are discussed in Chapter 6, and scheduling in the storage subsystem is discussed in Part 3. In the remainder of this chapter, we first consider methods by which applications can specify their QoS requirements to the resource manager. Note that each component needs to be aware of its capacity before it can set aside sufficient resources for guaranteeing continuous delivery for a playback stream. Because the multimedia server must be able to support arbitrary components from different vendors, it is not possible to prespecify component capacities in the form of a configuration table. Additionally, the bandwidths of two components of the same type will vary due to the configuration—the adapter used, for example. Hence, in practice, the usable capacities of the components need to be measured experimentally. For a complex system with interconnected components, measurement of useful capacity is a nontrivial task. In Section 4.3, we describe a novel and elegant measurement approach that can handle any system with arbitrary interconnection complexity. Next, in Section 4.4, we describe how the resource manager coordinates reservations in each system component to set up a channel.

4.2   QoS Specification

In order to guarantee continuous delivery, applications need to specify their quality-of-service requirements to the resource manager. These requirements may be explicitly specified by the application [6]. Alternatively, the quality-of-service requirements for each multimedia file may be stored in an associated metafile [8, 16] in a specific part of the file (e.g., header) or as associated attributes. For example, in the case of videoconferencing, the QoS information may be stored with the videoconferencing devices. In the case of video-on-demand, QoS information may be associated with the multimedia file. This is feasible because the QoS requirements for each multimedia file are normally fixed at the time the file is created. The most flexible implementation would be to store the QoS attributes of each multimedia file, as well as allow the application to override the stored specification. We will compare both approaches and then describe the commonly used QoS parameters.

4.2.1   Explicit vs. Implicit QoS Specifications

Requiring the application to explicitly specify QoS parameters results in a simpler implementation because the responsibility for keeping track of the QoS information is put on the application, not the multimedia server. It also allows the application to override the QoS requirements associated with a multimedia file. This is particularly useful for applications that can dynamically adjust their QoS requirements based on the available network bandwidth [9, 11, 10]. Such applications may, for example, retrieve and display only key frames from the multimedia stream instead of the complete moving image if sufficient network bandwidth is not available.

Implicit storage of QoS attributes with the multimedia file simplifies the process of application writing because the application need not retrieve QoS information. It also provides a migration path for nonmultimedia applications because the multimedia server can provide QoS support based on the associated attributes. Finally, storage of associated attributes may be required to store the names of associated special files (such as files for implementing fast forward or reverse). Hence, storing associated QoS information is only a small extension.

4.2.2   QoS Parameters

A number of standards [35, 12, 30] have been proposed for specifying QoS parameters. We list some of the important parameters in these standards below.

- *Bandwidth requirement.* The most important characteristic of continuous media (e.g., video) is that it has to be delivered at a specific rate if users are not to experience glitches (e.g., 1.5 Mbps for MPEG-1 video). Hence, it is important to allow applications to specify a bandwidth requirement that indicates the rate at which data is to be delivered. Due to variations in compression ratios, the data rate required by applications may not be constant [8]. Applications may thus specify an average data rate.

- *Peak bandwidth requirement.* Applications that deal with variable data-rate video may specify a peak bandwidth requirement in addition to the (average) bandwidth requirement. To allow meaningful reservation, the application may be required to specify a maximum *duration* over which the peak bandwidth is required (as in ATM networks) [35]. An alternative specification is the *burst size* or workahead [6]. This specifies the maximum amount of data by which the stream can exceed a strictly constant rate flow.

- *Delay.* In videoconferencing applications, it may be important to specify the maximum delay between the time a speaker generates a video or audio frame and the time the frame is received by all the conference participants [6]. Thus, it may be important to allow applications to specify the maximum delay for transmission of multimedia data. However, as discussed earlier, this may not be important for video-on-demand applications.

- *Loss probability.* In lossy environments (e.g., wide area computer networks), applications may specify a maximum tolerable loss probability [35]. Note that some encoding formats, such as the DVI format, embed control information along with the data [39]. Loss of such control information is more disruptive than loss of actual multimedia data. Hence, it may be desirable to provide a flag indicating whether the data being transmitted contains control information. The server (or viewer) may ignore loss of multimedia data but attempt to recover packets containing lost control information.

4.3   Capacity Estimation

To guarantee the QoS specified by applications, the resource manager has to reserve sufficient resources on all the components needed to deliver the stream. This implies that the resource manager has an estimate of the capacities of all the components that make up the video server. An important parameter for components in a multimedia server is their bandwidth capacity. As explained earlier, this is really an abstract number and represents the utilization level for guaranteeing certain QoS requirements. It is impossible to avoid jitters altogether without making the utilization level very low. As will be seen later in this book, by using more than one buffer in the overall pipeline, the stringent delivery requirements can be somewhat alleviated. In general, higher component utilization can be achieved by tolerating a certain level of jitters or missed deadlines (say, 1 in 1000, etc.) [15, 46]. Controlling the admission of user requests so as to guarantee the combined QoS requirements of all concurrent requests is termed *statistical admission control* [46].

A naive method of admission control would be to include in the resource manager a table containing the rated bandwidth capacity of each component (e.g., a disk of a particular type could be rated as having a maximum bandwidth of, say, 5 MB/s). However, this method has a number of disadvantages. First, the processes used by different manufacturers for measuring components may not be consistent with each other. Additionally, the measurement procedure may not be suitable for use in a multimedia server. Providing a table also makes it impossible to support disk types whose bandwidth capacity is unknown. Finally, the bandwidth capacity of a device may depend upon its interconnection. For example, the maximum bandwidth of a disk may depend upon the adapter it is connected to. As a result, it is necessary to estimate the bandwidth capacity of multimedia server components by measurement [7, 19], a process referred to as *calibration*.

The calibration process takes as input the configuration of the video server [19]. It runs a benchmark that the multimedia server can support without violating QoS requirements to measure the capacities of the components in the multimedia server. Since this interferes with the normal operation of the multimedia server, it is desirable to calibrate the multimedia server only when necessary—when the multimedia server is first put into service and whenever the configuration changes. As we will see later, depending on the instrumentation points and multimedia server configurations, the calibration process may not be able to distinguish between the capacities of certain individual components (such as those in a pipeline configuration.) Such components can be aggregated into *logical components*. The output of the calibration process is thus a table of logical components and their associated capacities.

During normal operation of the multimedia server, it may be sufficient to reserve resources on the logical components. Hence, the resource manager need not keep track of the constituent components of each logical component during normal operation. However, the information regarding each component may be useful if the multimedia server configuration changes (e.g., due to component failure). The information can be then be used for recomputing the approximate bandwidth capacity of the logical component without expensive recalibration. Consider, for example, a video server where multiple identical network adapters are aggregated into a single logical adapter. If one of the network adapters fails, it is possible to (approximately) compute the aggregate bandwidth capacity of the remaining adapters using linear interpolation.

We illustrate the calibration process using the simple multimedia server system shown in Figure 4.2. The system consists of a CPU containing two disk adapters, each of which has two disks attached to it. Therefore, the system contains four disks. These disks are striped together to form a striping group. (Striping will be discussed in detail in Part 3. In the current context, it is sufficient to know that blocks of a single multimedia file are stored in a round-robin manner among the disks in a striping group.) The system also contains two network adapters that are connected to the network. The outline of the calibration process is as follows [19]:

1. Represent the components of the system as a component graph (the graph may be a directed graph if some components have a unidirectional data flow). The component graph for the example system is shown in Figure 4.3(a).

2. Aggregate components whose capacities cannot be distinguished by measurement. These are components whose interconnection is such that the ratio of data flowing between them is fixed. There are two major cases where this can occur: First, two components may be connected in tandem so that data always flows either through both components or through neither. In the

Striping group

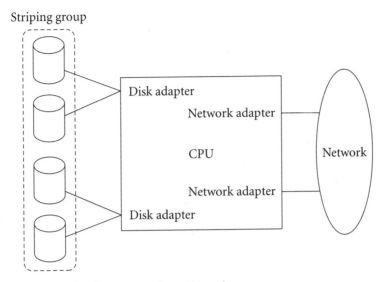

Figure 4.2 Example of a system to be calibrated.

example, this occurs in the disk adapter and the disks. The second case arises because of the semantics of the configuration (e.g., N disks are striped together, so each disk receives $1/N$ of the total data flow). Hence, a striping group can be reduced to a single node representing a single logical device.

The process of aggregation reduces the number of nodes in the component graph. Hence, it reduces the complexity of calibration—only the capacities of the smaller number of independent logical components need to be measured. In the example, the disks, disk adapters, and CPU can be aggregated into a single logical component. Figure 4.3(b) shows the aggregated component graph. Note that it has only three components, as opposed to nine components in the original graph. However, in a distributed server with many server nodes (e.g., front-end nodes connecting to the network and back-end nodes connecting to the storage devices, as illustrated in Chapter 3), multiple independent paths may share a common system component, and so the number of reduced logical nodes could be higher, even after the aggregation process.

3. Regard one set of nodes in the graph as source (e.g., reduced nodes that include the storage devices) and another set of nodes as destination (e.g., network adapters). For each source-destination pair in the system, enumerate all the paths in the graph connecting a selected source and destination pair. Compute the weight of each path as the fraction of the overall flow between

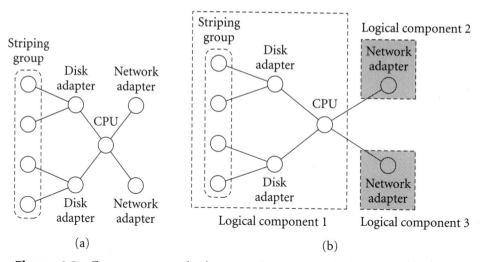

Figure 4.3   Component graphs for example system including an unreduced graph (a) and an aggregated graph (b).

the source-destination pair that flows through this path. There may be multiple paths connecting each source-destination pair, representing a logical channel during the establishment of a client session.

4. To measure the capacity of the logical components, systematically play back data streams by selecting appropriate source-destination pairs as well as controlling the data rate. The bandwidth capacity of each logical node is estimated by saturating it—that is, by creating the maximum possible flow without violating a given QoS level. To accomplish this, first order the paths passing through this selected node in terms of their weights. Next, select the path with the highest weight and drive it with a maximum flow. Note that a path may be saturated due to a bottleneck at a node other than the selected node. Additional flow through this selected node may be created by selecting remaining paths through it in order of their weights and driving each path to a maximum flow before selecting the next path in order. Note that the ordering for path selection is important for creating the maximum flow through the selected node. Two paths through the selected node may share one or more other common nodes (but with different flow fractions), and, hence, the wrong ordering of paths may result in the premature creation of a bottleneck in another node. Finally, the resulting bandwidth capacity of the selected node is the sum of the concurrent flows through all paths. As stated

earlier, the effective bandwidth depends on the server configuration. For example, a fast disk connected to a slow disk adapter may have a low measured capacity.

4.4   Logical Channel Setup

We next consider the policies used by the resource manager to reserve resources and guarantee QoS. As stated above, the resource manager views the multimedia server as an interconnected set of logical components. Each logical component is an abstraction of a possible aggregation of physical components. In order to set up a logical channel for a request, the logical components to service the video must be selected, followed by reservation of resources on these components. We discuss both of these operations next.

4.4.1   Component Selection

Selecting the components for servicing a request is nontrivial; there may be multiple sets of components that can service a given request. For example, it may be possible to play back a request through any one of multiple network adapters on the video server. Hence, the resource manager has to select one of the network adapters for servicing the request. We divide the criteria for component selection into three classes.

- *Optimization.* The choice of components may be driven by the desire to optimize server performance. For example, balancing the load on the components will clearly lead to more efficient server utilization by avoiding bottlenecks. Also, as discussed in a later chapter, the cache hit ratio of a distributed server can be improved by affinity routing, which routes requests for the same video to the same nodes. In this case, the choice of node may be based on the requested video.

- *Component characteristics.* Component characteristics may dictate the components that are selected. For example, switching network adapters may result in a large latency in serving a request. Hence, once a network adapter is selected for serving a client, it may be used to serve all other requests in the session.

- *Server topology.* Component selection may be based on component interconnection—that is, an available path through the selected component with sufficient capacity. For example, there may be more than one replica of a requested video on multiple data servers. However, the network configuration may be such that not all data servers are connected to all clients (e.g., the client may be on a T1 line and only some data servers may have T1 network adapters). The resource manager then has to select a data server that is connected to the client.

Even after multiple criteria for component selection are applied, there may still be multiple paths with different sets of components that can serve a request. The final selection among these sets of components can then be made so as to balance the load among the server components. Without load balancing, bottleneck formation will tend to limit the throughput of the system. We will describe next a policy that takes these issues into account, referred to as the *path-based component selection* policy [16, 14]. Other policies that influence component selection (e.g., affinity routing) are outlined in their respective chapters.

Figure 4.4 outlines the path-based component selection policy. A set of components that can service a request is referred to as a *possible data delivery path*. The calibration process outlined in Section 4.3 results in the enumeration of the set of all the data delivery paths in the system. From this set, the policy uses additional component selection criteria (as discussed above) to select a subset of paths to service this request. The selection is performed by the procedure getPaths and the results are stored in the variable PATH. The policy then considers each path in turn and invokes the function compBotBW to compute the bottleneck bandwidth on the path. The bottleneck bandwidth on the path is defined to be equal to the smallest available bandwidth of all the components on the path. Intuitively, the bottleneck bandwidth is the available capacity of the bottleneck component of this path and defines the maximum rate at which video data can be delivered on this path. The policy selects the path with the largest bottleneck bandwidth.

```
PATH = getPaths();
maxBotBW = 0;                   /* Maximum bottleneck bandwidth */
for ( each path in PATH )
  {
    botBW = compBotBW (path);  /* Compute bottleneck bandwidth */
    if ( botBW > maxBotBW )
      { /* Found better path */
        naxBotBW = botBW
        bestPath = path;
      }
  }
}
```

Figure 4.4 Path-based component selection.

4.4.2   Resource Reservation

After selection of a path—that is, the set of components for servicing the request—
it is necessary to reserve an appropriate amount of resource in each component to
create a logical channel. The objective of resource reservation is to ensure that the
application requirements (e.g., average bandwidth, end-to-end delay, burst size)
are satisfied [13]. It is always necessary to reserve at least the required average
bandwidth on each component. Sufficient buffer should then be reserved to handle the required burst size, and the total end-to-end delay should be partitioned
across the various components.

The set of possible reservations for satisfying certain QoS may not be unique,
even after the unique selection of path. This is because it may be possible to partition the total end-to-end delay in many different ways across the components.
Each such partitioning may lead to a different resource reservation plan. A unique
partitioning can be created by associating a cost function with each component
[6]. The cost function may reflect the actual cost or may reflect a performance objective (e.g., the cost of a component may increase as its utilization increases). The
cost of a logical channel can be defined as the sum of the costs of the individual
reservations. The resource reservation problem can be reduced to the problem of
finding the logical channel with the smallest cost [6]. In practice, once a path is selected, the resource reservation problem can be a simple task in many video-on-
demand servers where videos are typically encoded for playback at a constant
bit-rate. Hence, a constant bandwidth is reserved in all components for serving
this request.

4.5   Summary

In this chapter, we considered the issue of QoS specification for satisfactory presentation of a multimedia document and subsequent reservation of resources for
satisfying this QoS requirement. We provided an overview of how various components in a complex multimedia server are selected for servicing a request with a
specific QoS requirement. The criteria include finding a delivery path with available capacity from a data source containing a copy of this document to the network adapter, connecting the requesting client, and load balancing for proper
utilization of components. The set of reserved resources for delivery of a single
stream is referred to as a *logical channel*. Resource reservation in each component
requires knowing a priori its effective capacity—that is, the number of streams it
can support while satisfying a certain level of QoS. Typically, this capacity is measured experimentally by a process referred to as *calibration*. We described a novel
and elegant algorithm for determining the capacities of the components using a

graphing theoretic approach. The algorithm first aggregates components into logical nodes whose capacities can be experimentally measured and sets up the appropriate data flow for measuring the maximum capacity of each logical node. In the next two chapters, we elaborate on the process of selecting a client request to serve when the resources are available for achieving certain client satisfaction objectives and the details of the scheduling policies for ensuring jitter-free delivery of data.

5

Client Request Scheduling

5.1   Introduction

In the previous chapter, we described how a client session is established by reserving sufficient resources and setting up a logical channel. If the server utilization is low, all incoming requests for starting a new session or playback of a multimedia document can be satisfied immediately. However, if enough resources are not available, the client has to wait to be served. The channel scheduler is responsible for allocating a logical channel in the system to a client request for a multimedia stream. It determines when and which client request will be served to ensure a certain fairness across clients and to achieve certain client satisfaction objectives.

The simplest policy for a multimedia server would be to preconfigure the server with a sufficient amount of resources and to allocate channels on demand—that is, to allocate a logical channel upon receiving a playback request. Under this policy, the number of viewers a server can support is at best equal to the capacity of the server measured in the number of channels. This simple policy may not always be efficient, however. Consider a multimedia database application where clients retrieve short video clips based on queries. The network overhead and latency for setting up a connection may be significant. Hence, it may be desirable to allocate a logical channel for the duration of the session instead of for each individual clip. This will result, however, in wastage of server resources in the interval between clip displays, when the user may be formulating the next query. Resource reservation in the server typically involves little overhead and latency. Hence, it may be more efficient to use a static reservation policy for the networking component of the logical channel and a dynamic reservation policy for server resources. Due to statistical sharing of resources during the time that users are inactive, the total number of active users supported by the server may be greater under this system than its capacity in channels.

5.2　Client Scheduling Issues

Customer behavior is an important parameter that has to be considered by channel scheduling policies. For example, it is likely that client dissatisfaction will increase with increasing wait time. Long delays before video playback is started may cause clients to leave the system or renege [22, 23]. Hence, channel scheduling policies that have a wide variation in request service times are likely to have a high customer loss. Therefore, channel scheduling policies have to consider customer behavior while also addressing other issues—for example, handling VCR control operations, data stream sharing across clients, and providing consistent system behavior under time-varying load.

- *VCR control operations.* In a multimedia server environment, clients may also request pausing and restarting of videos (VCR control operations). In general, this will require a new logical channel upon resume, which, however, may not always be available. Similarly, interactive video applications, where a succession of small clips are viewed, can also be considered to fall into the same class. This is because playback is repeatedly paused and resumed, and resources may not be available for the resumed request. Other VCR control operations (e.g., fast-forward) also result in unpredictable demand in resource requirements. The contingency channel policy is a general policy for handling such requests [22, 27, 17]. It sets aside a small number of statistically shared contingency channels for handling unpredictable demands due to VCR control operations. Alternatively, specific algorithms can be used to handle VCR control operations either through reoptimization or alleviating the higher demand for one resource type by use of another available resource type. For example, if a viewer of a popular video pauses, the data blocks brought in by another closely following viewer can be buffered in anticipation of a resume [22, 24]. This allows the resume request to be serviced (from the buffer) even if there is no available disk bandwidth for retrieving video blocks.

- *Common data streams.* In a large multimedia server environment, it may be possible to share all or part of a logical channel (i.e., a data stream carried over this channel) among multiple clients requesting the same video material. The distribution of requests for videos are, in general, skewed [44], with some videos being much more popular than others. Hence, combining requests for the popular videos can result in a large reduction in the required server capacity [22, 17]. We refer to such policies as *batching* policies. Such policies exploit the multicast capabilities of modern communication networks, which allow the same message to be sent to multiple clients without any extra server overhead [35].

Conventional channel scheduling policies can be considered to be user-centered because they allocate users to logical channels. In a sense, batching policies can be considered to be data-centered because they allocate logical channels to popular videos, with each user assigned to the channel showing the requested video [46]. Batching policies have the advantage that the server capacity required is proportional to the number of videos, not the number of viewers. Adding users for a popular video does not result in increased server capacity requirements. Multiple clients can also share the same disk I/O stream if the data blocks in the intervals between successive requests are cached in the server. This policy, referred to as *interval caching,* trades off disk bandwidth for cache storage [18, 21]. A combination of dynamic batching and caching can also be used for data stream sharing [34]. Caching policies are further discussed in a later chapter.

- *Time-varying workload.* The arrival rate of client requests to a video-on-demand system may vary with the time of day [45]. For example, the request rate may peak during prime time; that is, the request rate may be much higher than during other parts of the day. Consider a simple channel scheduling policy that allocates channels on demand during a low-load period just preceding the peak time. Each client will be allocated a channel of its own because there will be no significant batching. As a result, server resources may be exhausted just at the beginning of the peak period. Additionally, since video playout times are long, these channels will be unavailable for a long period of time (typically two hours). Hence, the period of exhaustion may last for a significant length of time in the peak period. Because a waiting client may renege if it has waited too long [22], there will be a high rejection rate of client requests at the start of the peak period.

  A further complication is that these allocated channels may be freed all at once (within a short time period if the service times are nearly the same). The on-demand channel allocation policy will again allocate a large number of channels, after which there will be another period of low channel availability and high rejection [5]. Such cyclic behavior is extremely undesirable, not only for the high rejection probability during peak period but also for the non-uniform rejection probability throughout the day (even for a nonbatched environment).

5.2.1   Client Behavior

The choice of which request to serve by the channel scheduling policy is heavily influenced by client behavior. Clients independently select a video from the available videos according to a nonuniform access distribution. A typical access

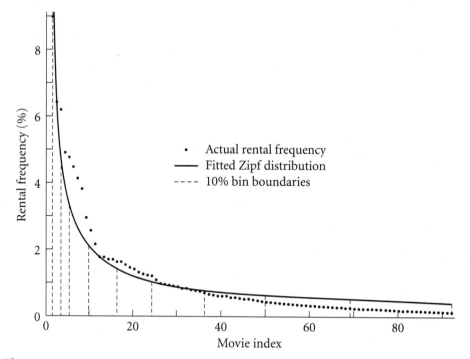

Figure 5.1 Video access distribution.

distribution, shown in Figure 5.1, is based on the frequency of rentals for various videos in a particular week in video stores [44]. This empirical distribution can be closely approximated by a Zipf[1] distribution with the parameter 0.271 [22].

Clients may renege or leave if they have to wait too long before video playback. However, the reneging time, or the exact length of time users will wait before reneging, is not known. Client reneging time, T_{ren}, may be modeled as a random variable with a general distribution. Clearly, the longer a client has to wait, the greater the probability of reneging. However, the reneging time may also depend upon the channel scheduling policy. The channel scheduler can attempt to influence reneging behavior through prior negotiation (e.g., by guaranteeing a maximum delay). Two different models of client reneging behavior have been proposed in [22].

---

[1] In a Zipf distribution, if the videos are sorted according to the access frequency, then the access frequency for the ith video is given by $p_i = c/i^{(1-\theta)}$, where θ is the parameter for the distribution and c is the normalization constant.

- *Minimum reneging time.* All clients are assumed to be willing to wait at least $T_{ren,min}$ amount of time, with the remaining reneging time being distributed exponentially. Formally, $T_{ren} = T_{ren,min} + T_{exp}$, where $T_{ren,min}$ is a constant and T_{exp} is a exponentially distributed random variable. A scheduling policy may preallocate capacity for hot videos by multicasting hot videos at time intervals of $T_{ren,min}$. The reneging probability for such videos will then be 0.

- *Maximum waiting time guarantee.* Under this model, clients agree to wait if a maximum waiting time, $T_{wait,max}$, is guaranteed. This can be achieved for particular videos by starting streams for those videos every $T_{wait,max}$ amount of time. The reneging probability of requests with dedicated streams is thus 0. The other clients still follow the general reneging time model. If the general reneging time includes any minimum reneging time ($T_{ren,min}$), then $T_{ren,min}$ is assumed to be smaller than $T_{wait,max}$. A variant of this model is proposed in [43]. Under the variant, customers agree to wait if $T_{wait,max}$ is less than a pre-specified threshold, T_{thresh}, and follow the minimum reneging time model otherwise.

5.2.2 Channel Scheduling Objectives

Channel scheduling policies have to trade off among various objectives when selecting a request for service. Because different scheduling policies may result in different waiting times for requests, their reneging probabilities may be different. Minimizing reneging probability is clearly, therefore, a desirable objective. However, scheduling policies may attempt to minimize reneging by giving preferential treatment to some videos—for example, popular videos. Such policies are unfair. In [22, 17, 5], the following five primary objectives have been proposed for scheduling policies:

1. *Minimize long-term reneging probability.* The long-term reneging probability is the average fraction of clients that reneges. A policy that has a low long-term reneging probability will require a low server capacity to achieve a target maximum overall reneging probability, α_1.

2. *Minimize short-term peak reneging probability.* If the total load on a VOD system is nonuniform with time, client reneging may also vary with time. The reneging probability may be high when the load is high (due to higher waiting times). The short-term peak reneging probability is the peak value of the fraction of clients that reneges measured over a short time interval.

3. *Minimize average waiting time.* Minimizing the average and/or variance of the waiting time of the clients improves client satisfaction.

4. *Fairness.* Intuitively, a scheduling policy is fair if the reneging probability for all video requests is equal. Unfairness can be defined as the standard deviation of the reneging probabilities for each video. In practice, the reneging probability for cold videos may be difficult to compute because the number of requests for cold videos is small. As a result, the standard deviation of the reneging probabilities is also difficult to compute. A measure of unfairness that is easy to compute can be derived by first dividing the videos into N_{bin} bins. The unfairness is defined as [22]

$$U = \frac{\sum_{i=1}^{N_{bin}}(p_{i,\text{ren}} - p_{\text{ren}})^2}{N_{bin}},$$

where $p_{i,\text{ren}}$ is the long-term reneging probability of the ith bin videos and p_{ren} is the average long-term reneging probability over all bins.

5. *Resume delay.* For workloads that include VCR control operations, no more than a fraction, α_2, of the resume delays are greater than T_{resume}.

5.2.3   Channel Scheduler Architecture

The architecture of the channel scheduler is dictated by the necessity for dealing with this set of issues and objectives. For scheduling under time-varying load, a hierarchical scheduler is required. Even complex single-tier policies that use the queue status can only optimize channel allocation across currently waiting requests. Hence, such policies will exhibit cyclic exhaustion and high short-term reneging (as we have discussed) once channels are depleted. Only hierarchical policies that conserve channels for peak loads by controlling the allocation rate can solve the problem. The structure of such a two-level hierarchical scheduler is as follows [17, 5]. The first level controls the channel allocation rate based on anticipated future load. The future load includes not only the load imposed by requests for new videos but also the anticipated load due to VCR control actions. The lower level allocates channels to waiting requests (including VCR control requests) and deals with the issue of batching.

In the remainder of this chapter, we first discuss channel scheduling policies for dealing with the issues posed by VCR control and then give a detailed description of the policies that aggregate client requests for serving via a single stream (referred to as *batching*). We conclude by addressing the issue of time-varying load and discuss policies that take a much broader perspective.

5.3 VCR Control Operations

Channel scheduling policies attempt to deal with issues of VCR control, batching, and scheduling under time-varying load based on client behavior. After discussing client behavior and the objectives of channel scheduling, we consider in detail channel scheduling policies for dealing with the issues of VCR control, batching, and scheduling under time-varying workloads. In video-on-demand systems, it is quite likely that viewers will want to perform operations such as pause, resume, fast-forward, and reverse that are commonly available on VCRs. Without special policies for handling such operations, there may be a high probability of denial due to unavailable bandwidth. Interactive video sessions, where many small clips are viewed in succession, also fall into this category. This is because it is undesirable that a request to play a clip be rejected in the middle of an interactive session. We refer to such operations as *VCR control operations.*

In this section, we focus on general techniques that can be used by the channel scheduler to handle arbitrary VCR control operations. Special techniques for handling specific cases (e.g., pause and resume in batching systems) are discussed in the appropriate subsection. We divide the discussion into two parts: (1) how to actually implement the VCR control function, and (2) how to ensure sufficient server resources to implement the function.

5.3.1 Implementation of VCR Control Operations

The implementation of pause and resume requests is fairly simple: it requires pausing the video upon receiving a pause request and resuming playback once a resume request is received. The problem of support for interactive video is also similar. The major complexity in the implementation of pause and resume arises from ensuring that sufficient bandwidth is available once the resume request is received. This is discussed in Section 5.3.2.

The other common VCR control operations (fast-forward and reverse) can be implemented using similar techniques, some of which we discuss next.

- *Special files.* It is possible to preprocess video files off-line to create special files that, when played back, give the appearance of fast-forwarding or reversing the video. The main advantage of this technique is the relative simplicity of the implementation, since the server and the client will continue to transmit and receive a standard video stream. However, the bandwidth required to play back the special file may be different from that required by the original video file.

  Because the special file gives the appearance of fast-forwarding or reversing at a particular speed, only a discrete set of speeds can be supported.

Storing the required special files results in storage overhead (although for a speedup of 10 times, it is likely that the overhead may be around 10%). Additionally, when the user requests a VCR control operation in the middle of the original file, the video server has to know the corresponding location in the special file. Hence, cross-indexes between the original video file and the special files are required, which results in additional storage overhead.

- *Fast playback.* An alternative technique is to play back the video forward or reverse at a higher speed. The client then displays either selected frames or the entire video at a higher speed. The main disadvantage of this technique is the increased client implementation complexity. Furthermore, it is not supported by any of the current decoding standards.

- *Scan.* In this technique, selected frames are transmitted from the server to the client. Displaying these frames gives the feeling of fast-forwarding or reversing the video. This mode can be supported by video decoders that provide a mode for displaying successive still images. This technique is suited to pull systems, where the client can read the video file nonsequentially and request the needed frames. In push systems, the technique requires the multimedia server to understand the details of the encoding format, which may limit the number of formats in which fast-forward and reverse can be supported.

5.3.2   Bandwidth Allocation for VCR Control

In discussing how the channel scheduler can ensure that possible increases in bandwidth requirements can be met, we first outline the contingency channel policy and then describe its performance.

A simple way to ensure that clients can proceed without rejection is to always reserve the maximum required resources at the start of every session. For example, in the case of pause and resume, server resources can be dedicated to the client even when the client is paused. However, this is wasteful of server resources, particularly if, on average, the client resource requirements are low for long periods of time. A more efficient alternative is to release server resources when they are not needed and reacquire them as needed. For ensuring client satisfaction, the server then has to guarantee that the delay for resource reacquisition is small. The probability that the delay is less than a prespecified limit can be used as a measure of client satisfaction [22, 17]. This is equivalent to providing a statistical guarantee of satisfactory service as opposed to the deterministic guarantee provided by reserving the maximum required resources. In the case of pause and resume, client satisfaction can be measured by the probability that the resume delay is less than a certain duration, say, T_{resume} [22, 17]. As an example, a system may be configured to guarantee that 95% of the resume delays are less than 30 seconds.

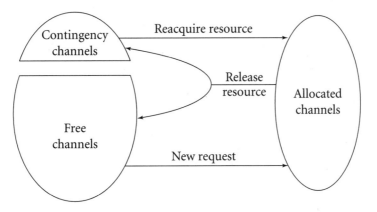

Figure 5.2 Channel allocation under contingency policy.

Figure 5.2 illustrates the operation of the channel scheduler with set-aside resources (contingency channels) for VCR control operations [22, 27]. The channel scheduler maintains a constant pool of contingency channels for VCR control actions. Hence, it starts a new request on a free channel only if sufficient contingency channels have been set aside. When resources are released (e.g., when a pause request is received from a client and the stream is not a multicast stream), the channel scheduler returns the resource to either the free or the contingency pool. If the contingency channel pool is depleted, the freed channel is returned to the contingency pool.

Upon receiving a resource acquisition request for VCR control operations, the channel scheduler attempts to allocate the resources from the contingency pool. Before performing this step, the channel scheduler may undertake special processing for VCR control actions. For example, in the case of resume, a sufficiently close ongoing stream can be used to satisfy the request if such a stream exists. In case the resources are not available in the contingency pool, the channel scheduler queues this request with high priority. As a result, the request will be serviced before channels are allocated new streams. This reduces the worst-case delay for the resume request.

5.3.3 Performance of the Contingency Channel Policy

The performance of the contingency channel policy for pause and resume requests has been studied in [17] using an analytical model. The model computes the reduction in server capacity (measured in logical channels) resulting from the use of

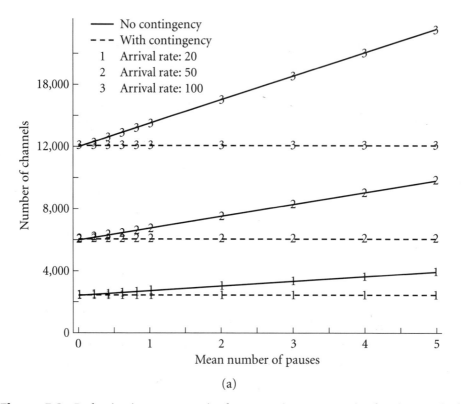

(a)

Figure 5.3   Reduction in server capacity due to contingency capacity showing required server capacities (a) and required contingency capacity (b).

the contingency capacity policy for pause and resume. The reduction is computed with respect to the server capacity using the simple policy of reserving the logical channel even during a pause.

The study in [17] assumes the workload described in Section 5.2.1 and a system that stores 100 videos. The arrival rate to the system is assumed to be 50 requests/min, which corresponds to a server with an average of 6000 active customers. Customers are assumed to pause once per video on the average, and the average duration of pauses is assumed to be 15 minutes. The system is configured to meet two design objectives. The first is that the reneging probability should be less than 5%; additionally, 95% of the requests for VCR control operations (pause and resume) are to be satisfied in less than 30 seconds.

Figure 5.3 compares the required server capacity under the contingency policy and under the no-contingency policy, where requests hold on to a channel while they are paused. Figure 5.3(a) studies the variation in the required number of channels as the mean number of pauses increases for three different arrival

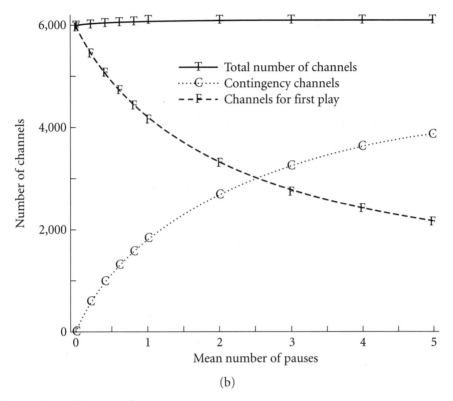

(b)

Figure 5.3 (Continued)

rates. Under the no-contingency policy, the required server capacity increases approximately linearly with the mean number of pauses. This is because as the mean number of pauses increases, the time a request holds a channel increases linearly. In contrast, the required number of channels under the contingency policy remains almost constant. The reasons for this can be seen from Figure 5.3(b). The figure plots the breakup between required contingency and noncontingency channels for the case where the arrival rate is 50. As the mean number of pauses increases, the arrival rate to the contingency queue increases, causing the number of required contingency channels to increase. However, increasing the mean number of pauses also causes the viewing time of new requests to go down. This results in a decrease in the number of required noncontingency channels. Hence, the total number of channels remains almost constant, varying between 6036 and 6124.

The study [17] also examines the sensitivity of the required server capacity to variation in workload parameters. As above, the required capacity under the contingency policy is also insensitive to the average duration of pauses. Additionally, the required server capacity under the contingency capacity does not vary greatly with T_{resume}, the maximum time allowed to service 95% of the resume requests. This is because the waiting time in the contingency queue is very small (because the contingency pool is rarely exhausted). As a result, reducing T_{resume} even to very small values has negligible effects on the required server capacity.

5.4 Batching Policies

The VCR control policies we have described exploit statistical properties of customer behavior to reduce the server capacity required for providing VCR controls. Batching policies take advantage of other facets of customer behavior. In many environments, most of the customer requests will be for a small subset of the videos. When a channel becomes available, batching policies may allocate the channel to multiple viewers who request the same video. This can lead to dramatic reductions in the required server capacity.

A simple batching policy is for the multimedia server to periodically transmit popular video material at preannounced times. Such systems are referred to as *near video-on-demand (NVOD)* systems. Pyramid broadcasting schemes [46, 3] are a refinement of NVOD systems where client storage is used to provide more efficient use of logical channels than is possible with the basic NVOD policy. In contrast, under dynamic batching systems [22, 23, 43], there is no predetermined list of popular videos. Instead, the server may delay one or more requests for the same video for a short amount of time by displaying some filler material such as previews. The delayed requests can be served using a single-disk I/O stream by sending the same data pages to batched clients. An alternative dynamic batching scheme is to start display of videos without any delay. By slowing down leading streams and/or speeding up lagging streams, it is possible to merge requests for the same video [32, 1].

Batching policies start users watching a video in synchronization. However, once a batched user performs any VCR actions (`pause` or `resume`), a different stream for service will be required. Hence, in estimating the reduction in server capacity achieved by batching policies, it is necessary to account for the impact of VCR actions. We will describe in detail the batching policies we have outlined and compare them to show their ability to reduce the required server capacity, taking into account the impact of VCR control actions.

5.4.1 Simple NVOD

Figure 5.4 illustrates two well-known NVOD policies. The basic NVOD policy is shown in Figure 5.4(a). In this scheme, each video is subdivided into N_{seg}

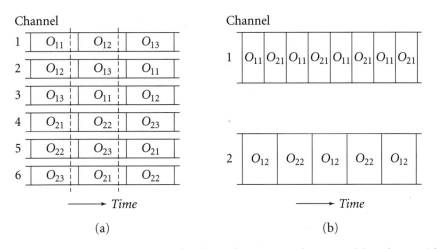

Figure 5.4 Near video-on-demand policies showing simple NVOD (a) and pyramid broadcasting (b).

segments. The segments are periodically broadcast over the available logical channels at different times. Viewers tune into the channel that is closest to their desired viewing time. Figure 5.4(a) shows an example with two videos subdivided into three segments each. As shown, the three segments of video 1 (O_{11}, O_{12}, and O_{13}) are broadcast in sequence over channel 1. The same segments are broadcast at different times on channel 2. A viewer who requests video 1 at the time shown by the first dotted line would tune to channel 3 at the time that segment O_{11} is broadcast on that channel.

The contingency capacity policy can be integrated with simple NVOD to provide full VCR functionality [17]. Viewers requesting a `pause` stop tuning in to the logical channel they were viewing. After executing a `resume`, they are allocated a contingency channel. Other VCR functionality (`fast-forward` and `reverse`) can also be handled similarly. As discussed later, substantial reductions in required server capacity are still possible. However, limited VCR functionality (limited `pause` and `resume`) can be provided without the use of contingency channels. After executing a `pause`, the viewer stops tuning to the current logical channel. For `resume`, the viewer tunes in to the logical channel that shows the desired portion of the video. However, the `resume` may not be instantaneous. For example, consider a viewer who had paused during O_{21} and requests a `resume` at the second dotted line. This viewer may be able to resume instantaneously if channel 6 is showing O_{21} before the desired point of `resume`. Otherwise, the viewer will have to wait.

5.4.2   Pyramid Broadcasting

As discussed earlier, customer behavior is an important influence on channel scheduling policies. The longer customers have to wait, the more likely it is that they will renege or leave the system. In the simple NVOD policy, we show here that the maximum time a customer has to wait for a selected video is $N_{obj}T_{play}/N_{serv,ch}$ [46], where N_{obj} is the number of videos, T_{play} is the time to play a video, and $N_{serv,ch}$ is the total numbers of logical channels in the server. The pyramid broadcasting scheme utilizes client storage to reduce this waiting time.

The upper bound on customer waiting time in an NVOD system can be derived as follows. The number of logical channels per video is $N_{serv,ch}/N_{obj}$. This is equal to $T_{play}/T_{playint}$ where $T_{playint}$ is equal to the interval between successive playbacks of a video. Equating the two yields $T_{playint} = N_{obj}T_{play}/N_{serv,ch}$, the maximum customer wait time, because the largest wait time for a customer for a movie will be the interval between successive playings of the movie. In Figure 5.4(a), the waiting time for a video is 33% of the time to play a video because the videos are divided into three equal segments.

We now explain the pyramid broadcasting scheme. Under this scheme, the total server bandwidth is subdivided into $N_{pyr,ch}$ logical channels. In Figure 5.4(b), there are two logical channels, each with three times the bandwidth needed to playback the video. Each video is also subdivided into $N_{pyr,ch}$ segments whose sizes increase geometrically by a factor α_{pyr}. In the example, the videos are divided into two segments where the second segment is 1.5 times as large as the first. We describe the rationale behind the choice of $\alpha_{pyr} = 1.5$ below. Note that if $N_{pyr,ch}$ is increased, the size of the first segment decreases. This is because the sizes of successive segments increase according to a geometric progression with factor α_{pyr}.

The ith segment of all videos is repeatedly broadcast on channel i. Thus, segments O_{11} and O_{21} are broadcast on channel 1 and segments O_{12} and O_{22} are broadcast on channel 2. To play video i, the client set-top starts download and play of O_{i1} when available. Because the first segments are small (due to the geometric increase in the size of the segments), the interval between successive broadcasts of the first segments is also small. In the example, segments O_{11} and O_{21} each contain 40% of the video and total data equal to 80% of a video. The logical channel has three times the bandwidth needed to play a video. Hence, the total time interval between broadcasts of the segments (which is equal to the time for the broadcast of the segments) is 26% of the time required to play a video. In comparison, the time interval between successive broadcasts for simple NVOD was shown earlier to be 33% of the playback time.

Because the bandwidth of the logical channels is greater than that needed to play the video, the downloading can be completed in less time than needed to play the segment. Hence, part of the segment needs to be stored on the client set-top (perhaps on an attached disk). After starting display of the current segment, the set-top starts downloading and storage of the next segment whenever it becomes available. Hence, the pyramid scheme requires sufficient local storage of the order of the size on the largest video segment.

As the segments increase geometrically in size by α_{pyr}, the overhead is dependent on α_{pyr}. The value of α_{pyr} is determined as follows. For display to be uninterrupted, it must be possible to start download of the next segment before display of the current segment is completed. It can be shown that this leads to a maximum value of α_{pyr} of $N_{serv,ch}/(N_{obj}N_{pyr,ch})$ [46]. This is equal to $6/(2 * 2) = 1.5$ in the example.

Because part of the video is stored on the set-top, the pyramid scheme is able to offer better VCR functionality than pure NVOD without the use of contingency capacity. In particular, the pyramid scheme can offer instantaneous pause and resume by pausing the display of the video while continuing to download it. Resume is handled by resuming the display from the stored video. The storage overhead of the pyramid scheme can be as high as half the storage space for a video for typical workloads [3]. By subdividing the segments into blocks and transmitting the blocks in a prespecified permutation order, it is possible to reduce the required storage overhead [3].

5.4.3 Dynamic Batching Policies

The NVOD policies we have described assume knowledge of the access patterns of the video objects stored in the server. However, the access patterns may fluctuate unpredictably or may not be known with sufficient precision. For example, children's movies may become suddenly popular during school hours if schools are unexpectedly closed. Certain videos that are expected to be popular may not meet expectations; other videos may be more popular than expected. Finally, the demand for all videos may change with time. To deal with these uncertainties, it may be desirable to develop batching policies that can dynamically detect popular videos and serve multiple users of such videos with a single stream. Such dynamic policies may be used by themselves or in conjunction with NVOD policies that serve popular videos with a stable demand. We describe proposed dynamic batching policies next and then discuss their relative performance.

- *FCFS policy.* The first come, first served policy [22] is a policy that attempts to serve customers who have been waiting for a long time because these are the customers who are likely to renege. Under this policy, video requests are put into a single request queue. When a channel becomes available, the scheduling policy services the request at the front of the requests queue, the longest-waiting request. All other queued requests for the same video are also served using the same data stream. Intuitively, FCFS seems a fair policy because it selects a video request independently of the popularity of the video. Additionally, under the FCFS policy, it is possible to consider the projected completion times of requests in the system and provide a time-of-service guarantee to waiting customers [43]. Hence, the FCFS policy can influence customer-waiting behavior under the maximum waiting time model.

- *MQL policy.* The maximum queue length policy [22] is a greedy policy that attempts to maximize the number of accepted viewers. Under the policy, each video is associated with a unique queue that contains all requests for that video. The policy allocates available channels to the video with the maximum number of queued requests. Under this policy, cold videos may not receive service very frequently due to their low queue length. Hence, there may be a high reneging rate for these videos leading to an increase in unfairness. However, for small server capacities, such a policy may have a low long-term reneging probability.

- *GGCS–FCFS policy.* The group guaranteed server capacity–FCFS policy attempts to minimize the average wait time for requests [43]. If object O_i has a playback time $T_{i,\text{play}}$ and is allocated $N_{i,\text{ch}}$ logical channels, its playback interval is $T_{i,\text{play}}/N_{i,\text{ch}}$. The average client waiting time T_{avwait} can be minimized by minimizing $\sum_{i=1}^{N_{\text{obj}}} p_i T_{i,\text{play}}/N_{i,\text{ch}}$, where p_i is the access probability to video i. This is to be minimized subject to the constraint $\sum_{i=1}^{N_{\text{obj}}} N_{i,\text{ch}} \le N_{\text{serv,ch}}$, where $N_{\text{serv,ch}}$ is the number of channels in the server. The optimal solution[2] is given by $N_{i,\text{ch}} = \sqrt{p_i T_{i,\text{play}}} / \sum_{j=1}^{N_{\text{obj}}} \sqrt{p_j T_{j,\text{play}}}$.

5.4.4   Impact of Dynamic Batching Policies

The different batching policies vary in terms of their ability to satisfy the scheduling requirements enumerated earlier. We first compare the three batching policies and then study the substantial reductions in server policy that are achievable using batching.

---

[2]A solution that is correct for the case where all the $T_{i,\text{play}}$ are the same but incorrect in general is found in [2]. The resulting policy, called the maximum factored queue length policy, is inferior to GGCS–FCFS [43].

The three batching policies differ in terms of their ability to influence quantitative measures such as customer reneging and unfairness. Additionally, a qualitative difference among the three policies is that FCFS and GGCS–FCFS can provide time-of-service guarantees to customers, whereas MQL cannot. Under the FCFS policy, the status of current customer requests can be used to provide a time-of-service guarantee to waiting requests. The waiting time can be explicitly computed under the GGCS–FCFS policy using the playback time of the video and the number of dedicated channels. This is not possible under the MQL policy. Hence, FCFS and GGCS–FCFS can influence customer behavior by negotiation.

FCFS vs. MQL. A surprising result is that FCFS is not only a fair and easy-to-implement policy but results in a lower reneging probability than the MQL policy for most operational ranges in the workload. The long-term reneging probabilities of the two policies are compared in Figure 5.5(a) [22]. Assumed is the minimum reneging time model, where viewers wait for a minimum of $T_{ren,min}$ minutes followed by an exponentially distributed time with the mean of 5 minutes. User requests are modeled as a Poisson arrival process with arrival rate λ. Each movie is assumed to be 2 hours in length. For modeling a commercial movie-on-demand installation with between 300 to 3000 users, λ is varied between 2 to 25 per minute.

As expected, when the server capacity is small, the MQL policy has a lower long-term reneging probability than the FCFS policy. However, the relative order of the two policies is reversed for higher server capacities. This will be the operating range for most systems, as the long-term reneging probability in this range is realistic (below 5%). This is because at higher capacities, the MQL policy does not take the amount of time clients have been waiting into account. As a result, it schedules requests for hot videos that have waited only a short time and ignores requests for cold videos that have waited longer. This causes higher reneging. The unfairness of the two policies is compared in Figure 5.5(b). Due to the reasons already discussed, MQL has greater unfairness than FCFS. Further details can be found in [22].

FCFS vs. GGCS–FCFS. We next compare the FCFS and GGCS–FCFS policies. For a large number of workloads, FCFS has lower reneging probability and unfairness compared to GGCS–FCFS [43]. The system environment is similar to that studied in [22]. A typical result shows that for the minimum waiting time model with an arrival rate of 40 requests per minute, the FCFS policy requires a server with 1000 channels to achieve a loss of 1%, whereas the GGCS–FCFS policy requires approximately 1200 channels. For a server with 1200 channels, the FCFS reneging probability is approximately 1% for all videos, whereas the GGCS–FCFS reneging probability can range up to 8%. However, GGCS–FCFS and FCFS appear to have different average waiting time characteristics. GGCS–FCFS has an overall lower

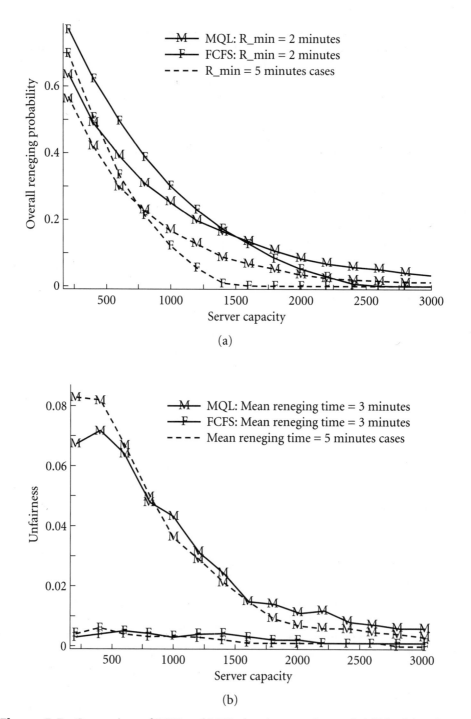

Figure 5.5 Comparison of FCFS and MQL showing reneging probabilities (a) and unfairness (b).

average waiting time than FCFS, while FCFS has a lower variability in waiting time across videos. The lower waiting time characteristics of GGCS–FCFS may be important in a captive audience environment such as universities and industrial organizations [43].

Reduction in server capacity. Because a large number of requests will be for hot videos, batching should substantially reduce server capacity. Depending upon the workload, the reduction can be as high as 70%, and the reduction is higher for larger servers [22]. VCR control operations require the dedication of individual streams to clients and, hence, result in increased capacity requirements. However, substantial reductions in server capacity can still be achieved [17]. This can be seen from Figure 5.6, which plots the required channel capacity against the number of VCR control operations [17]. The simulation environment is the same as that described earlier in Section 5.3.2. The figure plots the results for three different arrival rates. The reduction in required server capacity decreases as the number of VCR control operations increases, since more contingency capacity is required. However, the reduction is greater for greater arrival rates (larger servers). For the highest arrival rate, the reduction is greater than 30% over the entire range of number of VCR control operations considered.

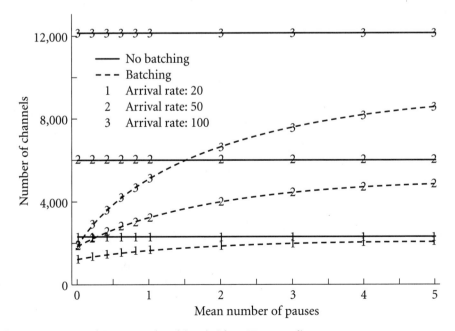

Figure 5.6   Batching vs. no batching (with VCR control).

5.5   Time-Varying Workloads

VCR control and batching are implemented by the low-level scheduler. As discussed earlier in Section 5.2.3, a high-level scheduler that controls the rate at which channels are allocated is required for dealing with time-varying workloads [5]. We discuss and compare various channel rate allocation policies next.

5.5.1   Channel Rate Allocation Policies

Three simple channel rate allocation policies [5] are the on-demand allocation policy, which does not control the allocation rate; the forced-wait policy, which attempts to control the rate implicitly; and the pure rate control policy, which controls the rate explicitly. We will describe the details of these policies.

- *On-demand allocation.* Under this policy, channels are allocated to requests on demand as soon as possible. Arriving requests are allocated channels if one is available; otherwise, they are queued. Freed channels are allocated immediately to the request at the head of the queue under an FCFS policy. As shown later, the policy does not solve the problem of cyclic periods of high reneging.

- *Forced-wait.* Under the forced-wait policy, the first queued request for each video is forced to wait for a minimum wait time. This results in implicit control of the channel allocation rate. Increasing the minimum wait time increases client reneging, while a low minimum wait time reduces to on-demand allocation. Hence, the minimum wait time is a critical parameter. We will show that the performance of this policy is critically dependent upon this parameter, and that correct estimation may be difficult.

- *Pure rate control.* The pure rate control policy explicitly sets a uniform channel allocation rate. The policy allocates a maximum number of channels, N_{delta}, over a fixed time interval called a *measurement interval.* N_{delta} is chosen so that the number of channels available in the server is never exhausted after setting aside the required contingency capacity. Details are found in [5].

5.5.2   Comparison of Rate-Based Allocation Policies

The performance of these three policies has been compared for a system with 1000 channels and 100 movies [5]. The system is modeled over a 24-hour period, ranging from 8 AM of one day to 8 AM the next, with the period between 6 PM to 12 PM being the peak period. The load during the peak period is modeled as being five times greater than that during the nonprime period. Client reneging behavior is assumed to follow the minimum wait time model, with a minimum wait time of 5 minutes and an exponentially distributed mean of 2.5 minutes.

On-demand allocation: The on-demand allocation policy is shown to have undesirable behavior—that is, periods of extremely high reneging probability and large oscillations in waiting time. Hence, it is not considered further.

Forced-wait vs. pure rate control: Figure 5.7 compares the forced-wait and pure rate control policies [5]. The *x*-axis in all of the graphs represents time of day and runs from 8 AM of one day to 8 AM the next. The individual points on the graph are 6-minute averages; the dotted lines represent cumulative averages. The period of 6 minutes is referred to as a *reporting interval.*

Figure 5.7(a) shows that the forced-wait policy is very sensitive to fluctuations in the minimum wait time of clients. The first graph plots the arrival rate, and the next three graphs illustrate the reneging probability for the minimum wait time of clients for three different values of 4, 5, and 6 minutes. The corresponding long-term reneging probabilities are 8.9, 6.2, and 17.6%, respectively. It can be seen that small changes in client behavior (e.g., minimum waiting time increases from 5 to 6 minutes) cause large changes in reneging probability (an increase of 300%). Additionally, when the forced-wait time is larger than the minimum wait time, large numbers of clients renege, causing the system to be underutilized. Hence, the system becomes underutilized even though the reneging probability is high. Furthermore, the system still exhibits undesirable cyclic behavior. Finally, even during periods of low load, the forced wait causes high average wait times. In contrast, the pure wait policy exhibits better behavior. The second graph shows that the reneging probability stays low at all times, while the fourth graph shows that the average wait time of client requests is high only in the peak period.

The forced-wait and pure rate control policies can also be compared with regard to the server capacity needed to meet specified target reneging probabilities [5]. For a specified long-term reneging probability of 5%, and assuming an optimal choice for the forced-wait time parameter for the forced-wait policy, both policies require a server capacity of 1000 channels. However, if an additional objective of a maximum short-term reneging probability in any reporting period of 15% is imposed, the forced-wait policy requires 25% more channels. The pure rate control policy, on the other hand, requires negligibly more channels. This is a consequence of the fact that even if the forced-wait policy has a low long-term reneging probability, it still has peaks in short-term reneging probability.

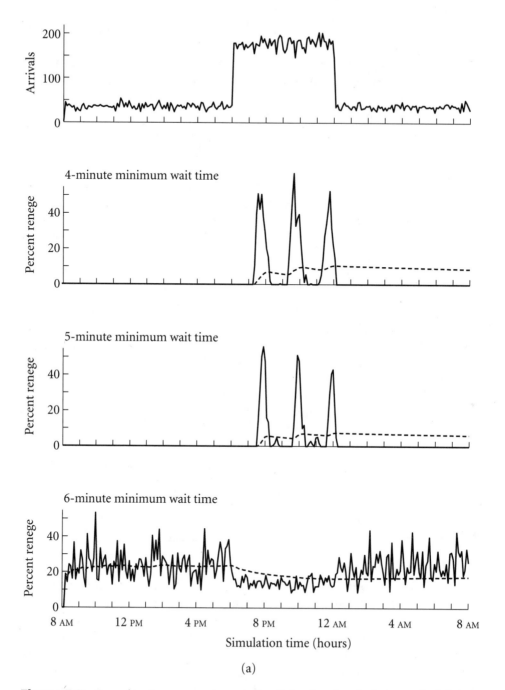

(a)

Figure 5.7 Forced wait vs. pure rate control policies showing the impact of minimum wait times on forced-wait systems (a) as compared to reneging probabilities in pure rate control systems (b).

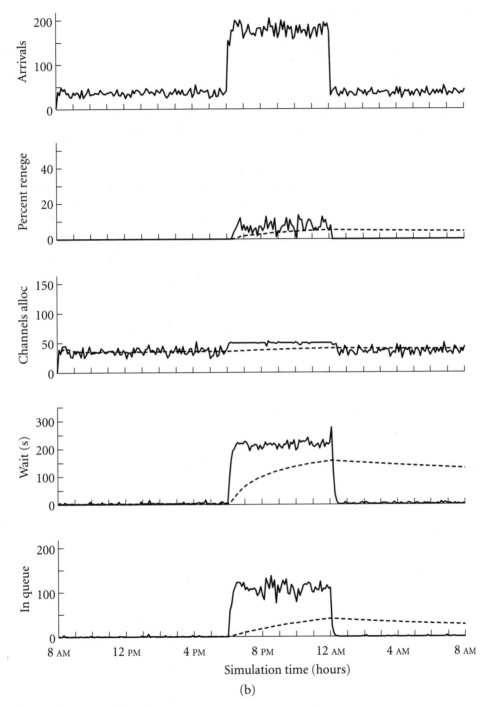

(b)

Figure 5.7   Continued

5.6   Summary

In this chapter, we addressed the issue of when and which client request to serve when the component resources become available to set up a logical channel. The client request scheduling policy takes into account many different issues and objectives in making this decision, including client request distribution, client reneging behavior, likely access patterns within a video and VCR control operations, fairness, anticipated future load, and broad objective measures—for example, average and/or peak waiting time, reneging probability, and so on. The channel scheduler selects a client request to serve and requests that the resource manager set up a logical channel. The resource manager, however, may also interact with the channel scheduler to ensure that sufficient bandwidth is available for VCR control operations (such as interactive playback of a video). The channel scheduler may batch multiple requests together for the same long video, thereby significantly reducing the server capacity required. In a near video-on-demand system, a client request is served by the closest prescheduled stream, whereas under a video-on-demand system multiple client requests are dynamically grouped to be served via a new single stream. Finally, the scheduler controls the rate of channel allocation for dealing with anticipated future load.

Further Reading

Further details on batching policies and their objectives can be found in [22]. The batching policies that take into account long-term objectives and channel conservation are detailed in [4]. Channel allocation for handling VCR control is detailed in [17]. Use of bridging and the merging of two nearest streams by appropriately speeding up or slowing down is addressed in [32].

6

Scheduling in System Components

6.1   Introduction

In the previous two chapters, we described how a logical channel is set up prior to playback (i.e., data delivery) of a multimedia document and how to select a client request to be served when resources become available. Because multiple channels may share a system component or resource, an operational scheduling policy is required to determine at every moment which channel is to be served next so that the QoS requirements of all channels are not violated. The operational scheduling policies and the principles detailed in this chapter are applicable to all system components. However, as mentioned earlier, system components other than the CPU may have additional constraints—for example, the disk storage system needs to consider the physical constraint of disk arm movement and the overhead of seek time in switching from one data stream to another. Hence, further details of the constraints and the adaptation of the scheduling policies for specific system components will be detailed in appropriate chapters. The current set of policies is primarily focused on CPU scheduling.

In video-on-demand servers, the CPU is one of the important resources needed for setting up a logical channel. An important use of the CPU is for executing the instructions necessary for delivering the video stream. For example, the CPU is used to execute the disk scheduling policies necessary to retrieve the data from disk and deliver it to the network. Hence, without CPU scheduling that allows execution of the disk scheduler, the stream may be unable to retrieve the needed blocks even though disk reservation may be implemented. In addition to execution of instructions for multimedia stream delivery, the CPU may be used by complex multimedia applications (as discussed in Part 1) for other processing of data. For example, a virtual reality application may generate a moving image by retrieving parts of the image from storage and computing part of the image. Such an application will require the CPU not only for data retrieval but also for real-time processing of data. Alternatively, in a multimedia application that retrieves composite documents [42], the higher-level scheduler with a detailed knowledge of the application may determine when and at what playback rate various components are to be retrieved, while the lower-level tasks may actually perform delivery of continuous and noncontinuous data streams. The higher-level application processing may involve interactions with databases and other application servers as well as dynamic processing of data. In future applications (e.g., e-commerce such as storefronts and marketplaces), multimedia interactions will become an essential embedded component and not a stand-alone activity, as in simple applications such as playback of a single, long video.

In a simple VOD application where, once the client playback streams are started, the CPU performs only the periodic tasks of transferring data from disks to the network and the system may be I/O bound, it may be argued that the best-effort scheduling of the CPU is sufficient. However, in most environments considering complex application requirements, either the CPU demand is unpredictable (other than the requirements for continuous media support) and/or the system may not be extremely I/O bound. Complex CPU scheduling policies are essential in such environments.

To satisfy these application requirements, the CPU subsystem has to reserve the required CPU resources for both continuous media and other tasks as well as appropriately schedule requests for the CPU. CPU reservation has been described in Chapter 5 as part of the policy for setting up a logical channel. Here, we focus on scheduling requests for the CPU to ensure continuous delivery and other objectives.

CPU scheduling for continuous media differs from scheduling in other contexts because, in general, supporting continuous delivery requires scheduling of periodic requests for the CPU with hard deadlines. The scheduling of periodic requests so as to satisfy hard real-time requirements has been studied in a series of classical papers [37, 38]. We first discuss these papers to provide a background for the scheduling policies. Subsequently, we discuss the extensions of these policies to multimedia servers, where both continuous delivery and other usage of the CPU need to be supported. Finally, we discuss system implementation issues.

6.2   Scheduling of Periodic Tasks

The classical papers on the scheduling of periodic tasks [37, 38] studied tasks with the following characteristics:

1. The only tasks with hard real-time deadlines are periodic tasks.

2. The deadline for a task is the next time a request for that task is generated.

3. The tasks are independent of each other.

4. The execution time for a task is constant and does not depend upon time or the execution sequence.

5. Nonperiodic tasks do not have deadlines.

6. Tasks can be preempted before completion.

As noted earlier, these characteristics apply better to CPU scheduling than to the scheduling of other components (e.g., disk scheduling violates characteristic 4). Such tasks can be scheduled using either a static priority policy or a dynamic priority policy [37]. These lead to the two policies below.

- *Rate monotonic scheduling.* This static priority policy associates one of a fixed set of N_{pr} priority levels to each task. The priorities are assigned such that tasks with greater frequency (lower interrequest times) are assigned higher priority. Formally, if $T_{i,\text{period}} \leq T_{j,\text{period}}$, then $N_{i,\text{pr}} \leq N_{j,\text{pr}}$, where $T_{i,\text{period}}$ and $T_{j,\text{period}}$ are the interrequest times of tasks i and j, respectively, and $N_{i,\text{pr}}$ and $N_{j,\text{pr}}$ are the associated priorities. The rate monotonic policy schedules the tasks in priority order. Within a priority, tasks can be scheduled in arbitrary order.

- *Deadline scheduling.* As noted, the deadline for a task is the time at which the next request for the task will be generated. The deadline scheduling policy sets the priority of each task to its deadline. Hence, it is a dynamic priority-based policy. The task with the lowest priority (deadline) is scheduled first. Tasks with the same deadline are scheduled in arbitrary order.

The rate monotonic policy is easier to implement [37]. This is because it is a static priority policy that associates priorities with tasks, whereas the deadline scheduling policy associates deadlines with requests. Hence, the deadline scheduling policy requires a computation each time a request is made, while the rate monotonic policy can associate a priority at the time the task is started. Additionally, computation of deadlines may be complicated.

These two approaches have also been studied with regard to their worst-case utilization bound (WUB) [37]. This is the lowest utilization at which a set of periodic tasks can be found that cannot be scheduled. The rate monotonic policy has been shown to be the optimum static priority assignment policy, in the sense that no other static scheduling policy has a higher WUB. Similarly, the deadline scheduling policy is the optimum dynamic scheduling policy. The WUBs for the deadline scheduling policy and the rate monotonic policy were shown to be 100% and 70%, respectively.

It is clear that the deadline scheduling policy should outperform the rate monotonic scheduling policy because the rate monotonic policy does not take the time that a request was submitted into consideration. In practice, the rate monotonic policy does not perform as badly as the analysis would suggest, and much higher utilizations are achievable [38]. The average case behavior of the rate monotonic policy can be studied by considering the achievable utilization under randomly generated workloads [38]. For a large number of tasks, the achievable utilization for the rate monotonic policy approaches 88%. Hence, both policies continue to be used for component scheduling.

6.2.1   Relationship to CPU Scheduling in Multimedia Servers

The classical policies we have described may not be adequate for scheduling in a multimedia server environment. This is because the workload may include a mixture of real-time applications with periodic requests, as well as non-real-time requests (which will generally be nonperiodic). The rate monotonic and deadline scheduling policies assume that nonperiodic requests are scheduled in the background. However, this could result in unnecessarily long response times for such requests. Consider a situation where a number of video requests with long deadlines are queued for the CPU. In such a situation, it may be possible to schedule a nonvideo request without causing any of the video requests to miss a deadline. Policies that schedule nonvideo requests in the background also cannot provide any sort of guarantee (e.g., response-time guarantee) for such requests. Hence, it is necessary to extend the classical policies for use in multimedia servers.

In the next two sections, we describe two different alternatives for augmenting the classical policies. The first approach is to modify the scheduling policies to handle non-real-time requests. The second approach explicitly recognizes that a multimedia server may contain a number of application types, each with its own scheduling requirements. This leads to a hierarchical scheduling structure where each task group can schedule its own tasks.

6.3   Hybrid Rate Monotonic Policy

The hybrid rate monotonic (HRM) policy [40] supports a wide range of request types using a mixture of round-robin scheduling and rate monotonic scheduling. The policy classifies tasks into three types: isochronous, guaranteed-service, and background. (The three task classes are referred to as *isochronous, real-time,* and *general purpose* in [40].) These are illustrated in Figure 6.1 together with some of the associated data structures required by the policy. Isochronous tasks are real-time periodic tasks, such as video streams. Guaranteed-service tasks are tasks that require a guaranteed throughput and bounded delay (e.g., polling device drivers).

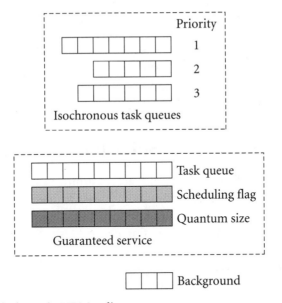

Figure 6.1 Task classes in HRM policy.

Background tasks are low-priority tasks with no guarantees of service. However, the scheduler grants the background class a minimum quantum to ensure that the class as a whole is not starved.

As in the rate monotonic policy, tasks are assumed to be preemptible. Background tasks may be preempted at any time. To avoid preempting isochronous and guaranteed-service tasks at an arbitrary time s, the tasks are made to allow (in software) for the existence of preemption windows. These are time intervals during which isochronous and guaranteed-service tasks may be safely preempted.

The basic operation of the HRM policy is as follows [40]. A new task may be scheduled when the task queue becomes nonempty, during a preemption window, or when the current task ends. During each scheduling instant, the scheduler first examines the isochronous tasks. Each isochronous task has associated with it a rate monotonic priority. When it is ready to run, it is inserted into the task queue corresponding to its priority (see Figure 6.1). The scheduler services the isochronous tasks in priority order until all the isochronous task queues are empty. To guarantee that each isochronous task can run at the required frequency, the scheduler will accept a new isochronous task only if it can reserve sufficient capacity (as described below). Next, the scheduler examines the guaranteed-service tasks. Each such task has associated with it a quantum size that specifies the amount of time the task is allowed to execute. As described later, the quantum sizes are chosen to satisfy the required throughput and delay bounds for the tasks. As in the case of isochronous tasks, the scheduler may reject a guaranteed-service task if sufficient resources are not available. Finally, after the isochronous and guaranteed-service task queues are empty, the background tasks are scheduled round-robin for a total execution time of one quantum.

6.3.1   Admission Control for HRM Policy

As stated earlier, the HRM policy cannot accept arbitrary sets of isochronous and guaranteed-service tasks for execution. This is because due to the finite capacity of the CPU, it may not be possible to schedule the tasks to meet their requirements. We now describe informally the admission control tests used by the HRM policy to decide whether to accept a new task [40].

The HRM policy uses two tests to determine whether to accept a new task. The first test checks to see if addition of the new task will cause any of the guaranteed-service tasks to miss their delay bounds. This is done by first calculating the delay due to execution of isochronous tasks (including the new task, if it is isochronous). To this, the delay due to other guaranteed-service tasks (including the new task, if it is guaranteed service) and the delay due to the background quantum is added. The second test needs to be carried out only for new isochronous tasks. It checks if addition of the new task will cause any isochronous task to miss its deadline. This is accomplished by computing the frequency with which each isochronous task of equal or lower priority is executed after addition of the new task.

6.4   Hierarchical Scheduling

The HRM policy is a single-level scheduling policy that attempts to support the diverse requirements of the applications that exist in a multimedia server. An alternative is a hierarchical scheduling policy that partitions the processor among task groups. Each group either further partitions the processor among subgroups or schedules tasks in the group. This allows each application to implement an appropriate scheduling policy. An additional advantage is that a hierarchical scheme is relatively easier to implement in a traditional operating systems environment (e.g., Unix) [20]. This is because only the higher level scheduling policy needs to be implemented in the kernel.

Figure 6.2 shows an example of a hierarchical task structure [28, 33]. The tasks in the system are subdivided into two groups, G_1 and G_2. Group G_1 contains four tasks, K_1 through K_4. Group G_2 is further subdivided into subgroups G_{21} and G_{22}. Group G_{21} contains no active tasks; group G_{22} contains tasks K_5 and K_6. Each

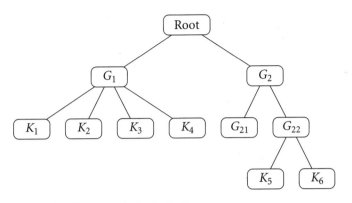

Figure 6.2 Example of hierarchical scheduling.

group can have associated with it a scheduling policy. In the case of G_1, the associated policy schedules the tasks K_1 through K_4, while in the case of G_2, the associated policy further partitions the resources between groups G_{21} and G_{22}.

In general, the lower-level policies that schedule between tasks will be application dependent. Hence, we consider only the higher-level policies that partition the processor between task groups. Before discussing the policies, we consider the objectives for such policies. Finally, we consider implementation issues, such as the implementation overhead.

6.4.1   Hierarchical Scheduling Objectives

The motivation for the high-level scheduler is to allow related tasks to be scheduled by an application-dependent scheduler. Hence, an important requirement for such policies is that they isolate different subgroups from each other. This implies that the partitioning of the CPU among the various groups should be independent of the load on the other groups; that is, it should not be possible for tasks in any group to maliciously or accidentally monopolize the CPU (e.g., by spawning many tasks). For generality, it should be possible to allocate each group, G_i, a fraction, ρ_i, of the CPU. Furthermore, since CPU times for threads are difficult to estimate, the policy should not require precise estimates of the CPU time required.

An ideal policy for achieving these objectives would be the perfect fair-share policy that services the various groups round-robin using an infinitely small quantum of CPU time. The quantum for group G_i would be proportional to ρ_i. But such a policy would not be realizable due to the overhead of context switching, and any policy that used a finite quantum would deviate from perfect sharing. The extent of the deviation of the policy can, therefore, be used as a measure to compare various policies. If $C_i(t_1, t_2)$ is the amount of CPU time used by group G_i in the time interval (t_1, t_2), $C_i(t_1, t_2)/\rho_i - C_j(t_1, t_2)/\rho_j$ is a measure of unfairness between the scheduling of groups G_i and G_j [31].

6.4.2   Fair-Share Policies

The perfect fair-share policy is unrealizable in practice. Achievable fair-share policies are those that attempt to approximate the perfect fair-share policy. The weighted fair queuing (WFQ) policy [26] is the first known proposed fair-queuing policy. The start-time fair queuing (SFQ) policy is a computationally more efficient policy that has greater fairness and behaves better under variable load [33].

Weighted Fair Queuing. The WFQ policy attempts to simulate the execution of a perfect fair-share policy. The concepts behind the policy are shown in Figure 6.3, which shows the hypothetical execution of five tasks, K_1 through K_5. (For simplicity, we discuss the scheduling of individual tasks; the same concepts apply to scheduling of groups.) Task K_i has a start time of $t_{i,st}$ and a finish time of $t_{i,fi}$. An important concept in the WFQ policy is the round number, $N_{ro}(t)$, at time t. In the figure, it can be seen that task K_1 receives a quantum of service during rounds 1 and 2. Task K_2 arrives during round 3. Tasks K_1 and K_2 both receive service during round 3. Similarly, tasks K_1, K_2, and K_3 receive service during round 4.

Under a perfect fair-share policy, the CPU is shared equally among all the ready tasks. Let W_{CPU} be the capacity of the CPU and *Ready* be the set of threads that are ready to run. It can be seen that under a perfect fair-share policy, $N_{ro}(t)$ satisfies the equation $dN_{ro}(t)/dt = W_{CPU}/\sum_{\epsilon Ready}\rho_i$. Consequently, the round number in which task K_i finishes its jth quantum of service is given by $N_{i,j,fi} = N_{i,j,st} + L_{i,j,q}/\rho_i$. Here, $N_{i,j,st}$ is the round in which the task starts its jth round of service, and $L_{i,j,q}$ is the length of the quantum. Note that both the starting and finishing round numbers can be fractional to indicate that the task started or finished its quantum in the middle of a round. The starting round number of the jth quantum for task K_i is either the finishing time of the previous quantum or the current round number when the task arrives (for the first quantum). Hence, it is given by $N_{i,j,st} = \max(N_{ro}(t_{i,ar}), N_{i,j-1,fi})$.

The details of the WFQ policy are

1. Compute $N_{ro}(t)$, $N_{i,j,st}$, and $N_{i,j,fi}$ for the current quantum j for all tasks.

2. Schedule the task with the lowest $N_{i,j,fi}$, with ties being broken arbitrarily.

Computation of $N_{ro}(t)$ in the WFQ policy is complex [31]. The self-clocked fair queuing (SCFQ) policy [25] reduces the complexity of WFQ by approximat-

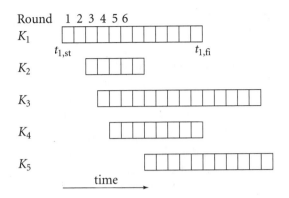

Figure 6.3 Weighted fair queuing policy.

ing $N_{ro}(t)$. An additional disadvantage of both the WFQ and SCFQ policies arises in the computation of the finish times for a quantum, which requires knowledge of the length of the quantum. In CPU scheduling, this may not be known because tasks may relinquish control of the CPU. The fair queuing based on start time (FQS) policy attempts to eliminate this disadvantage by scheduling tasks according to their start times. However, it still requires the complex computation of $N_{ro}(t)$.

Start-time fair queuing. The WFQ policy has the disadvantages of computational complexity and requiring knowledge of the execution times of tasks. Both of these disadvantages are addressed by the SFQ policy [33]. Instead of the round number, the SFQ policy uses a quantity referred to as the *virtual time at time t*, $t_{vir}(t)$. The details of the SFQ policy are

1. Initially, set $t_{vir}(t) = 0$. During execution of quantum j of task K_i, set $t_{vir}(t) = N_{i,j,st}$. If the CPU is idle, set $t_{vir}(t)$ to the maximum of $N_{i,j,fi}$.

2. Set $N_{i,j,fi} = N_{i,j,st} + L_{i,j,q}/\rho_i$, and $N_{i,j,st} = \max(t_{vir}(t_{i,ar}), N_{i,j-1,fi})$.

3. Schedule the thread with the lowest $N_{i,j,st}$, with ties being broken arbitrarily.

The SFQ policy has a number of advantages as a fair scheduling policy. First, like the SCFQ policy, its computational complexity is low compared to WFQ as it does not require the computation of $N_{ro}(t)$. As in the FQS policy, it does not require knowledge of the amount of CPU time required by a task. Finally, it has significantly better fairness than WFQ, particularly in the case of variations in the server capacity [33]. Such variations could be caused by unanticipated nonmultimedia load, such as interrupts.

6.5   Summary

Multiple playback streams or logical channels may share common resources. An operational scheduling policy determines how to mediate access to these resources at every point. The policies described in this chapter are most applicable to scheduling the CPU; scheduling policies for other system components need to address additional constraints. CPU scheduling needs to consider not only periodic tasks for retrieving multimedia data but other application tasks as well—for example, processing/generation of image data. There are two approaches to CPU scheduling in multimedia servers. Single-tier policies [40] extend traditional real-time CPU scheduling policies to handle mixtures of multimedia as well as nonmultimedia data. Alternatively, hierarchical scheduling policies [33] partition the CPU among various applications according to a fixed ratio, while allowing each application to use an application-specific policy for scheduling tasks belonging to that application. Retrieval of composite documents, where retrievals of multiple (continuous and noncontinuous) objects need to be synchronized, requires an additional level of scheduling. The higher-level scheduler with the knowledge of the document structure determines which next object fragment and/or data block should be retrieved as the CPU becomes available to this application [42]. Retrieval of composite documents concerns additional prefetching, buffering, and caching issues as well. These issues will be discussed further in Part 4.

Further Reading

Hierarchical scheduling issues discussed in this chapter are further explored in [5]. The scheduling of retrieval of composite documents is detailed in [42].

Part 2 References

[1]   C. Aggarwal, J. Wolf, and P. Yu. Adaptive piggybacking schemes for video-on-demand systems. Technical Report RC-20635. IBM Research, Yorktown Heights, NY, November 1996.

[2]   C. Aggarwal, J. Wolf, and P. Yu. The maximum factor queue length batching scheme for video-on-demand systems. Technical Report RC-20621. IBM Research, Yorktown Heights, NY, November 1996.

[3]   C. Aggarwal, J. Wolf, and P. Yu. Permutation-based pyramid broadcasting. Technical Report RC-20620. IBM Research, Yorktown Heights, NY, April 1996.

[4]   K. Almeroth and M. Ammar. On the use of multicast delivery to provide a scalable and interactive video-on-demand service. *IEEE Journal of Selected Areas in Communication,* pp. 1110, April 1996.

[5]   K. Almeroth, A. Dan, D. Sitaram, and W. Tetzlaff. Long-term channel allocation strategies for video applications. Technical Report RC-20249. IBM Research, Yorktown Heights, NY, 1995.

[6]   D. Anderson. Metascheduling for continuous media. *ACM Transactions on Computer Systems,* 11(3):205–225, August 1993.

[7]   D. Anderson et al. A distributed computer system for professional audio. In *Proceedings of ACM Multimedia Conference.* ACM, 1994.

[8]   M. Baugher, S. French, A. Stephens, and I. V. Horn. A multimedia client to the IBM LAN server. In *Proceedings of ACM Multimedia Conference.* ACM, 1993.

[9]   V. Bove and J. Watlington. Cheops: A modular processor for scalable video coding. In *Proceedings of SPIE.* SPIE, 1991.

[10] CCITT. Codec for audiovisual services at px384 Kb/s, CCITT recommendation H.261. CCITT, Melbourne, 1988.

[11] CCITT. Frame structure for a 64 Kb/s channel in audiovisual teleservices, CCITT recommendation H.221. CCITT, Melbourne, 1988.

[12] CCITT. ISDN frame relay standard, CCITT recommendation Q.933. CCITT, Melbourne, 1988.

[13] G. Coulson and G. S. Blair. Micro-kernel support for continuous media in distributed systems. *Computer Networks and ISDN Systems,* 26:1323–1341, July 1994.

[14] A. Dan, M. Eshel, J. Hollan, M. Kienzle, J. McAssey, R. Rose, D. Sitaram, and W. Tetzlaff. The research server complex manager for large-scale multimedia servers. Technical Report RC20705. IBM Research, Yorktown Heights, NY, January 1997.

[15] A. Dan, D. Dias, R. Mukherjee, D. Sitaram, and R. Tewari. Buffering and caching in large scale video servers. In *Proceedings of IEEE CompCon.* IEEE, 1995.

[16] A. Dan, P. Shahabuddin, D. Sitaram, and D. Towsley. Channel allocation under batching and VCR control in video-on-demand servers. *Journal of Parallel and Distributed Computing,* 30(2):168–179, November 1995.

[17] A. Dan and D. Sitaram. Buffer management policy for an on-demand video server. Technical Report RC-19347. IBM Research, Yorktown Heights, NY, January 1994.

[18] A. Dan and D. Sitaram. Calibration of video servers. Internal IBM memo, 1994.

[19] A. Dan and D. Sitaram. Resource allocation for multimedia support in a non-realtime environment. *IBM Technical Disclosure Bulletin,* May 1995.

[20] A. Dan and D. Sitaram. A generalized interval caching policy for mixed interactive and long video environments. In *Proceedings of Multimedia Computing and Networking.* SPIE, 1996.

[21] A. Dan, D. Sitaram, and P. Shahabuddin. Scheduling policies for an on-demand video server with batching. In *Proceedings of ACM Multimedia Conference.* ACM, 1994.

[22] A. Dan, D. Sitaram, and P. Shahabuddin. Dynamic batching policies for an on-demand video server. *Multimedia Systems,* 4(3):112–121, June 1996.

[23] J. Davin and A. Heybey. A simulation study of fair queuing and policy enforcement. *The Computer Communication Review,* 20(5):23–29, October 1990.

[24] S. Deering. Host extensions for IP multicasting. Technical Report RFC 1112. IETF, 1989.

[25] A. Demers, S. Keshav, and S. Shenker. Analysis and simulation of a fair queuing algorithm. In *Proceedings of ACM SIGCOMM*. ACM, 1989.

[26] J. Dey, J. Salehi, J. Kurose, and D. Towsley. Providing VCR capabilities in large-scale video servers. In *Proceedings of ACM Multimedia Conference*. ACM, 1994.

[27] B. Ford and S. Susarla. CPU inheritance scheduling. In *Proceedings of the second USENIX symposium on operating systems design and implementation*. ACM, 1996.

[28] E. A. Fox. The coming revolution in interactive digital video. *Communications of the ACM*, 7(32):794–801, July 1989.

[29] B. Furht, S. W. Smoliar, and H. Zhang. *Video and Image Processing in Multimedia Systems*. Kluwer Academic Publishers, Norwell, MA, 1995.

[30] S. Golestani. A self-clocked fair queuing scheme for high speed applications. In *Infocomm*, 1994.

[31] L. Golubchik, J. Lui, and R. Muntz. Reducing I/O demand in video-on-demand storage servers. In *Proceedings of the ACM SIGMETRICS Conference*. ACM, 1995.

[32] P. Goyal, X. Guo, and H. Vin. A hierarchical CPU scheduler for multimedia operating systems. In *Proceedings of the OSDI Symposium*. ACM, 1996.

[33] M. Kamath, D. Towsley, and K. Ramamritham. Buffer management for continuous media sharing in multimedia database systems. Technical Report 94-11. University of Massachusetts, February 1994.

[34] A. Laursen, J. Olkin, and M. Porter. Oracle media server: Providing consumer based interactive access to multimedia data. In *Proceedings of the ACM SIGMOD International Conference on Management of Data*. ACM, May 1994.

[35] J.-Y. Le Boudec. The asynchronous transfer mode: A tutorial. *Computer Networks and ISDN Systems*, 24:279–309, May 1992.

[36] J. Lehoczky, L. Sha, and Y. Ding. The rate monotonic scheduling algorithm: Exact characterization and average case behavior. In *Proceedings of the IEEE Real-time Symposium*. IEEE, 1989.

[37] C. Liu and J. Layland. Scheduling algorithms for multiprogramming in a hard real-time environment. *Journal of the ACM*, 20(1):46–61, 1973.

[38] Microsoft Corporation. *Multimedia Authoring and Tools Guide, Microsoft Windows Programmer's Reference Library.* Microsoft Press, Redmond, WA, 1991.

[39] K. Ramakrishnan, L. Vaitzblit, C. Gray, U. Vahalia, D. Ting, P. Tzelnic, S. Glaser, and W. Duso. Operating system support for a video-on-demand file service. *Multimedia Systems,* 3(2):53–65, May 1995.

[40] P. Rangan, H. Vin, and S. Ramanathan. Designing an on-demand multimedia service. *IEEE Communications Magazine,* 30:56–65, July 1992.

[41] J. Song, A. Dan, and D. Sitaram. Efficient retrieval of composite multimedia objects in the JINSIL distributed system. In *Proceedings of the ACM SIGMETRICS Conference.* ACM, June 1997.

[42] A. Tsiolis and M. Vernon. Group-guaranteed channel capacity in multimedia storage servers. In *Proceedings of the ACM SIGMETRICS Conference.* ACM, June 1997.

[43] D. Venkatesh and T. Little. Prospects for interactive video-on-demand. *IEEE Multimedia,* pp. 14–23, Fall 1994.

[44] *Video Store Magazine.* Advanstar Communications, Inc., December 1992 (published weekly).

[45] H. Vin, P. Goyal, and A. Goyal. A statistical admission control for algorithm multimedia servers. In *Proceedings of ACM Multimedia Conference.* ACM, October 1994.

[46] S. Vishwanathan and T. Imielinski. Metropolitan area video on demand multimedia service. *SPIE,* 24(17):66–77, 1995.

PART 3

The Storage Subsystem

7

Storage Management Overview

7.1   Introduction

The storage subsystem in a multimedia server is responsible for the storage and retrieval of multimedia data from storage devices. As described in Chapter 1, multimedia data is generally more voluminous than nonmultimedia data. Additionally, the multimedia data has to be delivered according to the stringent QoS specifications of multimedia applications. Satisfying these requirements makes the design of the storage manager very challenging.

Unlike other subsystems in the multimedia server, the storage subsystem deals with additional issues related to data storage (data placement and organization) apart from the main QoS issues (resource reservation and data delivery). The interactions among the two sets of issues dealing with both finite bandwidth and storage capacities of the storage devices make the management of the storage subsystem a complex and difficult task. Consider the case where all the frequently accessed multimedia data is stored on the same storage device. During playback, the storage device may not have sufficient bandwidth to satisfy all the requests [13]. Conversely, placing only infrequently accessed material on a storage device may result in the device being underutilized. Therefore, the storage management subsystem has to take into account both the storage as well as bandwidth capacity of the storage devices. A good set of abstractions and organization principles is needed to address these complex issues.

7.1.1   Storage Manager Functions

The storage manager is responsible for coordinating and managing the operations of all the storage devices. The primary functions of the storage manager are

- *Storage of multimedia data.* The storage manager is responsible for the allocation and storage of multimedia files on the various storage devices. To locate these files, the storage manager needs to maintain metadata that maps logical blocks of files to physical blocks on the storage devices.

- *Retrieval of multimedia data.* Chapter 4 described the session scheduler, which reserves bandwidth on all the resources needed to deliver a stream, including storage subsystem components. Because the session scheduler is invoked only when starting or stopping streams and not during block-by-block playback, the reservations are ensured not by the session scheduler, but by the data retrieval functions. Thus, the mainline operational function of the storage manager guarantees that the data needed by each stream is retrieved at the required rate. Consequently, the storage manager also has to enforce bandwidth reservations on storage devices to ensure that devices are not overloaded.

- *Recovery from failure.* In many multimedia applications, failure of hardware components may incur a very high cost. For example, in a movie-on-demand system serving a large number of viewers, failure of a hardware component in the storage subsystem may lead to interruption in the viewing of a very popular movie. This may lead to a large cost in terms of lost revenue as well as loss of goodwill among the viewers. Therefore, it is important for the storage manager to recover from hardware component failure.

- *Storage server optimization.* A large-scale multimedia server may contain a very large amount of multimedia data. As discussed earlier, for cost-effectiveness the storage subsystem may be organized as a storage hierarchy consisting of secondary and tertiary storage devices. The storage manager decides which data is to be stored on tertiary storage and manages the transfer of data from tertiary storage devices to secondary storage devices. Additionally, a multimedia server will generally contain multiple logical secondary storage devices. The storage manager is thus responsible for the placement of multimedia data among the multiple devices so as to avoid load imbalance during playback while fully utilizing the capacities of the devices.

In the rest of the chapter, we discuss the overall architecture of a storage subsystem and provide an overview of the issues in dealing with the placement and retrieval of multimedia documents. In subsequent chapters, we consider these issues in more detail.

7.2   Storage System Architecture

A typical storage subsystem, illustrated in Figure 7.1, may contain physical storage devices of varying speeds, capacities, and cost (e.g., disk, tape, and CD-ROM). We summarize (from Chapter 3) some of the characteristics of these devices and their impact on multimedia server design. Subsequently, we discuss the logical inter-

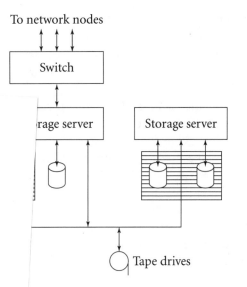

To network nodes

Switch

rage server   Storage server

Tape drives

multimedia server.

storage subsystem. The actual physical inter-
described in Chapter 3.

eristics

ess time and high bandwidth are important re-
s used to store multimedia data to be delivered
servers, these requirements can be satisfied pri-
VD. Since these secondary storage devices also
per byte, they are not suitable for storing infre-
is more cost-effective to store infrequently used
data on tertiary storage devices with a low storage cost per byte (e.g., tape). The
multimedia server needs policies to retrieve data from tertiary storage and deliver
it to the user [19, 28, 14, 22, 7]. These issues are discussed in detail later in
Chapter 10.

7.2.2   Storage Subsystem Topology

Storage devices in the storage subsystem are connected to storage servers that
manage the storage devices. The total bandwidth required from a multimedia

server may be greater than that obtainable from storage devices connected to a single server. Therefore, a large multimedia server may contain multiple storage servers. In this case, some storage devices may be connected to multiple servers. Connecting secondary storage devices to multiple servers improves the reliability of the system because it allows a backup server to serve streams that were being served by the failed server. If tertiary storage devices are connected to multiple servers, infrequently retrieved data can be retrieved from multiple servers. This relieves bottlenecks in the system. The storage servers, in turn, may be interconnected by switches to other components of the system (e.g., network servers), as shown in Figure 7.1.

The different secondary storage devices in a multimedia server are likely to store different multimedia data. Due to the nonuniform access to such data, load imbalance is likely to arise between the devices. Load imbalance can be reduced by combining the storage devices into striping groups and interleaving the data among the devices [33, 36]. For example, in a striping group consisting of four disks, blocks 0, 4, 8, . . . of each file can be stored on disk 0, blocks 1, 5, 9, . . . on disk 1, and so on. (Striping patterns are discussed in more detail in Chapter 9.) By storing parity data in striping groups, it is possible to prevent failure [36, 9, 4, 49]. The striping group can be considered to be a logical device with storage and bandwidth equal to the combined storage and bandwidth of the individual devices.

Because striping eliminates load imbalances among the devices in a striping group, it is natural to try to stripe all the secondary storage devices in a multimedia server into a single group. However, as discussed in more detail in Chapter 9, this is not possible in practice. First, it is difficult to combine devices with different capacities in the same striping group. For example, the simple striping pattern we have described requires all devices to have the same storage capacity. This would not be the case if the devices were different (i.e., from different vendors or a mixture of different disk types from the same vendor). Additionally, it is simple to reconfigure a server with multiple striping groups because only the affected group needs to be taken off-line. For eliminating load imbalances among different striping groups and storage servers, good multimedia data placement policies [13, 31, 20, 6, 5] are required. Because the access patterns at run time will fluctuate unpredictably, adaptive load-balancing policies are also required [12].

Striping can also be applied to tertiary storage devices. As discussed, striping results in the creation of a logical device with a bandwidth equal to the sum of the bandwidths of the individual devices. When an infrequently used multimedia object is requested from tertiary storage, it is desirable to retrieve the object to secondary storage as quickly as possible. Striping of tertiary storage creates a logical device with a very large bandwidth that has a retrieval time smaller than that of an unstriped device [23, 7].

7.3 Placement of Multimedia Data in Storage Devices

We now consider issues arising out of storage of multimedia data. As stated earlier, infrequently used data can be stored on tertiary storage and retrieved as needed [28, 14, 22]. Because the most frequently accessed multimedia data resides on secondary storage, policies for storage of this data have an important impact on server performance. We consider these issues in this section.

Much multimedia data, such as video and audio streams, consists of a sequence of frames. However, the storage manager may consider this data as being made up of a sequence of data blocks belonging to various multimedia objects. Therefore, it is necessary to map these frames into storage blocks. The storage manager is responsible for allocation and placement of these storage blocks on storage devices, as well as placement of multimedia files on various logical devices. Finally, many multimedia presentations may consist of multiple multimedia files to be played sequentially or in parallel. Because data placement has an important impact on performance, it may be possible to exploit this knowledge to improve the performance of the storage subsystem.

7.3.1 Grouping of Frames into Storage Blocks

Video and audio data consists of a sequence of logical frames. These frames have to be retrieved in sequence to ensure continuous display. As discussed in Chapter 3, on many secondary storage devices, data is stored in the form of fixed-size storage blocks. Hence, the media frames need to be mapped into storage blocks [16]. As we will see later, the characteristics of the storage blocks (e.g., size) are influenced strongly by the requirements for efficient retrieval. Hence, a simple one-to-one mapping between media frames and storage blocks will be inefficient. The other possibilities are to force storage blocks to contain an integral number of media frames or to view the multimedia data as a sequence of bytes that are broken arbitrarily into storage blocks. We discuss the advantages and disadvantages of both approaches next.

A multimedia server may need to support a variety of compression standards. As a result, multimedia data with different structures may have to be mapped into storage blocks. For example, a video stream encoded using the DVI standard contains a header, a number of I frames followed by D frames, and a trailer containing a frame index. The D frames are decoded using the preceding I frame, whereas the I frames can be independently encoded. This structure differs from the structure of an MPEG-encoded video, which contains I, B, and P frames. Here, the I frames can again be decoded independently, while the P frames depend on the previous I frame, and the B frames depend upon the preceding and following I frame or P frame. The problem is made more complex by the fact that frame sizes differ significantly even within a single standard. In the case of MPEG, the B and P frames are significantly smaller than the I frames. Additionally, even the sizes of the individual I, B, and P frames can vary significantly within a single video. If each storage block is to contain an integral number of media frames, the storage manager can be designed to be explicitly aware of the various standards. Storage can then be allocated for a video file based on the compression structure. For example, MPEG-compressed video files could be stored in a format that is optimized for MPEG files. However, this may lead to undesirable complexity in the storage manager, as well as make it difficult to support new compression standards.

The alternative of viewing the multimedia file as a stream of bytes is simpler. The multimedia file can then be partitioned into fixed-size storage blocks without taking the structure of the data into account. Under this approach, the storage block size is selected based on the physical characteristics of the device. Because the frame sizes are variable, each storage block may contain a variable number of frames. Extracting the frames from the storage blocks is normally left to the decoding software because the decoding software is specific to the compression standard. Continuous delivery can be guaranteed by converting the frame rate into an average storage block delivery rate using the average compression ratio. Fluctuations in the average compression rate can be smoothed by the use of buffering.

7.3.2   Placement of Data Blocks and Files

After grouping frames into storage blocks, the storage manager has to decide which logical devices to place the various multimedia objects on, as well as where on the devices to place each storage block. For optimizing performance, the storage manager should exploit the knowledge of access rates to each multimedia object and device characteristics. For example, it may be desirable to place frequently accessed multimedia data on a relatively high-bandwidth, small logical device, while less frequently accessed data may be placed on a relatively large, low-bandwidth device. Good data placement policies ensure high operational efficiency of the multimedia server by ensuring high utilization of the storage space as well as the bandwidth of the storage devices [13, 31, 20, 6, 5].

Once the storage manager has decided on the storage device on which to place a multimedia object, it has to decide where on the device to place the storage blocks of the object. As discussed earlier in Chapter 3, secondary storage devices incur various kinds of overhead in retrieving storage blocks. This overhead can be minimized by proper data placement [34, 50, 15, 47, 25, 35, 45]. These policies are reviewed in greater detail in Chapter 8. For layout of the data on the disk, the storage manager may use fixed-size blocks or variable-size blocks. As mentioned in Chapter 3, data is stored on magnetic disks in concentric tracks, which may be subdivided into sectors. In single-zone disks, all tracks can store the same amount of data. In multizone disks, data is stored on the disk at a constant linear density. Hence, the outer tracks contain more data than the inner tracks. For single-zone disks, very high space utilizations can be achieved using fixed-size blocks that are a fixed multiple of the track size. Very high space utilizations are also possible using variable-size blocks that are variable multiples of the track size. More complex policies are required for efficient management of space in multizone disks.

7.3.3 Placement of Media Threads

In the previous section, we considered the allocation of storage for a single stream. However, many multimedia presentations may consist of multiple video and/or audio streams. An example is a movie, which may consist of a single video track and multiple audio and music tracks. For handling such cases, some compression standards (e.g., MPEG) explicitly specify methods for interleaving multiple streams into a single stream. After receiving the multiplexed stream, the decoder demultiplexes it into the individual streams. In such cases, the file containing the multiplexed video and audio streams can be treated as a single stream. This allows using the earlier approach to storage and retrieval, but this may be inefficient in some situations. For example, in the case where multiple language versions of a movie are needed that differ only in one audio track, to avoid storing multiple copies of the multimedia data, it may be preferable to dynamically multiplex the movie with the selected language track. Dynamic multiplexing may also be required if the presentation is composed of distinct streams. In many such cases, information about the relationship between the different streams is available. The storage manager can store related blocks of the individual streams close together so as to increase the efficiency of retrieval. Chapter 12 details the issues in storage and retrieval of composite documents where multiple short clips may be played back simultaneously along with text and images.

7.4 Multimedia Document Retrieval

Retrieval of multimedia data to satisfy an application's QoS requirements is one of the most important functions of the storage manager. Data retrieval by the storage manager starts after resource reservation for transmitting the data is complete. As detailed in Chapter 4, the resource manager sets up a logical channel by reserving the required resources on all components on the delivery path, including the storage subsystem. For example, the resource manager may request the storage manager to reserve 1 Mbps for a stream that requires a bandwidth of 1 Mbps. However, reservation by itself is not sufficient. It is necessary for the storage manager to schedule the I/Os to ensure that the stream actually is able to read at the rate of 1 Mbps from the disk. By scheduling the I/Os, the storage manager also ensures that no stream is able to exceed its bandwidth reservation unless there is unutilized bandwidth in the storage device.

Scheduling in the storage subsystem differs from session scheduling and CPU scheduling discussed earlier in Chapters 4 and 6 in two important respects. First, as we will see later, the overhead incurred in the storage subsystem for servicing a sequence of requests depends upon the sequence in which the requests are served. In fact, it is an explicit objective of storage scheduling policies to minimize these overheads. Second, scheduling policies need to consider the storage subsystem architecture (discussed in Section 7.2) for optimal performance.

In the following sections, we provide an overview of the issues that arise during I/O scheduling in the storage subsystem. We start with a discussion of the access patterns to the storage blocks because they have an important impact on scheduling policies. Next, we provide an overview of the operation of the retrieval subsystem. Finally, we provide an overview of issues that arise during scheduling.

7.4.1   Document Access Patterns

Because multimedia data primarily consists of image, video, or audio, access patterns are primarily sequential. As a result, techniques for efficient support of sequential access (e.g., read-ahead) are very useful in designing the storage manager. It is also normally not necessary for the storage manager to support indexing or nonsequential access to the multimedia data. Support for interactive applications that require browsing or retrieval of random media segments can be provided by using a database that keeps track of the starting and ending blocks of the required fragments. If required by applications, such databases can also store semantic information about the contents of the multimedia data (e.g., color and texture of the various objects). After locating desired clips or segments, the database can interface to the multimedia server storage manager to display the required clips.

Because storage patterns are primarily sequential, the storage manager can be optimized for sequential accesses. However, access patterns are not purely sequential, and so the storage manager should be capable of efficiently supporting nonsequential access patterns as well. Two important instances of nonsequential access arise from VCR controls and accessing nonmultimedia files. As discussed in Chapters 1 and 4, VCR controls (e.g., `pause` and `resume`) constitute an important class of functions that need to be supported by multimedia servers. The `fast-forward` or `rewind` functions are typically supported by using a separate file of appropriate quality and data rate. Because the need to support VCR controls arises in all components of the multimedia server, not just in the storage manager, the techniques for dealing with VCR control operations, described separately in Chapter 4, can be applied in the storage manager as well. In addition, many multimedia applications may require nonmultimedia files (e.g., index files), which are accessed nonsequentially. It may be convenient for applications to store such files on the same storage devices used for multimedia files. Therefore, the storage manager needs to support access to nonmultimedia files as well as multimedia files.

7.4.2 Data Delivery

The storage manager needs to interact with other components of the multimedia server to deliver data to clients. Figure 7.2 shows the relationships among components in a typical multimedia server during normal operation [10]. The storage manager reads multimedia data needed by the client into memory buffers (labeled *disk buffers*). However, as discussed in Chapter 1, the bandwidth requirements of multimedia applications are extremely variable. To mask the impact of these variations, the storage manager may prefetch data into the caching and prefetch buffers. (Prefetching policies are discussed in more detail in Chapter 12.) The communications manager then transmits multimedia data from the network

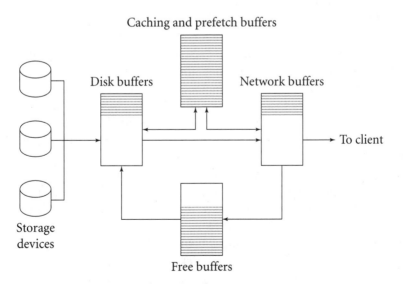

Figure 7.2   Normal operation of storage subsystem.

buffers' memory pool to the corresponding client processor across the network. The storage and network devices may be attached to the same physical node. In this case, the storage and communication managers can transfer data without copying. If they are on different nodes, it is necessary to physically transmit the data between the nodes. After transmission, the multimedia data may be either discarded or retained in the caching and prefetch buffers by the caching manager. (We consider caching policies for multimedia servers in Chapter 12.)

7.5   Issues in I/O Scheduling

Generally, scheduling policies for retrieving multimedia data have two objectives. The first objective is to maximize the efficiency of retrieval from the storage devices or, equivalently, to minimize the retrieval overhead incurred while retrieving the multimedia data. The second objective is to ensure that each multimedia stream (video or audio) is able to read at the desired rate. We consider these issues with respect to magnetic disks, which are the most widely used storage device in multimedia servers.

7.5.1   Minimizing Retrieval Overhead

To understand the overhead associated with various scheduling policies, we consider a simple model. Disks generally have a rated bandwidth, which represents the maximum rate at which data can be transferred from the disk. The effective read bandwidth of a disk will generally be less than the disk's rated bandwidth due to various overheads. Two important sources of overhead were discussed in detail in Chapter 3: the seek time, or the time required for the disk head to move to the desired track, and the rotational latency, the time required for the desired sector to come below the read head. As we shall see, detailed modeling of these and other overheads is difficult due to a number of complexities, but it can be demonstrated that large block sizes amortize the overheads associated with retrieval of multimedia data and that the effective read bandwidth of a disk will approach the rated bandwidth as block sizes get larger.

For simplicity, consider scheduling policies where all disk reads are for blocks of size B; that is, the file system stores files in blocks of size B. The conclusions can be generalized to blocks of varying sizes. The maximum effective throughput of a disk can be calculated as B/T_B, where T_B is the disk I/O time to read a block of size B. Figure 7.3 shows the components of T_B. We can see that T_B is the sum of the seek time, $T_{B,\text{seek}}$; the disk rotational delay, $T_{B,\text{rot}}$; and the transfer time, $T_{B,\text{Tr}}$. $T_{B,\text{seek}}$ and $T_{B,\text{rot}}$ are overheads; to compute the total overhead, it is necessary to estimate the overhead component of $T_{B,\text{Tr}}$.

I/O Number 1

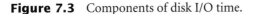

I/O Number 2

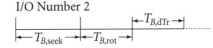

Figure 7.3 Components of disk I/O time.

As shown in Figure 7.3, the disk transfer time, $T_{B,\mathrm{Tr}}$, itself may be broken down into subcomponents. The actual subcomponents will depend on detailed modeling of the storage subsystem. In the SCSI systems typically used in workstations, the data is first read from the disk into the SCSI controller's internal buffers, taking time $T_{B,\mathrm{dTr}}$. It is then transmitted to the main memory of the system in time $T_{B,\mathrm{cTr}}$. The SCSI controller and main memory are generally connected by an I/O bus, as discussed in Chapter 3. Before transmission to main memory, there may be an additional delay due to contention on the I/O bus $T_{B,\mathrm{wait}}$. The effective throughput thus is $B/(T_{B,\mathrm{seek}} + T_{B,\mathrm{rot}} + T_{B,\mathrm{dTr}} + T_{B,\mathrm{wait}} + T_{B,\mathrm{cTr}})$. Because $T_{B,\mathrm{dTr}} = B/W$, where W is the rated disk bandwidth, we can see that the effective disk bandwidth will generally be lower than the rated disk bandwidth.

This argument also shows that $T_{B,\mathrm{dTr}}$ and $T_{B,\mathrm{cTr}}$ increase linearly with the block size. Typically, $T_{B,\mathrm{cTr}}$ is significantly smaller than $T_{B,\mathrm{dTr}}$ for most SCSI controllers. Hence, for large block sizes, $T_{B,\mathrm{dTr}}$ can be made to dominate the disk I/O time. Typical block sizes used in multimedia servers are in the range of 64 KB to 512 KB. This contrasts with block sizes of 4 KB used in conventional file systems. This large block size allows the effective disk read bandwidth to approach the rated bandwidth of the disk.

7.5.2   Ensuring Continuous Delivery

We next consider how the scheduler can ensure that multimedia streams are able to read at the required rate. If a stream has a playback rate of P, a block of size B contains sufficient data for display for B/P time units. If this is greater than the time between two successive reads for the stream, there will be no interruption in the display. As discussed, the retrieval time is T_B. Clearly, B/P should be greater than the sum of the retrieval times for all the reads for other streams scheduled between two successive reads of this stream. Otherwise, the client display may find that it is starved of data after B/P time units. Hence, the scheduler should choose

B to be large enough to satisfy this condition. In a general policy, the scheduler can choose a different read block size for different streams. For example, if *P* is small, the scheduler can choose a small size for *B* to avoid reading ahead very far into the future. This may be inefficient, however, if the user decides to pause or stop the display.

If the total bandwidth of all the streams reading from the disk is greater than the effective bandwidth of the disk, it will be impossible to choose read block sizes so as to ensure continuous delivery. This is also evident from bandwidth considerations because it is not possible for the total bandwidth of streams reading from the storage device to be greater than the available bandwidth. However, if the total bandwidth is less than the effective bandwidth, it is always possible to find read block sizes that will ensure continuous delivery [1, 48].

7.5.3   Impact of Block Size

It is clear from this discussion that block size is a very important parameter of the scheduling policy. Using very large read block sizes has a number of disadvantages. First, it results in a requirement for increased buffer space both in the disk controllers and in system memory. This may not be a significant consideration in many multimedia server configurations (e.g., [10]) in which disk storage is the most significant component of the cost of the server and memory cost is much less significant. An additional consideration is the impact on startup latency for new streams—that is, the time between requesting playback of a stream and the actual start of playback. Increasing the disk block size causes the disk I/O time to increase. Each new request for playback has to wait for the streams ahead of it to finish retrieving their next blocks. Hence, the larger block size directly translates into a larger startup latency. The increased latency may be masked in some applications by giving starting streams higher priority in disk scheduling. However, this may be difficult in interactive applications, where there are a large number of short clips.

7.5.4   Read vs. Write Scheduling

In many situations (e.g., while copying files from tertiary storage to disk), it is necessary to write multimedia files. Most storage management policies assume that the overheads for disk reads and writes are the same. This implies that the effective disk read and write bandwidths are identical. In actuality, the effective write bandwidth for a disk may be slightly lower than the effective read bandwidth because while writing, it is necessary to locate the block to be written with extra precision to avoid inadvertently overwriting existing data. Hence, some overheads (e.g., the disk head settling time) are larger in the case of disk writes, which results in a slightly lower effective disk write bandwidth. For simplicity, we shall treat disk reads and writes as being symmetrical.

7.6   Summary

The storage manager is responsible for the management of the storage subsystem in a multimedia server. The storage subsystem may consist of a large number of heterogeneous storage devices of varying cost and speed. Frequently accessed multimedia data may be stored on relatively expensive and fast secondary storage devices, while less frequently accessed data is stored in the less expensive tertiary storage devices. Striping groups may be used for load balancing across a set of homogeneous storage devices and enhancing the overall reliability of the system.

The two main functions of the storage manager are the storage and retrieval of data. For storage of multimedia data, the manager maintains metadata containing not only mapping information from logical data blocks to physical blocks but also QoS properties of the document. The storage manager also makes decisions on which file to place on which storage devices and where each logical block should be placed on the storage devices. These decisions have a strong impact on the performance of the system.

There are two major objectives of scheduling policies for retrieving multimedia data. The first objective is efficient retrieval of multimedia data while minimizing the retrieval overhead of the storage devices. The second objective is ensuring continuous delivery by guaranteeing that each multimedia stream is able to obtain the required bandwidth.

In the following chapters, we first consider the policies for management of secondary storage devices such as disks. In most multimedia servers, efficient management of the secondary storage devices is very important because they are used to store the most popular multimedia data. We also explore the issues of the handling of file system metadata, the placement of blocks, scheduling to guarantee continuous delivery, and bandwidth reservation. We next consider organizational issues arising from the use of multiple disks (e.g. striping), RAID organizations, and the placement of files across multiple disks. Finally, we describe policies for managing tertiary storage devices.

8

Single-Disk Issues

8.1   Introduction

As discussed in the previous chapter, storage bandwidth and space are critical resources in multimedia systems. Hence, storage management policies attempt to efficiently manage both of these resources in individual storage devices. As discussed earlier in Chapter 7, both the space and bandwidth utilizations are dependent upon many factors (e.g., the size of blocks stored on the device). In this chapter, we discuss these issues as they apply to individual storage devices, and because disks are by far the most popular secondary storage device, we focus on disks. However, the same types of policies can be applied to other secondary storage devices, such as CD-ROM.

The two main functions of the storage manager are the storage and retrieval of data. As described earlier in Chapter 7, the storage manager needs to efficiently place the blocks on the storage devices as well as create metadata for locating multimedia data. We first consider policies for management of storage and then retrieval policies.

8.2   Storage Organization

The basic requirements of multimedia file systems and traditional file systems differ greatly. Multimedia files tend to be much larger than conventional files. Additionally, the continuous delivery requirement of multimedia files makes efficient delivery a much more important concern in multimedia file systems than in conventional file systems. Thus, the storage organization of traditional file systems may not be suited to multimedia servers.

We consider two important aspects of storage organization for placement of data. Multimedia data is stored as data blocks on the storage device. However, from the application point of view, the data is organized into files. Therefore, the mapping between files and storage blocks is an important issue. This mapping is maintained by metadata, which may also keep track of the directory structure and special attributes of multimedia files. The challenge is that because multimedia files are much larger than conventional files, techniques used in conventional systems may not be efficient.

The other aspect of storage organization that we consider is the placement of blocks on the storage devices. As described in Chapter 3, a number of overheads can be incurred in the retrieval of blocks from secondary storage devices. This overhead can be reduced by appropriate block placement techniques.

8.2.1   Metadata Organization

The file system metadata is used during data retrieval to locate files and their blocks and during file writing to allocate blocks and locate free blocks. Multimedia servers offer the same hierarchical organization of multimedia files into directories as that offered by conventional file systems. Hence, the superblock and inode structure found in conventional file systems can be adapted for use in multimedia servers. These are described in detail later. We first discuss issues that need to be addressed in adapting the metadata organization from conventional file systems.

Access characteristics. In conventional file systems, both data and metadata have similar access characteristics. In multimedia servers, the access characteristics of metadata remain similar to those of traditional files but are unlike those of multimedia data. File system metadata does not have a continuous delivery requirement. Furthermore, metadata tends to be small and may be difficult to stripe over a large striping group. For both these reasons, it may be desirable to store metadata and multimedia data separately on a multimedia server. Different layouts tailored to their differing access characteristics can then be used. An alternative design is to store metadata on disks managed by a conventional file system.

Storage overhead of metadata. The design of the metadata may have a large impact on the efficiency of the storage of the multimedia data. Because multimedia files are large compared to conventional files, it is possible to optimize the design of the metadata for the support of large files. However, many multimedia applications may have small, associated nonmultimedia files (e.g., configuration files, indexes), and the multimedia server itself may need to store additional file attribute information about multimedia files (e.g., QoS data such as average and peak playback rate). Also, if operations such as `fast-forward` are implemented using specially encoded files, the names of these special files must be stored. File attributes may be stored together with the file system metadata, but adding additional file attributes then becomes difficult as it involves updating data structures used by the retrieval mechanism. A more flexible alternative is to store this information in associated metafiles [27, 11]. Therefore, the structure of the metadata has to be able to support the storage of both large and small files.

The metadata has to keep track of the location of every storage block, so the size and storage overhead of the metadata is proportional to the number of storage blocks. Using large block sizes reduces the metadata storage overhead for large multimedia files. However, this may result in storage fragmentation for the small nonmultimedia files. This can be avoided by supporting variable-size blocks in the file system or by allowing a single block to store fragments from various files. For efficiency in storage, therefore, the design of the metadata has to support one of these two alternatives. In the following subsections, we describe storage organizations that exemplify these design choices.

Unix-like organization. The Tiger Shark file system [26] uses a modification of the metadata structures used in conventional file systems. The modifications allow data blocks or metadata to be replicated for availability and files to be striped over multiple disks. We first describe a typical implementation of Unix-like file systems [2] that forms the basis for the Tiger Shark file system. In such systems, the file systems maintain a metadata structure (called an *inode*) associated with each file. The inode stores information about the file, such as the file size, type (e.g. directory, regular file), access rights, and ownership information. The inode also contains information used to locate the data blocks of the file (described next). Inodes are resident on disk and are copied into main memory (for efficient access) when a file is opened. On disk, inodes are stored as an array in a contiguous inode table. Directories also have associated inodes. The directories are simply special files interpreted by the file system that contain pointers to other files.

The inode contains a data structure that maps file blocks to corresponding disk blocks. This data structure has to allow arbitrarily large files to be stored, while efficiently storing small files. For this purpose, each inode contains space for a number of direct and indirect pointers (see Figure 8.1). The direct pointers point directly to file data blocks; the indirect pointers contain pointers to indirect blocks of pointers, which may contain other indirect pointers to additional indirect blocks or direct pointers. The number of direct pointers in the inode is selected so as to allow most small files to be stored without referencing the indirect pointers. The indirect blocks allow arbitrarily large files to be stored.

The file system itself has a superblock that contains global data about the file system. This includes such information as the number of blocks in the file system, the size of the inode table, the number of free blocks, and a list (or bitmap) of the free blocks and inode table entries. As with inodes, the superblock resides on disk and is cached in memory for efficient access.

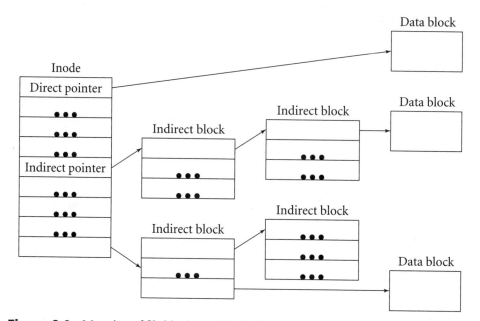

Figure 8.1 Mapping of file blocks to disk blocks.

As mentioned earlier, allowing multiple files to share a disk block reduces wastage of space when storing small files, while allowing the use of a large block size for efficient retrieval. In the 4.3 BSD Unix system [30], disk blocks are 4096 bytes long. Each block may be broken up into a system-dependent number of fragments (two, four, or eight). In addition to keeping track of free blocks, the file system keeps track of free and used fragments. When writing less than a block of data, the file system attempts to locate a contiguous set of fragments within a single block that can be allocated. The allocated single block may contain fragments with data from other files. If no such block can be found, a free block is partitioned into fragments. As files expand, noncontiguous fragments in different blocks may be coalesced by the file system into single blocks. This organization allows 4.3 BSD to retrieve large files efficiently and have a storage fragmentation overhead similar to those in systems with smaller block sizes [30].

Separate metadata disks. The Tiger Shark file system extends a conventional Unix-like file system. As mentioned earlier, an alternative design is to store metadata as well as nonmultimedia files on different devices from multimedia files. This approach is used in the implementation of the Lancaster Storage Server (LSS) [34]. Unlike a traditional file system, the LSS stores file system metadata on separate storage devices from multimedia data. The metadata also is organized differently from the multimedia data so as to efficiently support the differing access patterns. To avoid fragmentation and for efficient retrieval (described later), LSS supports variable-sized block sizes for different files.

The basic organization of the LSS metadata is similar to that of traditional file systems. Like the Tiger Shark system, the LSS metadata disk contains a superblock and an inode table; the superblock contains global data, such as the number of entries in the inode table, and a bitmap that indicates whether each inode entry is free or allocated. The inode structure, however, differs from that in conventional file systems. Each multimedia file has an associated inode entry, which consists of a file header and pointers mapping the data blocks for the file. The file header contains the disk block size of the file (because LSS supports variable file block sizes). It also contains some QoS information, such as the average playback rate.[1] As described later, the LSS selects the disk block size of the file based on the QoS information with the objective of efficient retrieval. However, unlike conventional file systems, to allow efficient retrieval and manipulation of the data block pointers, inodes in LSS contain no indirect pointers. Instead, the inode contains enough direct pointers to allow the file to span the entire storage device on which it resides. For multimedia files, which have a large block size, the storage overhead involved is not very large (on the order of 4 bytes per 64 KB).

8.2.2 Block Placement

We next consider block placement policies in a multimedia server. As discussed in Chapter 3, seek overhead is one of the major overheads incurred during disk block retrieval. In this section, we examine how this overhead can be reduced by appropriate block placement policies. As in the case of metadata organization, it is possible to adapt the block placement policies used in conventional file systems. Additionally, various constrained-placement policies that attempt to explicitly bound the seek distance between successive disk blocks of a multimedia file have been proposed for multimedia servers. We survey both types of policies next.

Traditional block placement policies. Traditional block placement policies have used knowledge of file access patterns to place blocks so as to minimize the seek overhead and, hence, the response time. We consider two such policies: The contiguous allocation policy attempts to eliminate intrafile seeks, while the organ-pipe placement policy reduces the interfile seek overhead.

Contiguous allocation. Under the contiguous allocation policy, all disk blocks for a file are placed contiguously on disk. This eliminates intrafile seeks during

---

[1]As discussed earlier, additional QoS information can be stored in metafiles [27, 11].

sequential reading of the file because successive blocks of a file that are to be read in one I/O operation are placed contiguously. It does not, however, eliminate interfile seeks that occur because successive reads against a disk are for different files. Seeks may also occur due to nonsequential access to the file (e.g., VCR control operations).

Contiguous allocation policies are very suitable for read-only media, such as CD-ROM. Under a read/write workload, contiguous allocation policies have to deal with fragmentation of storage device space. The large size of multimedia files makes compacting of files on disk difficult because compaction will take a long time during which the file may be unavailable. Additionally, the large size implies that compaction will incur a large overhead. For read/write workloads, many of the advantages of contiguous allocation can be realized by allocating storage device space in sizes that are an integral multiple of the block size for I/O operations.

The Everest policy [21], an adaptation of the contiguous allocation policy, addresses these issues of storage fragmentation under read/write workloads. The policy attempts to maintain contiguous allocation while minimizing the overhead due to compaction. Under the policy, blocks are allocated to files only in contiguous segments of size ω^i blocks, where ω is a tunable parameter and i is an integer. For example, if $\omega = 2$, then blocks can be allocated only in contiguous segments of size 1, 2, 4, 8, 16, . . . blocks. To allocate a file that requires L_f blocks, the policy represents L_f as a base ω number, $d_k d_{k-1} \ldots$, and allocates d_i segments of length ω^i. Hence, as shown in Figure 8.2, if $\omega = 2$, a file of length 5 blocks would be allocated as one segment each of lengths 4 blocks and 1 block (the representation of 5 in base 2 is 101). If $\omega = 3$, the same file would be allocated as one segment of length 3 blocks and two segments of length 1 block. Thus, the number of segments, which is an upper bound on the number of intrafile seeks, is always bounded by $\omega \lceil \log_\omega L_f \rceil$ [21].

The free blocks in the system are organized into free segments, which are maintained in a free segment list. The free list is actually subdivided into a number of sublists, one for each possible segment size ω^i. To simplify allocation, the policy enforces a bounded list length property such that there cannot be more than $\omega - 1$ segments in any sublist. If a file deletion results in the creation of more than $\omega - 1$ free segments of size ω^i, the policy first migrates allocated segments on disk until there are at least ω contiguous free segments of size ω^i. These contiguous segments are then collapsed into a free segment of size ω^{i+1}. Figure 8.2 illustrates an example of file deletion, followed by migration and compaction.

Block allocation under Everest uses a variant of the buddy algorithm [29]. To allocate a segment of size ω^i for a file, the policy first checks the sublist for segments of size ω^i. If there are none, it checks the sublists in turn for successively larger segments until a larger segment is found. This segment is then progressively subdivided into ω smaller segments until a segment of the required size is gener-

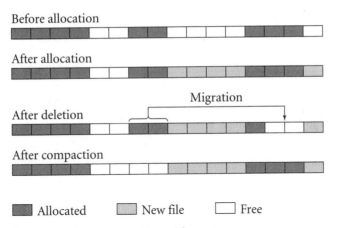

Figure 8.2 Everest contiguous allocation with $\omega = 2$.

ated. Note that because of the bounded list length property, if there is sufficient free space to satisfy the request, there must exist a contiguous free segment of a length larger than or equal to the required segment size. If the disk does not have sufficient free space, it is necessary to delete files in order to create space. As noted earlier, this may result in the migration of existing files in order to compact the free space.

Organ-pipe placement. Unlike the contiguous allocation policy, the organ-pipe placement policy attempts to minimize the interfile seek overhead incurred when seeking between successive I/O operations to a disk. The noncontiguous placement of blocks on storage media has been studied for magnetic disks in [50, 25] and for optical disks in [15]. These studies show that the optimal placement of blocks follows an "organ-pipe" arrangement, with the most frequently referenced blocks being placed together at the center of the disk and with less frequently referenced blocks being placed alternately around the hottest blocks (see Figure 8.3(a)). In a multimedia server, the most frequently referenced blocks will belong to the most popular multimedia files. Using block access probabilities computed from the file access frequencies, the organ-pipe placement can be used to place blocks within disks. The complementary problem of the choice of storage device on which to place a multimedia file (the file placement problem) is studied later in Chapter 9.

Log-structured placement. In a log-structured file system, the storage device is treated as a single circular log [35]. File blocks are updated by deleting the original block and writing a new block at the end of the list. Therefore, multiple writes, even to different files, will be written to consecutive storage blocks on the storage

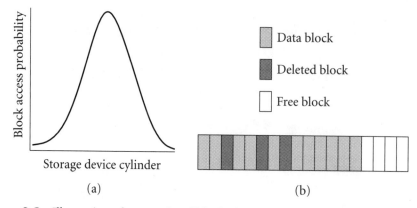

Figure 8.3 Illustration of conventional block placements showing the organ-pipe (a) and log-structured (b) placements.

device. Outstanding writes can be combined periodically into a single write, which incurs very little overhead. However, once the storage device is full, new blocks will have to be written into the space occupied by deleted blocks. These blocks will in general be noncontiguous, and overhead may be incurred in compacting these deleted blocks.

In the context of multimedia servers, the advantage of log-structured file systems is that they may achieve a greater degree of contiguous allocation than other methods. The LSS [34] adopts this organization for the storage of multimedia data. In contrast, the file system metadata is stored separately using a conventional Unix-like inode data structure. The multimedia data disks (referred to as *stripe disks*) contain a superblock and the log. The superblock contains a map table that maps logical log addresses to physical disk blocks and a log head pointer that points to the next free location in the log. This pointer is updated after every write operation. Deletion of blocks results in the creation of unreferenced disk blocks. These deleted blocks are detected by a background process that later compacts the log.

Constrained-placement policies. The policies described above are adaptations of conventional block placement policies. We now discuss two policies that take advantage of the sequential access of multimedia streams to bound the seek overhead incurred. The REBECA system [17] attempts to trade off the seek overhead against the startup latency for new streams. The strand-based allocation policy [38, 37] attempts to reduce the seek overhead incurred when retrieving multiple related streams that are part of the same multimedia presentation.

REBECA. The region-based block allocation method (REBECA) first divides the storage device into a fixed number of contiguous regions. The accesses to various

Region number	0	1	2	3	4	5
	block 0	block 1	block 2	block 3	block 4	block 5
	block 11	block 10	block 9	block 8	block 7	block 6
	block 12	block 13	block 14	block 15		

Center of disk   Disk periphery

Figure 8.4 Mapping of file blocks to regions under REBECA.

blocks within a single region are served by a single scan step. As we will show, increasing the number of regions decreases the seek overhead while increasing the initial latency seen by new streams. The number of regions is thus selected to provide an acceptable value for both the seek overhead and initial latency.

Under REBECA, the successive blocks of a multimedia object are allocated to different regions. The order of allocation is the order in which the regions would be visited by an elevator scan algorithm (see Figure 8.4 for an example with 6 regions and 16 blocks). The disk scheduling policy sweeps the disk starting from the center to the periphery and then back to the center. Each time it visits a region, it services all the requests in that region. Clearly, the worst-case seek occurs when the disk head has to move from the start of a region to the end of the adjoining region. This worst-case seek is equal to twice the size of a region. Hence, increasing the number of regions reduces the seek overhead.

Under REBECA, the display of a multimedia object cannot start until the scheduling policy considers the region that contains the starting block of the object. By considering the worst-case startup delay, it is shown in [17] that the worst-case latency increases with the number of regions. Hence, the REBECA policy reduces the seek overhead at the expense of increasing startup latency.

Strand-based allocation. An application may require the display of multiple media files (e.g., video and multiple sound tracks). The required multimedia data may be stored as a single file with multiplexing of the various media streams. MPEG [16], for example, specifies a standard for the multiplexing of multiple audio and video streams within the same media file. After transmission, the individual streams are extracted in the client station, which displays them in synchronized manner.

An alternative approach is to store the individual streams as individual files and to transmit these files to the client. In this case, it may be desirable to store the blocks of the files close together to facilitate easy retrieval [38, 37]. Such an approach may be particularly valuable on devices with limited bandwidth.

For an application needing a single video and audio stream, the continuous delivery requirement implies that the time taken to retrieve a single block of video and a single block of audio is less than the time taken for display. Hence, $T_{seek} + (N_v * B_v)/W + (N_a * B_a)/W \leq (N_v * B_v)/P_v$ [38, 37], where N_v and B_v are, respectively, the number of video blocks retrieved and the disk block size for video blocks, N_a and B_a are the corresponding values for the audio file, T_{seek} is the seek time overhead, and W is the disk bandwidth. If particular values are chosen for N_v, B_v, N_a, B_a (see the discussion of read-ahead buffering in Section 8.3.1), it is possible to compute a maximum value for T_{seek}. Placing the blocks of the multiple media files while restricting the seek overhead as computed above allows continuous delivery to be guaranteed. The approach has been generalized to devices with multiple simultaneous streams retrieved on behalf of different users [38, 37].

8.3   Retrieval

A major function of the storage subsystem is to guarantee that data needed by applications is retrieved on time so that there are no interruptions in delivery. The disk scheduling policy achieves this by scheduling requests for blocks such that each stream can retrieve its blocks before they are needed. Admission control limits the number of streams allowed into the system to ensure that requests for blocks can be scheduled in time. It does this by considering the resources available (e.g., buffer space, disk bandwidth) before accepting requests for new multimedia streams. The details of any admission control policy will depend upon the particular disk scheduling policy used. We discuss disk scheduling policies and their associated admission controls next.

The traditional objectives of disk scheduling policies are to maximize disk throughput and minimize disk response time. In multimedia servers, these objectives still have to be satisfied while ensuring that each stream is able to retrieve its blocks without missing deadlines.[2] As discussed in Section 7.5, the achievable disk bandwidth will depend upon the parameters of the disk and the block size used for retrieval.

Multimedia disk scheduling policies can be divided into two categories—round-based policies that schedule I/O requests only during periodic scheduling rounds and fixed block size policies that can schedule I/O requests aperiodically. Round-based policies typically assume that the playback rate is constant and attempt to guarantee continuous delivery deterministically. These assumptions may not hold in practical systems due to variability in compression rate and user interactions (e.g., pause, resume). Therefore, in practice, multimedia disk scheduling

---

[2]With statistical admission control or scalable media, some fraction of missed block retrieval may be permissible.

policies cannot provide deterministic continuous delivery. However, with sufficient read-ahead buffers the variations in the retrieval time can be masked [10].

We will describe examples of both types of policies. Under both policies, it is necessary to be able to support retrieval of nonmultimedia data as well as multimedia data from the same disks. Following the discussion of scheduling policies, we describe methods for supporting retrieval of nonmultimedia data without causing interference to retrieval of multimedia data.

8.3.1   Round-Based Scheduling Policies

Round-based disk scheduling policies attempt to take advantage of the periodic nature of I/O requests to multimedia files by scheduling I/O requests in rounds. In each round, exactly one request is serviced for each stream. Clearly, the amount of data read for each stream in a round has to be sufficient to ensure that the client's buffers are not exhausted before the start of the next round. For streams with different playback rates, a variable amount of data per request has to be read of different streams. If the file system supports only fixed-size blocks, issuing variable block reads may result in intrafile as well as interfile seek overhead. A solution is to allocate for each stream a buffer size that is an integral multiple of the block size and is greater than the amount of data that needs to be read for the stream. In each round, only the blocks that have already been transmitted to the clients are replaced using independent I/Os. In some rounds, no data may be retrieved for a stream if all blocks contain data that has not yet been transmitted.

In the following sections, we first describe the admission control policies associated with various disk scheduling policies, and then we discuss the disk scheduling policies themselves.

Admission control policies. As stated earlier, the admission control policy determines whether to accept requests for the starting of new streams, depending upon the availability of system resources and the disk scheduling policy. For example, it considers the available buffer space and allocates this buffer among the active streams. Thus, it also determines the amount of data to be read for each stream (recall that a variable amount of data is read for each stream in a round-based policy).

We will describe two admission control policies for round-robin disk scheduling, where streams are serviced repeatedly in a fixed order. A policy for determining the minimum amount of buffer that needs to be allocated for the streams is proposed in [1]. Such a policy may be suitable for servers with restricted buffer space. In contrast, the Quality Proportional Multi-Subscriber (QPMS) policy proposed in [39] partitions the available buffer among the various streams. Because the QPMS policy partitions the available buffer, it also has to reclaim buffer space from already existing streams when a new stream arrives.

Minimum buffer allocation. The Continuous Media File System (CMFS) [1] determines the minimum amount of blocks that needs to be allocated for each media stream in a step-by-step fashion. In the following description, the number of blocks allocated to each stream is computed in an array, N_i, that contains an entry for each stream i. Let $R(N)$ be the total retrieval time of a round given the current values of N_i, P_i be the playback rate of this stream, and $T_{i,\text{disp}}$ be the time to display the data retrieved by N_i.

1. Initialize each element of N_i to 1.

2. If the total buffer required by summing all the elements of N is greater than the total available buffer, N_{av}, exit with failure.

3. Estimate R as the sum of the retrieval time for all blocks. As discussed in Chapter 7, the retrieval time includes overheads such as the seek overhead and rotational latency. Because these cannot be known exactly, estimates of these quantities may be used.

4. For each stream i, estimate $T_{i,\text{disp}} = N_i/P_i$.

5. If $T_{i,\text{disp}} > R$ for all i, then stop with success.

6. Otherwise, add 1 to all N_i for which the test in step 5 fails and go to step 2.

QPMS buffer allocation. The requirement for continuous delivery of a media stream is that for each stream, the quantity of data retrieved in each round is sufficient to allow playback during the round. Mathematically, this can be expressed as $R(N) \leq \min(N_i/P_i)$. Values of the N_i have to be found subject to the constraint that $\sum_i N_i \leq N_{\text{av}}$ where N_{av} is the total available buffer space. In these equations, the only unknowns are the N_i. If it is assumed that $N_i = kP_i$, where k is some proportionality constant, the equations can be solved to find the value of k. It is shown in [48] that the resulting values of N_i are optimal in the sense that if a buffer allocation N_i exists such that continuity requirements are not violated, it will be found by the QPMS policy. A practical consideration is that the values of N_i found in general will not be integral. It is shown in [48] that by retrieving $\lfloor N_i \rfloor$ and $\lceil N_i \rceil$ on different rounds, the average amount of data retrieved for each stream will be N_i while satisfying the continuity requirement.

Under the QPMS policy, all the available buffer space is partitioned among the existing streams. Thus, when a new stream arrives, it is necessary to reclaim buffer space from the existing streams and allocate it to the new stream. Reclaiming the buffer reduces the amount of buffered data for a stream and could lead to violation of the continuity requirement. This can be avoided by modifying the QPMS policy to reformulate the continuity requirement as $R(N^+) \leq \min(N_i/P_i)$, where N^+ is equal to N with one block added to each element. The modified requirement implies that the amount of data buffered for each stream is greater than required for a round and that one block can be taken away from each stream without violating the continuity requirement. This modification allows buffer space to be reclaimed from existing streams in multiple steps without violating their continuity requirement.

8.3.2 Round-Based Disk Retrieval Policies

After computing the amount of data to be retrieved for each stream in each round, round-based policies need to schedule a single I/O for each stream in each round. We discuss three typical policies—round-robin, scan, and the group sweeping scheduling policy.

Round-robin. The round-robin scheduler orders the streams in a fixed order and performs I/Os for each stream according to this fixed order (Figure 8.5(a)). Due to its simplicity, such a method is used in, for example, [34]. A disadvantage of the round-robin policy is that because the streams are served in a random order, the policy does not optimize the seek overhead. Hence, the seek overhead may be greater under round-robin than under other disk scheduling policies, leading to greater buffering requirements.

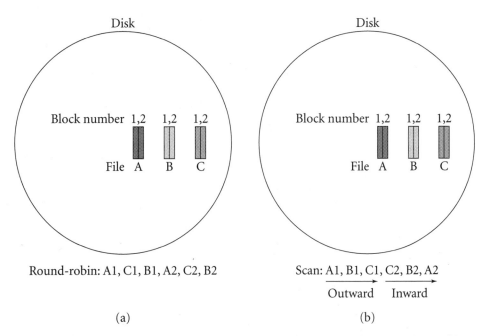

Figure 8.5 Round-based disk scheduling showing the round-robin (a) and scan (b) policies.

Scan. Figure 8.5(b) illustrates the scan policy. Under this policy, the disk head repeatedly sweeps outward from the center of the disk to the periphery and back to the center. The I/O requests are executed in the order that the disk blocks are encountered in the sweeps of the disk head. For example, during the outward sweep, the request closest to the center of the disk is executed first, followed by the next closest request, and so on. On reaching the furthest I/O request, the policy sweeps inward to the center, again servicing I/O requests in the order encountered.[3] The scan policy has lower seek overhead than any other commonly used disk policy [44], which tends to reduce its buffering requirements. Note, however, that due to the fact that the service order for streams may be different in each round, the stream served first in a round may be served last in the next round (see Figure 8.5(b)). The read-ahead buffer needed per stream is therefore equal to that needed for two rounds. This is in contrast to round-robin scheduling, which needs a read-ahead buffer per stream equal to only one round (though the length of the round under round-robin will be greater than under scan).

Group sweeping scheduling (GSS). The GSS policy [51] combines both scan and round-robin, resulting in a policy with low seek overhead (as in scan) but with buffer requirements of the length of one round (as in round-robin). The details of the GSS policy are as follows (see Figure 8.6):

1. Partition the V active streams into M_{gr} groups.

2. Service the M_{gr} groups in round-robin order.

3. Service the streams within each group using C-scan.

   In step 1, the GSS policy partitions the streams so as to minimize the total amount of buffer required. It first considers all possible values $1, \ldots, V$ for M_{gr}. For each possible value for the number of groups, the GSS policy computes the total amount of buffer required and the partitioning of streams among groups. This requires the solution of a complex optimization problem for each potential value of M_{gr}, details of which can be found in [51]. The value of M_{gr} that results in the lowest buffer requirement is the optimum value. Because the groups are served in a round-robin order, the amount of data that needs to be buffered is approximately equal to the data displayed in one round. However, since the streams in each group are serviced using scan, the seek overhead is low.

   Putting all the streams into one group causes the GSS policy to service the streams in scan order. At the other extreme of putting each stream in its own individual group, the GSS policy will service all streams in round-robin order. Hence,

---

[3]A variant of the scan policy, called *C-scan*, performs sweeps in only one direction (inward or outward). Its performance is very similar to the scan policy.

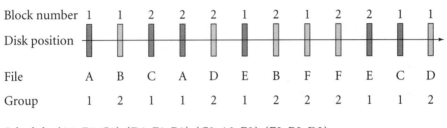

Block number	1	1	2	2	2	1	2	1	2	2	1	1
Disk position												
File	A	B	C	A	D	E	B	F	F	E	C	D
Group	1	2	1	1	2	1	2	2	2	1	1	2

Schedule: {A1, E1, C1}, {D1, F1, B1}, {C2, A2, E2}, {F2, B2, D2}

Figure 8.6 Group sweeping scheduling policy (with two groups).

the GSS policy can be made to reduce to either scan or round-robin by extreme values of partitioning. Experimentally, it has been found that under heavy load and with all streams having the same playback rate, the GSS policy and scan tend to service the streams in the same order [51].

8.3.3 Fixed Block-Size Policies

In the round-based policies described earlier, the amount of data retrieved for a stream by each I/O request is proportional to the stream's playback rate. Because the data retrieval size is variable and proportional to the stream's playback rate, the number of I/O requests queued for each stream in any time interval is independent of the stream's playback rate. However, implementation of variable-size disk blocks in the file system is complex. Hence, the file system may support only fixed-size blocks. This would require round-based schemes to map the logical variable-size I/O requests into the fixed block sizes supported by the file system. Additionally, variable compression rates can result in variations in playback rate.

An alternative when the file system supports only fixed block sizes is for the disk scheduling policy to read a fixed amount of data (the disk block size) per I/O request. In such policies, the number of I/O requests for a stream per unit of time is proportional to the playback rate of the stream. We will first discuss buffer allocation for such policies and then describe a variant of the well-known earliest deadline first policy [32], called *scan-EDF*, that has been proposed for multimedia disk scheduling.

Buffer allocation for fixed block-size policies. As shown in Section 7.5, the effective retrieval bandwidth for a disk increases with the disk block size. Larger amounts of buffering also allow variations in disk response time that can be tolerated without causing interruptions in data delivery to clients. As a result, disk utilizations can be very high. The number of read-ahead buffers required for fixed

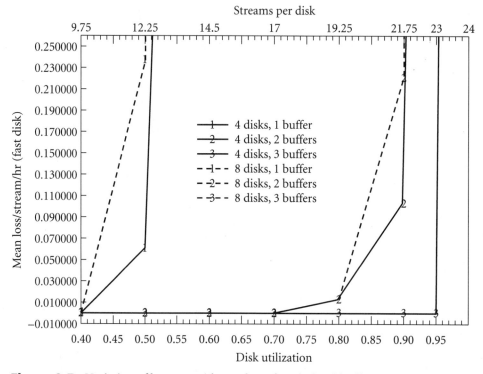

Figure 8.7 Variation of loss rate with number of read-ahead buffers.

block-size policies was studied in [10] using a simulation model, where it was found that triple buffering (three read-ahead buffers) with a sufficiently large block size (256 KB in the study) results in very high disk utilizations. The simulated environment consisted of a high-performance server node connected to a disk array. Successive blocks of each file were assumed to be placed on a random permutation of the disks (see Chapter 9 for a detailed discussion of disk arrays). Two types of disks were considered—a fast disk with 8 ms average seek, 20 MB/s transfer rate, and 3.96 GB capacity; and a slow disk with 9 ms seek, 10 MB/s transfer rate, and 1.05 GB capacity. Figure 8.7 shows the simulated rejection rates (number of streams rejected due to disk overload) for varying buffer sizes and disk utilizations. The solid lines represent a disk array of four disks and the dashed lines a disk array of eight. With three buffers, the utilization of both disks can be driven to 95%. The effective throughput of the disk (defined as the maximum throughput for a given rejection rate) can be computed from the figure.

Scan-EDF. The earliest deadline first (EDF) policy is a well-known real-time scheduling policy for tasks with deadlines. (See Chapter 6 for a detailed discussion

of scheduling.) Intuitively, giving priority service to tasks with the earliest deadline should result in fewer numbers of missed deadlines. It is shown in [32] that if
tasks are preemptable with zero preemption cost, the EDF policy minimizes the
number of missed deadlines. The EDF policy can be adapted for disk scheduling
in multimedia servers by associating a deadline with each disk I/O request and
servicing the I/O requests in deadline order. However, such a policy may have a
high seek overhead because the I/O requests will be served in random order.

The scan-EDF policy [42] reduces the seek overhead associated with EDF by
grouping requests with deadlines in a small time interval T_{group}. T_{group} is a parameter of the policy. The details of the policy are

- Upon arrival, associate a deadline with each I/O request that represents the
  time by which the request needs to be started in order to guarantee continuous delivery to the client. Note that this deadline will depend upon the
  amount of available read-ahead buffer. Using a larger buffer results in more
  efficient utilization of the disks.

- At each scheduling time, consider all requests with deadlines between the current time t_{cur} and $t_{cur} + T_{group}$. Schedule the nearest request in the current
  scan direction.

By servicing deadlines that are close together using scan, the scan-EDF policy reduces the seek overhead while giving priority to I/O requests with closer deadlines.

A number of interesting results comparing scan-EDF and other scheduling
policies are presented in [41]. The other policies considered are C-scan and EDF.
The results were obtained by simulating a single-disk system, with successive I/O
requests for a stream being for random disk locations. The number of streams that
could be supported with continuous delivery was used to compare the scheduling
policies. The simulations showed that the performance of C-scan and scan-EDF
were very close together, with EDF being significantly worse. However, with large
disk block sizes (200 KB), there was not much difference in the performance of
the various policies due to the increasing domination of the disk transfer time.

8.3.4 Non-Real-Time I/O Requests

Multimedia applications may access a mix of real-time (e.g., video and audio) and
non-real-time data. From a system administration point of view, it is desirable
that it be possible to store both types of data on the same physical disks. Additionally, as mentioned earlier, file system metadata has no continuous delivery requirement. Hence, it is important that multimedia disk scheduling policies retrieve
non-real-time data from disks containing real-time data without violating the continuous delivery requirement.

Two approaches have been proposed for solving this problem.

1. *Deadline.* In deadline scheduling systems, such as scan-EDF, a deadline based upon the estimated unused capacity of the disk or the desired response time can be associated with each non-real-time I/O request [42, 20]. The request can then be scheduled using the deadline scheduling policy.

2. *Priority.* In nondeadline systems, real-time requests can be given higher priority than non-real-time requests [11, 27, 34]. For example, non-real-time requests could be scheduled only if there are no waiting real-time requests. A variant used in the CMFS [1] is to compute the slack time, defined as the time in each scheduling round not used by real-time requests. Non-real-time requests are scheduled in the slack time of each round.

Under both approaches, starvation of non-real-time requests can be avoided by limiting the fraction of disk bandwidth that is allocated to real-time requests. The performance of the CMFS file system in handling non-real-time requests has been studied in [1, 24]. For moderate loads (less than 50% disk utilization by real-time requests), the response time for non-real-time requests is adequate. For higher loads, it may be necessary to associate deadlines with the non-real-time requests or to reserve a higher fraction of the disk capacity for non-real-time requests.

8.4 Multizone Disks

Advances in technology have led to the development of multizone disks (see Chapter 3). These are distinguished from conventional disks by their constant linear density. The disk transfer rate at the periphery of a multizone disk is higher than the transfer rate at the center. The effective bandwidth of the disk therefore depends upon the placement of blocks within the disk. Most disk management policies implicitly cater to conventional single-zone disks because they do not exploit the difference between access rates at the center and the periphery. We summarize policies for management of multizone disks in the next two sections. The modified organ-pipe block placement uses knowledge of block access rates to improve the throughput of the disk [47]. In contrast, the approach proposed in [18] attempts to place file blocks across multiple zones, thereby making the throughput independent of the placement.

8.4.1 Modified Organ-Pipe Placement

For single-zone disks, an organ-pipe arrangement, with the most frequently referenced blocks at the central cylinder, is optimal, as this tends to minimize the seek overhead. For multizone disks, placing frequently referenced blocks nearer to the outer cylinder of the disk reduces the time taken to transfer the data from the disk. However, moving the most frequently used blocks away from the center may increase the seek overhead. Therefore, the optimal cylinder for the hottest blocks is displaced outward from the center of the disk by an amount that depends upon the relative importance of the seek time and the transfer time. This leads to a skewed organ-pipe arrangement. A method for approximately computing the optimal placement for this skewed organ-pipe placement using the block access probabilities and disk parameters is given in [47].

8.4.2   Round-Robin Placement

The modified organ-pipe approach attempts to use knowledge of data access rates for block placement. However, this may lead to complex admission control policies because the maximum bandwidth available will depend on the zone in which blocks of a file are placed. This is an important parameter in admission control policies so the admission control policy will have to be aware of the files that are placed in each zone. It is possible to simplify the problem by using the bandwidth of the slowest zone; this will, however, result in poor disk utilization.

The round-robin placement proposed in [18] places blocks of a file round-robin across the zones of a disk, which allows the average transfer rate to be used in the admission control policies and results in full utilization of the bandwidth. However, the round-robin allocation implies that the maximum amount of data that can be stored in any zone is equal to the capacity of the smallest zone. Because the zones closest to the center of the disk hold less data than the zones at the periphery, there is significant wastage of space. The wastage can be reduced by aggregating multiple physical zones into larger logical zones [18] and setting the bandwidth of each logical zone to that of the slowest physical zone included in the logical zone. There will be some wastage of bandwidth as a result, but by varying the aggregation of physical zones into logical zones, it is possible to trade off between these two overheads. Depending upon whether space conservation or bandwidth conservation is more important, an appropriate aggregation can be chosen.

8.5   Summary

The major functions of the storage manager are the storage and retrieval of multimedia data. Two important issues in the design of storage policies are the structure of the metadata and the placement of storage blocks. For the metadata, methods used in conventional file systems can be adapted for multimedia servers. Retrieval overheads can be reduced by appropriate placement policies, such as the organ-pipe placement policy.

Real-time policies are required for retrieval of multimedia data. Retrieval policies may be either round-based or fixed block size. Round-based policies retrieve multimedia data in rounds in which data proportional to the stream's bandwidth is retrieved in each round. In contrast, fixed block-size policies retrieve a fixed amount of data for each stream with each I/O request. To increase efficiency of retrieval, both types of policies read large block sizes from the disk. The retrieval time from the disk can be variable so both types of policies use buffering to reduce jitters.

Further Reading

File system metadata in Unix systems is described in detail in [2, 30]. The organ-pipe policy for block placement has been discussed in [25]. Buffering requirements for multimedia servers as well as the impact of various factors such as disk speed have been studied in [10]. The GSS policy is described in [51], and the scan-EDF policy is described in [42].

9

Multiple-Disk Organization

9.1   Introduction

In Chapter 8, we considered issues arising in the management of individual storage devices in a multimedia server. We now consider policies required for the management of multiple storage devices in a coordinated manner. The bandwidth and storage of an individual storage device may be small compared to the total requirements of a large-scale server. Hence, servers may contain a very large number of storage devices, making management difficult. For easier management, the individual storage devices may be aggregated into a smaller number of logical devices, the device being formed from a set of physical storage devices by striping files over them. It is likely that large-scale multimedia servers will have multiple striping groups. Load imbalance may arise among the various striping groups due to the skewed access to multimedia objects and load fluctuations. Hence, a file placement policy is needed to balance the load among the various striping groups, and to reduce the impact of device failures, it is also possible to replicate multimedia objects or store redundant (parity) information.

9.2   Striping

Striping groups are created by interleaving blocks of multimedia objects across multiple physical storage devices (as shown in Figure 9.1). The bandwidth and storage capacity of a striping group is the sum of the bandwidth and storage of the component devices. Hence, large striping groups have a much larger aggregate bandwidth than is available with a single physical storage device. This is helpful in satisfying a large bandwidth demand for popular multimedia objects with a single replica and, thus, avoiding creation of multiple replicas. A larger multimedia library can be maintained on-line by avoiding this replication overhead.

The performance of such striping groups may depend upon various factors, such as the storage device characteristics, the striping pattern, and the number of storage devices in a striping group. We discuss the impact of these factors next.

9.2.1   Striping Patterns

Striping patterns proposed in the literature can be classified into two categories. The simple striping schemes use an interleaving pattern to place blocks of a multimedia object across the storage devices of a striping group. Failure of a single device thus affects the entire striping group. To reduce this risk, compound striping schemes divide storage devices in a striping group into subgroups, and use an interleaving scheme to place blocks across the storage devices of a subgroup.

Simple striping patterns. The block interleaving pattern in a striping group may be regular or random. Three such simple patterns and their impact on storage device throughput are considered in [46]. Under the scan striping pattern (Figure 9.1(a)), blocks of a file are assigned in a round-robin manner over the storage devices. The independent striping pattern (Figure 9.1(b)) uses a different round-robin pattern for each individual multimedia object. The random striping pattern (Figure 9.1(c)) uses a random allocation of blocks to storage devices while ensuring that each storage device receives the same number of blocks.

The study in [46] shows that the random striping pattern results in the lowest storage device throughput, both for long multimedia objects and for interactive workload. This is due to the random placement of blocks, which produces unpredictable peak loads on individual storage devices, leading to delayed delivery of multimedia data blocks. The scan striping pattern tends to be better than the independent striping pattern due to the clustering of streams into groups that move in approximate synchronism from one storage device to the next. This tends to balance the load on the storage devices in the striping group.

Compound striping patterns. Compound striping patterns divide the devices in a striping group into subgroups and maintain associate redundant information associated with each subgroup. Hence, varying the number of subgroups allows a trade-off between the reliability of the system and the associated redundancy overhead. (These issues are described in more detail in Section 9.3.) The staggered striping policy is an example of a compound striping policy [3]. Under this policy, each multimedia object, O, is divided into a variable number of subobjects. Each subobject is further declustered into a variable $M_{O,\text{frag}}$ number of fragments (disk blocks) of size B_O. $M_{O,\text{frag}}$ and B_O are chosen so as to satisfy the bandwidth demand for the object; B_O is chosen so as to allow efficient disk retrieval—that is, so that the seek and rotation overhead is comparatively small. After placing a subobject on a cluster of $M_{O,\text{frag}}$ disks, $D_{\text{stride},O}$ disks are skipped before placing the

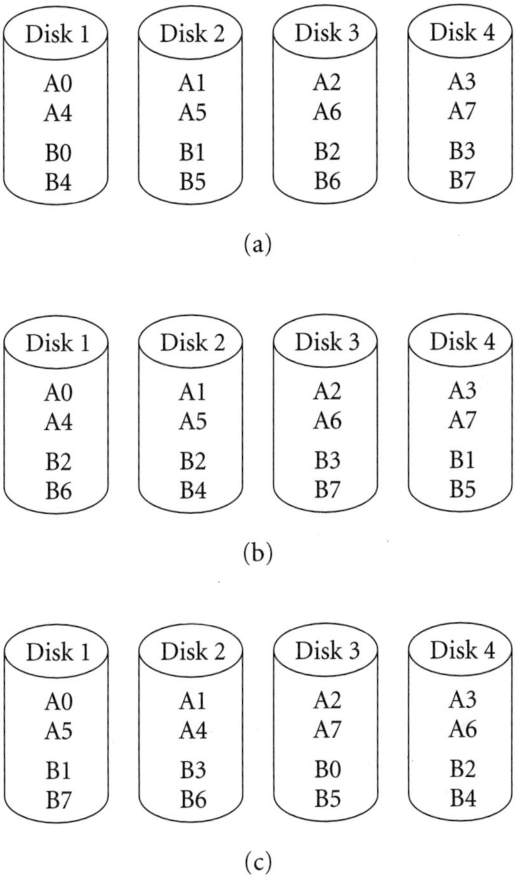

Figure 9.1 Illustration of simple striping patterns: scan (a), independent (b), and random (c).

next subobject (see Figure 9.2). Note that the clusters occupied by successive subobjects can overlap.

9.2.2 Striping Width

The block interleaving policies we have described uniformly distribute the blocks of a multimedia file among the devices in the striping group. Hence, they also balance the load among the individual devices in the group. However, random variations in stream playrate may lead to random instantaneous imbalances among the devices in the striping group. The extent of the imbalances will depend

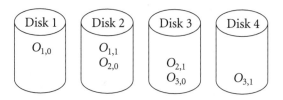

Figure 9.2 Staggered striping of an object: Object O broken into subobjects O_1, O_2, O_3; O_1, O_2, O_3 declustered into two fragments each; stride of 1, disk clusters = (1, 2), (2, 3), (3, 4).

on the striping width, the size of the read-ahead buffers, and the storage device characteristics. The relationship among these factors is studied in [10] using a simulation model (see Section 8.3.3 for a detailed description of the simulated environment). With a sufficient read-ahead buffer size, the maximum achievable disk throughput per disk is found to be independent of the striping width and approaches the maximum achievable disk bandwidth.

Figure 9.3 shows the effective throughput per disk of two different disk types for different buffer sizes and striping widths and a rejection rate of 0.1 blocks/hr. With a single buffer, the disk throughput drops dramatically with increasing striping width. This is because with random block placement, the number of streams to a disk at any time can vary, causing a large variance in response time. Increasing the number of read-ahead buffers to three (and delaying stream startup until two buffers are full) flattens the curves almost completely. Having more than three buffers is not cost-effective because the system is already operating close to maximum throughput.

Number of striping groups. Because striping balances the load on the individual devices in a striping group and the throughput is flat with the number of disks, it is natural to consider combining all the disks in a server into a single striping group. However, as we will discuss, there are many considerations that make multiple striping groups in a multimedia server desirable.

Heterogeneity of storage device types can be most easily handled through the use of multiple striping groups. Large-scale multimedia servers may contain various types of disks in a single system. For example, a system may grow with time such that newer devices (with different storage and bandwidth) may be introduced. If storage devices of different types are striped into a single group, it will be difficult to efficiently use the space and bandwidth of all of them. For example, a simple striping policy such as round-robin interleaves successive blocks of a multimedia object in different storage devices in order. The policy distributes the blocks of the multimedia objects evenly over the storage devices. As a result, all storage devices will contain the same number of multimedia data blocks. Because the same amount of data is stored on both the smallest and largest storage devices,

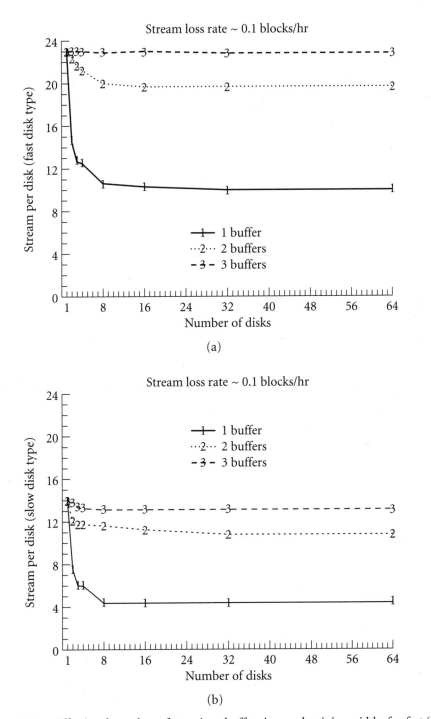

Figure 9.3 Effective throughput for various buffer sizes and striping widths for fast (a) and slow (b) disks.

there will be wastage of storage space on the larger storage devices. Striping schemes that use storage more efficiently can be devised. However, since the blocks are no longer evenly distributed over the storage devices, these schemes will lead to load imbalances among different storage devices. Overloading of individual devices also may result from different bandwidth capacities of the different types of disks. Thus, heterogeneity of storage device types naturally leads to grouping of different types of storage devices into separate striping groups.

Simple system reconfiguration, such as adding a storage device to the system, is also more difficult if there is only a single striping group. Because all multimedia objects will be striped over all storage devices, most of the blocks of every multimedia object will have to be moved. The time needed for system reconfiguration is hard to estimate (it depends, for example, on the load on the system), so all storage devices may be subjected to undesirable extra reconfiguration load for varying amounts of time. For any commercial system, it is not desirable to limit system reconfiguration to times when the system is not operational or is lightly loaded. If the system supports the use of multiple striping groups, only the affected striping group has to be taken off-line for quick reconfiguration, if desired. Additionally, as will be shown later, with a small amount of replication, any viewership loss due to the reconfiguration process can be made smaller even if the system is heavily loaded.

The use of a single striping group also complicates recovery in the event of the failure of a single storage device. If the recovery is made from backup tapes, the recovery overhead will be high in terms of either time or the number of backup tapes required. If the backup tapes contain copies of the multimedia objects, every multimedia object that does not have a storage device replica has to be read to extract the lost blocks, a process that could take a very long time. An alternative would be to store the images of every storage device on tape. This significantly increases the backup tape requirements. Additionally, this complicates the procedure for loading a multimedia object onto storage devices because a new storage device image backup tape has to be created each time a multimedia object is loaded onto a storage device. As shown in Section 9.3, high availability in the presence of failure can be ensured by the use of multiple striping groups and a small amount of replication overhead.

9.2.3   Disk Characteristics

In addition to the striping width, the effectiveness of striping may also depend on whether the disks are relatively fast or slow. A slower disk can only accommodate smaller queue lengths at the disk and thus support fewer streams, for a given loss rate. Hence, the impact of statistical fluctuations in playback rates may be larger, and the average achievable utilization may be lower. The impact of disk characteristics on striping group throughput is also studied in [10]. Recall that Figure 9.3 plots the effective throughput per disk as a function of read-ahead buffer size and striping widths for a rejection rate of 0.1 blocks/hr. Figure 9.3(a) shows a fast disk, while Figure 9.3(b) shows a slower disk with a peak bandwidth half the peak bandwidth of the faster disk. A comparison of the two figures shows that the maximum achievable throughput for the fast disk type is 1.7 times that achieved by the slower disk. However, the ratio between the effective throughput of the two disk types decreases with an increase in the read-ahead buffer size. This is because increasing the buffer size causes the sustainable throughput to be close to the maximum for both disk types. With one buffer, a larger queue length can be tolerated with a faster disk, and throughput is correspondingly higher.

9.3 Recovery from Failure

In many applications, interruption of service due to failure may lead to loss of customer goodwill and, hence, may be considered expensive. Consider, for example, an on-line news service, where timeliness of news delivery and recording is essential. Server failure may lead to loss of news material and may result in customer dissatisfaction. Such applications require the server to continue operation even in the presence of failure.

If the server contains multiple storage devices, it is possible to ensure operation in the presence of failure by the storage of redundant information and by reserving extra bandwidth. Two types of redundancy are possible. As in RAID devices, it is possible to store parity information along with the multimedia data, allowing the lost data to be reconstructed. An alternative approach, which is simpler, is to replicate some of the multimedia data. Both the parity-based and replication schemes attempt perfect recovery of the lost data. However, in the case of video, perfect reconstruction may not be necessary because adaptation via a small degradation in picture quality may be undetectable by customers. We thus describe partial reconstruction schemes, which attempt to encode the multimedia data so that a degraded reconstruction is possible in the event of failure.

9.3.1 Parity-Based Schemes

Parity-based recovery schemes such as RAID [36] associate extra parity blocks with sets of data blocks from different disks. The parity blocks are typically generated by performing an exclusive-or ($\oplus$) of the corresponding bits in the data blocks from all disks in the parity group. If a single data block becomes inaccessible due to a disk failure, it can be reconstructed by performing an exclusive-or of the parity block and the accessible associated data blocks. Multiple sets of parity blocks can be devised to deal with failure of multiple disks. However, because the time to failure of disks is typically very large (years), most schemes deal only with single-disk failures.

The set of associated blocks over which the parity is computed may all belong to the same object or different objects [36]. An example of the second case is the association of the corresponding physical bits of each disk in a striping group. If parity blocks are associated with sequential subsets of a single multimedia object, the retrieval overhead incurred during failure is limited to the retrieval of the parity blocks. However, in the second case, where parity blocks are associated with unrelated blocks of different objects, the retrieval overhead will additionally include the unrelated blocks of unrelated files. Parity schemes for multimedia servers hence have to compute parity over blocks of the same file [4].

From this discussion, it is clear that parity-based schemes require extra storage and bandwidth for storing and retrieving the data and parity blocks. As is shown later, buffering requirements are also higher during failure. Different parity-based schemes differ in the trade-offs between these two factors. We describe two striping parity schemes: the staggered striping parity scheme [4] and the segmented information dispersal (SID) scheme [9]. The SID scheme has a higher disk overhead but a lower buffer requirement. Both schemes require CPU overhead for recomputing the failed data blocks. The CPU overhead can be eliminated by performing the computation in a special controller. Such controllers, however, are typically very expensive.

Staggered striping. The disk layout policy for the parity-based recovery in staggered striping [3] is detailed in [4]. We first describe the placement of parity blocks under such a scheme and then discuss the operation of the scheme upon a failure. Finally, we discuss the associated overheads and show how reducing the disk storage overhead requires increasing the buffer requirements of the system.

The staggered striping policy associates a parity block with each subobject [4]. The parity block for each subobject is stored on a different cluster; specifically, if O_i, the ith subobject of O, is stored on cluster j, the parity block for O_i is stored on cluster $j + 1$. For balancing the load on cluster $j + 1$ during degraded mode,[1] it is necessary to disperse the parity blocks over the different disks in the cluster. This can be done by storing the parity block for the first subobject in cluster j on the first disk in cluster $j + 1$, the parity block for the second subobject on the second disk, and so on (as shown in Figure 9.4).

During normal operation, each stream retrieves blocks cyclically from the disks. If a disk in cluster j fails, the staggered striping policy needs to retrieve a

---

[1]The addition is done modulo the number of clusters.

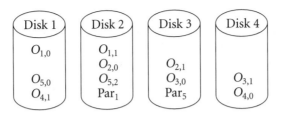

Figure 9.4 Staggered striping of an object: Object O broken into subobjects $O_1, O_2, \ldots,$ O_6 (O_6 not shown); $O_1, O_2, \ldots, O_6$ declustered into two fragments each. Stride of 1; disk clusters = $(1, 2), (2, 3), (3, 4), (4, 1)$. Par_i is parity block for O_i.

parity block from cluster $j + 1$. This operation is referred to as a "shift to the right." If no extra bandwidth for retrieving the parity block is available in cluster $j + 1$, the policy acts as though the disk on which the requested parity block resides has failed and performs a second shift to the right. This involves (a) canceling a scheduled read from cluster $j + 1$, (b) reading instead the requested parity block, and (c) attempting to reconstruct the canceled block from cluster $j + 2$. The failure thus propagates over all the clusters until a cluster with the needed extra bandwidth is found. If no such cluster is found, the stream suffers a failure in continuous delivery due to bandwidth exhaustion. Note that because parity blocks are associated with a cluster, the staggered striping policy can recover from a single failure in each cluster.

To reconstruct the block on the failed disk, it is necessary to exclusive-or the data from the accessible blocks of the subobject and the parity block. If the scheme uses a fixed small number of read-ahead buffers per stream (for example, three, as suggested in Section 8.3.1), the required blocks will, in general, not be available immediately after the failure. One solution is to buffer all the blocks of the current subobject for each stream in anticipation of a failure. However, this may be expensive in terms of the required storage. Alternatively, if all the blocks of a subobject are buffered only after a failure, there will be an interruption immediately after the failure while the remaining blocks of the accessed subobjects in the failed cluster are being read. In either case, after a failure it is necessary to buffer all the accessible blocks and the parity block for each subobject in the failed cluster.

It can be seen that the storage overhead of the staggered striping policy is inversely proportional to the cluster size. For example, if the cluster size is 10, the storage overhead is equal to 10% because there is a parity block for every 10 data blocks. The preceding discussion shows that the buffer space overhead is directly proportional to the size of the cluster. Hence, the appropriate cluster size has to be chosen to balance these two factors. The extra disk bandwidth required during failure can be found as follows. If the total idle bandwidth in the remaining clusters is equal to the bandwidth of the failing disk, all the streams accessing the failed disk can be successfully recovered by load shifts to the right. Hence, the bandwidth overhead is equal to the bandwidth of a disk. At high load, multiple shifts to the right may require multiple parity recomputations. The CPU overhead is therefore variable and increases with load. More complex policies with different trade-offs among these factors are also presented in [4].

Segmented information dispersal. The staggered striping parity scheme associates a parity block with the $M_{O,\text{frag}}$ fragments of a subobject. Hence, its disk storage overhead is proportional to $1/M_{O,\text{frag}}$, and the buffer overhead during failure is proportional to $M_{O,\text{frag}}$. If parity blocks are associated with a subset of the $M_{O,\text{frag}}$ fragments, the buffering requirements during failure will be reduced. However, the disk storage overhead will increase because there will be more parity blocks. This may be a reasonable trade-off if the cost of memory is high compared to disk cost [9].

The SID scheme divides each object O into a variable number of subobjects,[2] each of which is placed on a single disk. Additionally, the data blocks in each disk are divided into logical segments. The number of such logical segments, M_{dseg}, depends upon D, the total number of disks, and is chosen to minimize the disk storage overhead and buffering requirements. A table of M_{dseg} for $5 \leq D \leq 100$ is given in [9]; details of the derivation can be found in [8]. To construct the logical segments, each subobject is first divided into M_{dseg} fragments. The ith logical segment is then constructed by logically grouping together the ith fragment of each subobject on the disk. Under the SID scheme, the number of data blocks needed to compute the parity block is also equal to M_{dseg}.

Figure 9.5 illustrates a SID layout for a set of 5 disks. The SID layouts for $5 \leq D \leq 100$ can be found in [9] and the derivation of these layouts in [8]. The optimum number of logical segments, M_{dseg}, in this case is two. Each disk contains fragments of the objects together with parity data. For example, disk 1 contains fragments $O_{1,1}$, $O_{1,2}$, $O_{6,1}$, and $O_{6,2}$. The parity data on disk 1 is the exclusive-or of segment 1 of disk 5 together with segment 2 of disk 2.

We compare the overheads of the SID policy and the staggered striping policy using an example. To provide comparable failure tolerance, we assume that the staggered striping group contains only one cluster. With 25 disks, the SID policy would divide each disk into four logical segments [9]. Hence, each parity block is associated with four data blocks, and the buffer requirements are lower than those for the staggered striping policy. However, reconstructing a failed block requires the reading of four blocks, resulting in a 12% increase in bandwidth to read the three extra blocks. This is in comparison to the 4% extra bandwidth (the bandwidth of a single disk) required by the staggered striping policy. Additionally, be-

---

[2]Referred to as *slices* in [9].

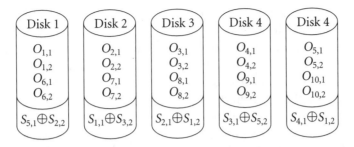

Figure 9.5 Segmented information dispersal recovery policy: Object O divided into 10 subobjects $O_1, \ldots, O_{10}$; each disk D_i divided into two logical $S_{i,1}$ and $S_{i,2}$; $S_{1,1} = \{O_{1,1}$ and $O_{6,1}\}$, $S_{1,2} = \{O_{1,2}$ and $O_{6,2}\}$, ...

cause each parity block is associated with four data blocks, the storage overhead is 25%. This compares to 4% for the staggered striping policy, where each parity block is associated with 25 data blocks.

9.3.2 Partial Replication

The parity-based recovery schemes we have discussed require recomputation of the multimedia data blocks from the parity data, which may be complex or computationally expensive. We will show that partial replication together with the use of multiple striping groups also significantly reduces the amount of storage overhead needed to ensure high availability [12].

Intuitively, if there is only a single striping group that includes all the disks in the server, failure of any single disk results in unavailability of all the multimedia objects. On the other hand, with the use of multiple groups, only the multimedia objects in the group containing the failed disk are lost. Hence, taking advantage of the skewed access patterns to multimedia objects, it is possible to replicate some of the popular multimedia objects to increase availability but with a low replication overhead. We present a simple model from [12] that computes the relationship between availability, the number of striping groups, and the replication overhead.

The availability of a multimedia system is defined in [12] as the fraction of viewers who can continue viewing the multimedia objects even in the event of a single disk failure. Hence, $A = 1 - V_{aff}/V$, where V_{aff} is the number of affected viewers and V is the total number of viewers in the system. Consider a system containing S striping groups and M_O multimedia objects, where the average number of viewers of the replica of multimedia object m on striping group s is $v_{m,s}$. Let C_s be the set of multimedia objects on striping group s and $v_{m,s,sh}$ be the number of viewers of multimedia object m that can be shifted to an alternate striping group if a disk in striping group s fails. Clearly, $v_{m,s,sh}$ will be zero for multimedia objects with a single copy on disk.

For replicated multimedia objects, $v_{m,s,sh}$ will depend upon the actual loads and capacities of the disks containing the additional replicas. Systems that have to operate reliably under failure of a disk have to be configured with enough spare capacity to ensure that none of the viewers of popular multimedia objects are lost on a disk failure. In this case, all the load for the replicated multimedia objects can be shifted to a nonfailed striping group (i.e., $v_{m,s,sh} = v_{m,s}$). This leads to a simple expression for the availability of such a system. The number of lost viewers for the nonreplicated multimedia objects in striping group s is then given by $V_{s,\text{aff}} = \sum_{m \in C_s} v_{m,s} - v_{m,s,sh}$. Let the probability of failure of striping group s be u_s. If all the disks are assumed to be identical, and D_s and D are the number of disks in striping group s and the total number of disks, respectively, $u_s = D_s/D$. The expected loss due to failure of a single disk is given by $V_{\text{aff}} = \sum_{s=1}^{S} u_s V_{s,\text{aff}}$.

The required replication storage overhead for replication to achieve a given availability requirement A can now be computed. Under the skewed access to multimedia objects normally expected in a multimedia server, high availability (say, 90%) can be achieved with only a small replication storage overhead using a small number (four to eight) of striping groups. Figure 9.6(a) shows the required replication overhead as a function of the number of striping groups for various availability requirements. The access distribution to various multimedia objects is the empirically derived distribution shown in Figure 5.1 in Chapter 5. The figure shows that increasing the availability requirement results in an increase in the required replication overhead. However, the replication overhead drops significantly as the number of striping groups increases. For certain combinations of availability requirements and numbers of striping groups, the replication overhead is zero. For example, to achieve 75% availability with eight striping groups, no replication is required because only 12.5% of the viewers are lost if a single disk fails.

The required replication overhead drops sharply with the increase in the number of striping groups because the expected loss from the failure of a single disk drops sharply as the number of striping groups increases. Figure 9.6(b) shows this relationship between the expected loss and the number of striping groups for different values of the replication overhead (number of replicated multimedia objects). With no replication, the expected loss V_{aff} falls as $1/S$. Replicating some popular multimedia objects causes V_{aff} to drop even lower.

9.3.3 Imperfect Reconstruction

Both the parity-based and replication schemes we have discussed attempt to perfectly reconstruct the blocks lost due to a storage device failure. However,

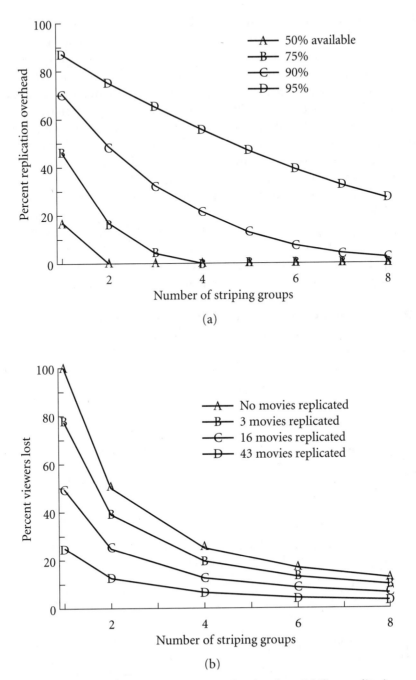

(a)

(b)

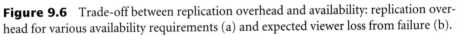

Figure 9.6 Trade-off between replication overhead and availability: replication overhead for various availability requirements (a) and expected viewer loss from failure (b).

limitations in human perception may make perfect reconstruction of lost multimedia data unnecessary. Instead, the redundancy in multimedia data may be exploited to produce an imperfect reconstruction that is of acceptable quality. Figure 9.7 illustrates the DRAD policy [43], which follows this approach. Recall from Chapter 1 that in the MPEG-1 encoding process, video frames are subdivided into 16×16 subimages, which are then transformed using interpolation and DCT transforms into fixed-length macroblocks. The transform process also produces motion vectors and headers associated with each macroblock. The macroblocks contain coefficients associated with the DCT for each subimage and are of comparable size to the original image. In the normal MPEG-1 compression scheme, these macroblocks are compressed using run-length and Huffman encoding.

The DRAD policy interposes a scrambling step in between the transformation and compression stages of MPEG-1 (see Figure 9.7). It scrambles sets of D macroblocks to produce D scrambled blocks, where D is the number of disks in the striping group. Each scrambled block contains some coefficients from each image in the set. These scrambled blocks are then compressed as in MPEG-1, and the compressed blocks are written to disk.

Decoding follows the reverse sequence of operations. First, a decompression phase generates scrambled blocks. Sets of D scrambled blocks are then unscrambled and used to generate the original image. If one of the disk fails, some of the compressed scrambled blocks are unavailable. The values of the coefficients in the

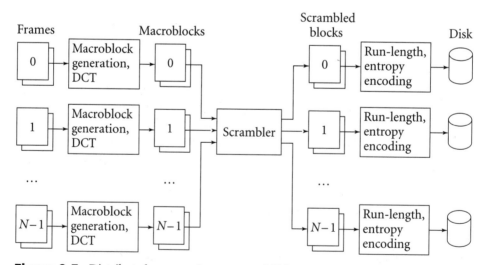

Figure 9.7 Distributed recovery in an array of disks.

inaccessible blocks are estimated from the accessible values in neighboring blocks or set to zero [43]. This results in the display of a slightly degraded image.

Because no extra disk reads are required, the DRAD policy does not require any extra bandwidth overhead during failure. Additionally, there is no loss in compression efficiency as the compression rate of the scrambled blocks is equal to that of the unscrambled blocks. A slight disk storage overhead is still incurred because the motion vectors and macroblock headers cannot be inferred if lost. These have to be replicated on every disk; the resulting disk storage overhead is on the order of 2 to 8% [43]. Buffer storage requirements are greater during normal operation because the unscrambling step requires reading blocks from all the disks in parallel.

Unlike the other schemes discussed, recovery under the DRAD policy has to be performed on the client. First, recovery (estimation of the inaccessible coefficients) is carried out during the unscrambling step. This step uses uncompressed (though encoded) data that is too voluminous to process on the server. Second, unlike the other schemes, the DRAD scheme is specific to the compression algorithm used, so it is preferable to implement it in the client decoding adapter. A version of the DRAD scheme for JPEG is also found in [43]. Performing recovery in the client may lead to greater scalability and also allow recovery from loss of blocks in the network.

9.4   File Placement

As discussed earlier, a large multimedia server is likely to contain multiple striping groups or logical storage devices. Hence, a file placement policy that selects the storage devices on which to place multimedia files is required. Storage devices in multimedia servers are limited both by their bandwidth (number of concurrent streams they can support) as well as by their space capacity (the number of multimedia objects they can store). The objectives of file placement policies in a multimedia server are to achieve maximum utilization of both space and bandwidth and, hence, efficient usage of these devices by avoiding load imbalance across the devices. To achieve these objectives, file placement policies have to consider the characteristics of both the storage devices as well as the multimedia objects. We discuss these factors in detail.

The multimedia objects stored in a multimedia server can be characterized by their access patterns and sizes. Accesses to these multimedia objects will in general be nonuniform; that is, some objects will be viewed more frequently (referred to as *hot* files), while others are viewed less frequently (referred to as *cold* files). Depending upon the supported applications, the server may have to store a mixture of both hot and cold large multimedia objects (e.g., long movies) as well as hot and cold short multimedia objects (e.g., objects in interactive applications such as shopping, medical, etc.). To support simultaneous viewing of popular multimedia objects by a large number of clients, it may be necessary to create multiple replicas of popular multimedia objects on multiple storage devices. Many interactive applications also may require the display of multiple objects (see Chapter 1). For such applications, it is desirable to place the objects so as to minimize switching between servers.

The parameters of the storage devices also are important factors in the placement decisions. In a clustered server, the logical storage devices may be individual storage servers, while in a single server, they may be striping groups. Storage devices can be classified as fast or slow depending on whether they have relatively larger bandwidth or space. Placing many large cold objects on a fast device will lead to wastage of the device's bandwidth because only a limited number of streams will be requested from the cold objects during operation. Similarly, placing many short hot clips on a slow device will result in wastage of the device space, as the lower bandwidth will permit access to only a few objects. Therefore, large and short, hot and cold objects have to be mixed properly both to balance the load across the devices and also to effectively utilize both the bandwidth and space of the devices.

The objective of balancing the load among storage devices can also be achieved by dynamic policies. For example, the dynamic segment replication (DSR) policy [12] uses dynamic partial replication of multimedia objects for load balancing in multimedia systems. Note that a good initial placement policy makes it easier for the dynamic policy to handle load fluctuations that may arise during actual operation of the system. Hence, dynamic policies are complementary to a good file placement policy. In real systems, about 5% of the total bandwidth may be set aside for the purpose of load balancing and dealing with these dynamic variations in load [12].

In the rest of this section, we first discuss the practical requirements of file placement policies that arise from the need for smooth operation of a multimedia server [11]. Finally, we describe the policies [13, 31] that have been proposed in the literature.

9.4.1   Operational Issues in File Placement

In addition to the objective of efficient usage of storage devices, practical considerations dictate a number of requirements for file placement policies [27, 11]. Multimedia objects may be very large, making migration and deletion of multimedia objects in general very time-consuming. It is thus very important to place multimedia objects carefully in advance based on the anticipated load. Even though the *expected load* or expected number of viewers of a multimedia object can be projected using historical data together with human input [31], the actual load may be affected by factors that are hard to predict or quantify. Examples of factors that may unpredictably increase demand for a movie are favorable reviews or discounted pricing. Such unexpected changes can be better handled by monitoring the demand for multimedia objects and initiating on-line changes in the placement of multimedia objects when needed. This adaptation can be carried out by an external agent in coordination with the file placement policy. Hence, the file placement policy should provide for interfaces by which changes in predicted load can be communicated by the agent, resulting in changes in placement.

The expected load on multimedia objects changes with time. The inputs to the placement policy can be updated periodically. It is important that system operation not be interrupted for placement, so the file placement policy should allow on-line reconfiguration. For adjusting quickly to the new predictions of future load, a necessary input to the placement policy should be the speed with which changes in placement have to be made. Also, if the predicted load on multiple multimedia objects changes, it is important for the file placement policy to allow a smooth transition from the current file placement to a new placement that minimizes disruptive migration and deletion.

The file placement policy needs to maintain the expected load for all multimedia objects in the system. As a result, instead of allowing explicit deletion and creation of replicas independently of the placement policy, it is preferable that all placement of multimedia objects be carried out in coordination with the placement policy. For example, if the expected load on a popular multimedia object with multiple replicas drops, it may be desirable to delete some of the replicas. This can be achieved by invoking the file placement policy with a lower expected load and allowing the policy to decide which replicas to delete. Similarly, the file placement policy should be allowed to decide on the placement and creation of new replicas based on the expected load.

Finally, it is important that a file placement policy be integrated with policies for managing the storage hierarchy, described later in Chapter 10. Hence, in addition to deciding where to place files being staged in from tape, an input to the placement policy should be the speed at which the newly retrieved file is to be written to disk. This feature would be useful in situations where a rarely used file is to be staged in within a predetermined amount of time (say, 5 minutes, for example). From the size of the file, the storage hierarchy manager can determine the speed at which the file needs to be read in and supply this as input to the placement policy. This will also allow the placement policy to support recording of real-time data that has to be written to disk at a particular rate (e.g., live news).

In the rest of this section, we survey file placement policies that have been proposed in the literature.

9.4.2   Popularity-Based Assignment

Popularity-based placement policy [31] is a policy that can be used to place multi-media objects on a set of identical disks. The policy attempts to minimize the average number of customers rejected due to storage device overload under high load conditions.

The policy uses the access probabilities $p_{i,t}$ to each file i on day t (referred to as *popularities*) for making placement decisions. Here, it is assumed that the access probabilities $p_{i,t}$ are fixed over a 24-hour period and that the system is reconfigured every 24 hours to reflect new access probabilities. The following method for predicting $p_{i,t+1}$ from historical data on days $t-1$ and t is suggested in [31]. If $\Lambda_{i,t}$ is the number of requests for multimedia object i on day t, a reasonable estimate for $\Lambda_{i,t+1}$ can be found by linear interpolation: $\Lambda_{i,t+1} = 2\Lambda_{i,t} - \Lambda_{i,t-1}$ (see Figure 9.8). The value of $p_{i,t+1}$ can be computed as $p_{i,t+1} = \Lambda_{i,t+1}/(\sum_i \Lambda_{i,t+1})$. These values of $p_{i,t+1}$ can be used at the end of day t to reconfigure the server off-line for day $t+1$.

For identical disks, it can be shown that the probability of rejection is minimized when the probability of access to all disks is the same [31]. Assigning multimedia objects to disks in a way that results in a uniform disk access probability distribution is a problem similar to the bin-packing problem, which is known to be NP-hard. An approximate solution can, however, be obtained by well-known heuristics, such as the greedy algorithm. In [31], it is shown that even assignments that deviate moderately from uniformity are very close to the optimal.

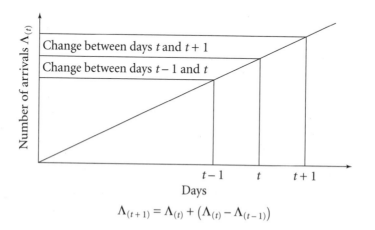

$$\Lambda_{(t+1)} = \Lambda_{(t)} + \left(\Lambda_{(t)} - \Lambda_{(t-1)}\right)$$

Figure 9.8   Projection of future demand in popularity-based assignment.

9.4.3 BSR Policy

The bandwidth-to-space ratio (BSR) [13] policy attempts to mix hot and cold as well as large and small multimedia objects on heterogeneous storage devices or striping groups so as to match the (bandwidth and space) characterization of these devices (see Figure 9.9). The policy characterizes each device by its bandwidth-to-space ratio (or actual BSR). Similarly, for placement decisions, each multimedia object is characterized by the expected bandwidth requirement on that replica (based on the expected number of concurrent viewers) and the space required to store that replica. Hence, during operation, the BSR policy needs to keep track of the bandwidth and space of each device as well as the expected load and size of each replica of a multimedia object. As discussed in Section 9.4.1, the BSR policy is an on-line multimedia object placement policy that dynamically creates and/or deletes existing replicas for better utilization of the storage devices in response to changes in the expected load on the multimedia objects and/or system configuration.

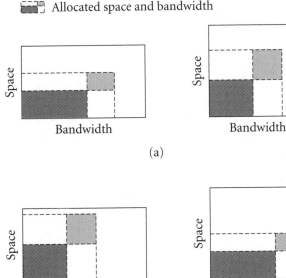

Figure 9.9 Illustration of the BSR policy showing matched (a) and unmatched (b) space and bandwidth requirements for an object.

The BSR policy may be invoked for modifying the placement of an existing multimedia object or for placing a new multimedia object. Changes to the expected load for multiple multimedia objects can be handled by repeated execution of the BSR policy for different multimedia objects in a certain order. First, the policy is invoked to modify the placement of multimedia objects that have reduced demands. This results in freeing bandwidth and possibly space on the system storage devices. Next, the policy is invoked for multimedia objects whose expected load has increased (including new objects). Performing the placements in decreasing order of expected load produces better placement [13]. In the following section, we describe the BSR policy in more detail, and summarize some of the experimental results regarding its performance from [13].

Details of the BSR policy. The BSR policy has two input parameters: the new expected load for the multimedia object to be placed, and the required bandwidth for creating replicas. For a new multimedia object, the new expected load is the expected load of the multimedia object. The bandwidth required for creation of replicas will depend on how quickly the replica is to be written (e.g., if the multimedia object has to be staged in from tape within a specified time or if it is from a real-time source).

The algorithm consists of four phases. In the first phase, the policy determines if additional replicas are needed. The determination takes into account an availability parameter that limits viewer loss by specifying the maximum number of viewers that may be allocated to any replica of any multimedia object. In the second phase, the BSR policy selects, if needed, additional devices on which to create new replicas. In the third phase, the expected load is then allocated to all the selected devices so as to match the actual BSRs of the devices. If the policy is unable to place all of the expected load, it enters a replica consolidation phase in which the policy deletes some of the existing replicas of other multimedia objects to place the new load. All four steps of the BSR policy may need to be followed only for increases in expected load—that is, for creating additional replicas. For a decrease in the expected load, only the third phase (the reallocation step) is executed.

The BSR policy implicitly determines the number of replicas for each multimedia object. In the first phase, the policy determines if additional replicas are necessary by determining the maximum additional expected load that can be placed on existing replicas. This is estimated from the free bandwidth of the devices on which the replicas reside, the limit imposed by the availability parameter, and the maximum allowable BSR deviation (defined below). If enough space and expected bandwidth is available on the storage devices, the BSR policy may create many replicas. A larger number of replicas increases the ability of the system to balance expected load during future placements because expected load may be shifted between replicas without any overhead. Unneeded replicas are marked for deletion in the third phase but are not deleted immediately; they are deleted only when the space is actually required.

In selecting additional devices to create new replicas, the BSR policy attempts to match the allocated and actual BSRs of a device. The allocated BSR of a device is defined as the ratio of the total allocated bandwidth to the total allocated space of that device (Figure 9.9). The BSR deviation of a device is defined as the deviation between the allocated and actual BSRs of a device. A device is classified as hot if its allocated BSR is greater than its actual BSR, and as cold otherwise. In selecting a device, the devices not containing a replica of the current multimedia object are considered, with devices having a high BSR deviation being considered first. A hot device is selected if placing a replica on that device will reduce the BSR deviation and make the device less hot. Otherwise, the multimedia object is placed on a cold device. Additionally, the device must have enough free space to create the replica and to free current bandwidth to satisfy the quickness criteria. If sufficient devices cannot be found, an emergency scan is initiated in which the availability limit and the classification of the devices into hot and cold are ignored.

Initial placement. The performance of the BSR policy was studied in [13] using a simulation of a video-on-demand system. The simulated system was assumed to have four striping groups of 8, 16, 32, and 64 identical disks. Each storage device was assumed to have 2 GB of storage space and sufficient bandwidth to support 6.25 units of load (i.e., streams). Hence, the striping groups had space and bandwidth capacities of (16 GB, 50), (32 GB, 100), (64 GB, 200) and (128 GB, 400). The video access distribution used was the empirically derived distribution with parameter 0.271 (shown in Chapter 12). The system was assumed to store 64 multimedia objects. As there was sufficient space to store only at most one copy of each video, only under the ideal placement of files could all the bandwidth be utilized. Hence, this configuration was a stress test for the BSR policy.

Figure 9.10 shows the allocated space and bandwidth under the BSR policy. The system is assumed to be empty initially. Each figure contains four sets of bars, one for each striping group. The two different allocations are for different availability parameters (30 and 50) that specify the maximum units of load per replica affected by a single failure. As can be seen, very little bandwidth and space are wasted by the policy.

Changing load. The BSR policy also adapts well to changes in the access frequency of the multimedia objects [13]. Starting with the initial placement just described, the policy was used to change the multimedia object placement in response to a change in load. To generate the load change, a K-shifted folded Zipf distribution is used (see Figure 9.11(a)). Under the folded Zipf distribution, the relative access frequencies to various multimedia objects are still given by the Zipf distribution. However, the video access distribution is indexed so that the video with the high-

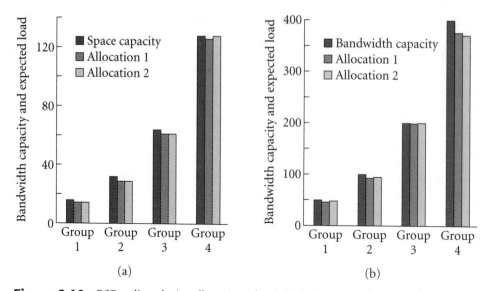

Figure 9.10   BSR policy: device allocation after initial placement showing allocated space (a) and bandwidth (b).

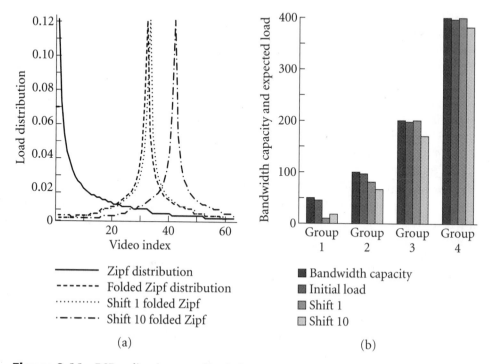

Figure 9.11   BSR policy: impact of load change on access distribution (a) and bandwidth allocation (b).

est load is in the middle, the second highest load is on its immediate left, and the third highest is on its immediate right, and so on. The K-shifted distribution is created by shifting the indices by K (e.g., the peak load is on a video earlier indexed as peak plus K). Shifts of 1 and 10, representing a small and large change in the access frequencies, respectively, were simulated. Figure 9.11(b) shows the bandwidth allocation after the load shift. It can be seen that the BSR matches are still excellent.

9.5   Summary

Issues regarding the organization and management of systems consisting of multiple disks were studied in this chapter. Multiple physical disks can be combined by striping into a single logical disk whose space capacity and bandwidth is equal to the sum of the space capacities and bandwidths of the component disks. Striping balances the load among the individual disks in the group. However, due to practical considerations such as the difficulty of striping together different kinds of disks, it is likely that there will be multiple logical disks in a system. Striping can also provide recovery from failure by storing parity blocks in the striping group. However, recovery from failure can also be achieved by replicating popular multimedia objects on other striping groups or by exploiting the redundancy of image data to reconstruct failed blocks.

Because there are multiple logical disks in a multimedia server, a file placement policy is needed that decides where to place multimedia objects. For very popular multimedia objects, the placement policy should also determine the number and placement of replicas. The placement policy makes its decision based upon the anticipated demand for multimedia objects, as well as the space capacity and bandwidth of the logical disks in the system. For consistency, it is desirable that all creation, replication, and deletion of multimedia objects be carried out in conjunction with the file placement policy. This includes on-demand retrieval of infrequently used multimedia objects from tertiary storage. Because placement policy cannot achieve perfect load balance at run time (due to fluctuations in demand for multimedia objects), a complementary dynamic load-balancing policy is also desirable.

Further Reading

Striping policies to allow recovery from failure are described in [3, 8]. Recovery from failure through imperfect reconstruction is described in [43]. Failure recovery by replicating popular multimedia objects is described in [12]. File placement policies are discussed in [13, 31].

10

Storage Hierarchy

_____

10.1   Introduction

Many applications require storage of a large amount of data. For example, military planning and digital battlefield computing require storage and efficient access to millions of detailed terrain, weather, and satellite images [22]. These images may need to be displayed in real time by applications. On-line storage of such large amounts of data on disks or memory may not be feasible. Even where on-line storage is feasible, an alternative approach that takes advantage of the differing costs and characteristics of different storage devices may be more economical. This naturally leads to a storage hierarchy where frequently accessed data is stored on faster, more expensive devices and infrequently accessed data is stored on slower, less expensive devices. A common storage hierarchy found in multimedia servers and other computer systems consists of tertiary storage (e.g., tape) to hold the most infrequently used data, secondary storage (e.g., disk) to hold more frequently used data, and memory to hold the most frequently used data. Such policies exploit the uneven data access rates to reduce the total storage cost of the system.

The choice of which data to store on secondary storage or memory and which data to store on tertiary storage depends upon the individual storage device characteristics. The feasibility of storing multimedia data on tertiary storage necessitates development of policies for real-time retrieval of data. Many of the techniques used in the management of secondary storage devices (e.g., striping) may be applicable to the management of tertiary storage devices. In this chapter, we first discuss the characteristics of tertiary storage devices and the choice of which multimedia objects to store on them. We then describe policies for the management of tertiary storage devices.

10.2   Overview of Tertiary Storage Devices

Two commonly used types of tertiary storage devices are optical jukeboxes and tape drive systems (see Chapter 3 for details). Optical jukeboxes consist of an optical library that stores CD-ROMs together with one or more CD-ROM drives. A robotic arm allows any CD-ROM in the library to be mounted. Tape drive systems similarly contain a tape library for storing tape cartridges, one or more tape drives, and a robot.

Tertiary storage devices have playback characteristics that are significantly different from those of secondary storage devices. In both optical jukeboxes and tape libraries, a storage element (CD-ROM or tape) has to be retrieved mechanically from the library and inserted into the storage drive. This introduces a relatively long delay, or latency—typically, on the order of seconds—between the time the request for a multimedia object is made and the time playback can begin. This latency has to be masked by tertiary storage management policies. Some tertiary storage elements (e.g., tape) have an extra latency due to their access characteristics. Tapes can be accessed only sequentially, so there is an access latency after the tape is mounted while the playback device is positioned for accessing the required data. Additionally, the playback bandwidth of some devices (e.g., slow CD-ROM or tapes) may not be much larger than that of a single stream. Hence, it is difficult to play multiple streams from the same storage drive, making it necessary to dedicate a storage drive to each stream. This can significantly increase the cost of the system, nullifying the advantage of the lower cost per byte. Finally, unlike disks, CD-ROM systems are read-only devices, which precludes reorganization of the multimedia data as well as the use of such devices for archiving.

10.3   Staging Issues

The policies for the management of tertiary storage devices depend upon the playback characteristics we have described. We first consider staging issues that deal with the real-time retrieval of data from tertiary storage devices. Following this, we consider issues relating to the organization of tertiary storage devices.

Retrieval policies for tertiary storage devices can be classified into two categories (see Figure 10.1). Direct playback policies retrieve multimedia data from CD-ROM or tape into the memory buffers in the multimedia server and then directly transmit it to the client. Alternatively, it is possible to first retrieve the data to secondary storage devices and subsequently to play back from these secondary storage devices. These are referred to as the *staged playback* policies. Direct playback policies always operate on demand because the memory in a multimedia server is normally too small to hold a large amount of multimedia data. In con-

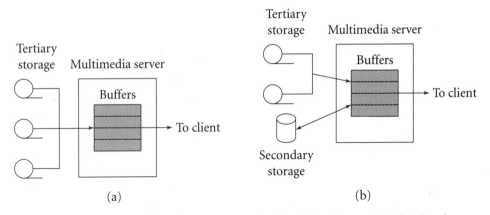

Figure 10.1 Alternative tertiary storage retrieval policies: direct playback (a) and staged playback (b).

trast, the staged playback policies may choose to retrieve the multimedia data on demand from tertiary storage or to prefetch the data before it is needed. In both cases, either all the multimedia data or only part of it may be retrieved. We discuss these alternatives in the next section.

10.3.1 Direct vs. Staged Playback

Direct and staged playback policies have been compared in [28]. The direct playback policy is simpler and may be less expensive because no additional staging to disk is needed. However, the long latency of tertiary storage devices implies that the storage drive cannot be multiplexed among multiple multimedia objects. Hence, the storage drive is occupied for the entire length of time it takes to play the multimedia object and is freed only when the multimedia object is completed. On the other hand, the staging policy can stage the multimedia objects to disk at a high speed. By increasing the number of streams that can be served from a tertiary storage drive, it can reduce the system cost per multimedia object.

These characteristics can be quantified using a simple model. The cost of storing a multimedia object, i, on the tertiary storage is the cost of the storage element plus the amortized cost of the player. Under direct playback, the storage drive is occupied for the duration of the multimedia object, after which it is freed for subsequent requests. Hence, the amortized cost of the storage drive is $v_i c_{drv}/\rho_{drv}$, where c_{drv} is the cost of the storage drive, v_i is the average number of active streams of multimedia object i, and ρ_{drv} is the maximum achievable utilization of the drive. Typically, ρ_{drv} will be much lower than 1 for reducing queuing delays. Let $c_{i,stor}$ be the cost of the storage element (CD-ROM or tape) storing this multimedia object. The cost of storing a multimedia object i on tertiary storage can thus be represented as $c_{i,\mathrm{drv}} = c_{i,\mathrm{stor}} + v_i c_{\mathrm{drv}}/\rho_{\mathrm{drv}}$ when direct playback is used.

The cost of storing multimedia objects under staged playback can be computed similarly. If γ is the ratio of the speed at which the data is staged onto secondary storage to the playback rate of the multimedia object, the amortized cost of the tertiary storage drive is reduced to $\gamma v_i c_{\mathrm{drv}}/\rho_{\mathrm{drv}}$. However, it is necessary to include the amortized cost of the staging disks. If c_{disk} is the cost of storing the multimedia object on the staging disks, and ρ_{disk} is the maximum achievable utilization of the staging disks, the amortized staging disk cost is $2 v_i c_{\mathrm{disk}}/\rho_{\mathrm{disk}}$. The factor of 2 is required as the staging disk is accessed twice per multimedia object. The total cost under staged playback is thus given by $c_{i,\mathrm{stg}} = c_{i,\mathrm{stor}} + \gamma v_i c_{\mathrm{drv}}/\rho_{\mathrm{drv}} + 2 v_i c_{\mathrm{disk}}/\rho_{\mathrm{disk}}$.

The direct and staging policies are compared using this cost model in [28] for different tertiary storage devices. For values typical of slower CD-ROM systems, the direct model yields a lower cost. Direct playback is thus preferable for CD-ROM systems. For values typical of high-speed tape systems, the staging policy is less expensive, as the increased cost of the staging disks is more than offset by the reduced amortized cost of the tertiary storage drive.

10.3.2   Staging Policies

We now consider the different types of staging policies. A simple staging policy is the pure on-demand policy, where multimedia objects are fetched from tertiary storage upon reference. Such a policy has the advantage that no previous knowledge of multimedia access patterns is required. However, on-demand staging may not be practical for short multimedia objects due to the relatively large latency in accessing tertiary storage devices. Hence, popular short multimedia objects should be prestaged to disks. Even larger popular multimedia objects may be economical to prestage to disks, because on-demand staging incurs various overheads, such as the overhead of reading the object from tape and storing it on disk. Staging may also incur queuing delays for accessing the tertiary devices.

Pure on-demand staging and prestaging of popular multimedia objects to disk are compared in [28] using the cost model we have outlined. Considering only the popular multimedia objects, the disk storage configuration (i.e., number of disks required) is determined by the bandwidth required for playback and not the storage space. Hence, the cost of prestaging a multimedia object i to disk is given by $c_{i,\mathrm{disk}} = c_{\mathrm{disk}}$ because the multimedia object is permanently staged to disk. Comparison of $c_{i,\mathrm{disk}}$ and the staging cost, $c_{i,\mathrm{stg}}$, in [28] shows that for popular multimedia objects, prestaging to disk is preferable to pure on-demand staging.

Prestaging policies may also be better suited to handling time-varying loads than pure on-demand policies. The expected demand for a multimedia object may change with time of the day (e.g., children's videos may be popular during the daytime). Due to the large sizes of multimedia objects, staging may take a long time. The time taken to stage a multimedia object may also depend upon the system load. At times of peak load, it may not be possible to stage many objects from tertiary storage. In such situations, a policy that prestages popular multimedia objects in anticipation of high demand may perform better than an on-demand policy.

As mentioned in Chapter 9, it is important that the staging policy be integrated with the file placement policy. This can be achieved if the staging policy allows the file placement policy to select the location to which the multimedia object is to be staged [13, 11, 19]. The staging policy can supply the parameters needed by the file placement policy such as the expected demand for the multimedia object. An alternative policy is to dedicate a part or the whole of selected secondary storage devices for staging [28]. The file placement policy can then be modified to select a secondary storage device only from the staging pool.

10.3.3 Partial Staging

In the earlier discussion, it was assumed that multimedia objects are completely staged to disk. However, in some multimedia servers, the disk configuration may be determined by the storage space required to store the multimedia object rather than the bandwidth for delivering the multimedia object. Disk space may be the bottleneck resource in such systems rather than disk bandwidth. In such storage-limited systems, it may be desirable to stage fragments rather than the entire multimedia object. Such an approach is more suited to pure sequential viewing of multimedia objects because it may limit VCR control actions (e.g., skip).

We next describe the PIRATE policy [19], which stages segments of multimedia objects. The partial replacement technique (PIRATE) policy focuses on minimizing the average latency for retrieved requests as well as the variance in latency. Unlike the approaches in the previous sections, it does not focus on the efficient usage of tertiary storage devices. The PIRATE policy divides each multimedia object O_i into M_{seg} segments. Since PIRATE retrieves multimedia objects one segment at a time, it has to ensure that the jth segment of the object is retrieved before it needs to be displayed. This is ensured by pipelining, as illustrated in Figure 10.2. Under pipelining, the retrieval time for the jth segment is overlapped with the display time of the $j - 1$th segment. The initial latency is equal to the time needed to retrieve the first segment. The segment sizes are selected so as to ensure that pipelining is achieved. The choice of segment size depends upon the production consumption ratio (PCR), which is defined to be the ratio, W_t/P,

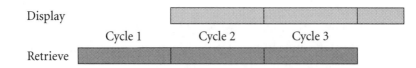

Figure 10.2   Pipelining under PIRATE.

where W_t is the bandwidth of the tertiary storage device and P is the playback rate of the multimedia object. If $PCR > 1$, data can be retrieved from the tertiary storage faster than it can be displayed. If the staging disk bandwidth is not a bottleneck, any arbitrary value can be selected as the segment size. However, if $PCR < 1$, the segment sizes have to be carefully chosen so as to allow pipelining to occur. For example, consider the case where the segment sizes are chosen to be equal. The first segment will then be displayed in a shorter time than it takes to retrieve the second segment. This results in a violation of pipelining. Let $T_{i,\text{disp}}$ and $T_{i,\text{ret}}$ be the times taken for display and retrieval of the ith segment, respectively. The pipelining condition can then be stated as $T_{i,\text{ret}} \leq T_{i-1,\text{disp}}$; for example, $T_{2,\text{ret}} \leq T_{1,\text{disp}}$. It can be shown that the size of the first segment is given by $N_{O,i} - \lceil PCR(N_{O,i-1}) \rceil$, where $N_{O,i}$ is the number of blocks in the multimedia object O_i. After determining the size of the first segment, the size of the second segment can be determined by applying the formula to the rest of the object O_i minus the first segment. Similarly, the sizes of succeeding segments can be determined.

When the secondary storage is full, the PIRATE policy may need to delete an already staged segment in order to retrieve a new segment. This is done by the PIRATE policy in two passes. In the first pass, PIRATE deletes blocks not in the first segment. Under a sequential access model, this ensures that future requests for those objects can be serviced without any latency. If this does not free sufficient blocks, PIRATE deletes blocks from objects with lower frequency of accesses. It can be shown [19] that this replacement policy guarantees that the PIRATE policy minimizes the average latency for requests. However, the PIRATE replacement policy may restage previously deleted segments.

The performances of the PIRATE policy and the policy of staging complete multimedia objects are compared in [19]. Under a skewed workload, the average latencies under the two policies are not very different. However, because the PIRATE policy maintains the first segment of popular objects in the secondary storage, the variance in latency is significantly lower. A variant of the PIRATE policy, called the *extended PIRATE policy*, that requires a minimum fraction of the popular objects to be resident has been proposed [19]. It can be shown that by appropriately selecting the minimum fraction, the average latency can be traded off against the variance in latency.

10.3.4 Prefetching

An important problem faced by these staging policies is masking the latency in accessing tertiary storage devices. In video-on-demand systems, where a video is viewed sequentially after it is started, the latency will occur only at the start of the request. This consists of the delay required to mount the tape and to stage the initial section of the video. However, in some applications, the data may be too large to store on secondary storage devices [22]. An example of this is a virtual reality application that digitally renders a battlefield using satellite images. Motion over the battlefield requires retrieval of the appropriate images from tape and their display in real time. In such applications, tape latency can occur at any time during the display because the data has to be continually staged in from tape.

A simple solution for such video-on-demand systems is to store the initial parts or leaders of multimedia objects on secondary storage devices [19, 14]. This may, however, result in an increase in the secondary storage requirements of the system. If the total number of multimedia objects in the system is M_O, and the size of the leader is I, the total storage required for storage of the leaders is $M_O I$. The total storage required by disk-resident multimedia objects is $M_{O,\text{disk}} l_{\text{disk}}$, where $M_{O,\text{disk}}$ is the number of disk-resident objects and l_{disk} is the average size of a disk-resident object. Because generally $M_O I \gg M_{O,\text{disk}}$, the storage required for leaders can quickly begin to dominate the storage required [14]. It may be appropriate, therefore, to store on the secondary storage only the leaders of a few of the videos.

This technique cannot be used for virtual reality applications where the amount of data to be stored exceeds the capacity of secondary storage. This is because there is no leader and viewing of the images is not sequential (i.e., after viewing an image, any of the adjacent images may be viewed). However, if the next image to be displayed can be anticipated, prefetching can be used to mask tertiary storage access latency [22]. In the battlefield rendering application mentioned earlier, geographically adjacent images can be grouped together into sequences. These sequences of images are then divided into superblocks whose size is determined by the characteristics of the tape drive. The size is chosen to be large enough to utilize the bandwidth of the tape effectively. The superblocks are then striped over a selected set of tapes. During playback, the image sequence containing the desired image is retrieved. As a result, images adjacent to the desired image are prefetched for display, resulting in masking of the latency in accessing the tertiary storage devices.

10.4 Storage Organization

The organization of tertiary storage devices is dictated by the device characteristics. Tertiary storage devices may be organized into a strict hierarchy; that is, data may always be staged from tertiary storage to secondary storage before playback. As shown earlier, depending on the device characteristics, either staging or not staging from tertiary storage to secondary storage may be preferable. Generally, staging or strict hierarchy is preferable for expensive, high-speed tertiary storage devices, where minimizing occupancy of the device is important. A mixed hierarchical organization, where data is transmitted directly from the device to the client, may be preferable for less-expensive, slower devices. These may include CD-ROMs, DVDs, and low-speed tape drives.

As with secondary storage devices, tertiary storage devices also can be striped together to provide a higher effective bandwidth as well as more availability [7, 23]. Consider, for example, the retrieval of a 3 GB video file representing approximately one and a half hours of MPEG-2 video at 0.5 MB/s. The time to transfer such a file would be approximately 6 minutes using a tape drive with a transfer rate of 8 MB/s. The total retrieval time would additionally include the tape latency, which consists of the time to eject and store the previous tape from the drive as well as the time to fetch and mount the required tape (see Figure 10.3). The time to transfer the file can be reduced by striping. Figure 10.3 illustrates this for the case of four-way striping. As shown, the four tape drives simultaneously eject the currently mounted tape. Each tape is then successively retrieved and mounted (assuming that there is only one robot). After the final tape is mounted, the drives begin to transmit the multimedia data concurrently. In the earlier example, if the file is striped over eight tapes, the transfer time can be significantly reduced to approximately one-eighth of the earlier value—that is, 45 seconds.

Unlike striping over secondary storage devices, striping over tertiary storage devices increases the overheads in the system. If all multimedia object files have a

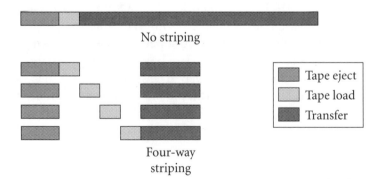

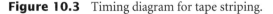

Figure 10.3 Timing diagram for tape striping.

striping degree of M_{stripe}, then the total number of tape switches is increased by the same factor. This increased overhead tends to lower the throughput of the striped system. Additionally, striping increases the contention for the robot arm that mounts the requested tape because the number of mounts required is increased by the striping factor. Finally, Figure 10.3 shows that though the transfer time is reduced, the time to mount the tape is increased. Hence, the total retrieval time may be increased if very wide striping is used. The mount time can be reduced if multiple robots are present. However, this may significantly increase the cost of the library system, as robots are expensive.

The complexity of the issues involved in the analysis of tape striping can be seen in [23] where a simulation model is used to study its performance (see Figure 10.4). Requests to the system arrive according to a Poisson process and enter the request queue. Each request may belong to class j with a probability p_j, where the class determines the size (i.e., number of bytes) of this request. Each request is assumed to require between 1 and M_{tape} tapes, where M_{tape} is the number of tape drives in the system. The request exits the request queue after a sufficient number of drives is available. It then enters a queue for the robot. After the robot mounts all the required tapes, the request is serviced and the tapes are rewound and ejected.

Simulation results are presented in [23] for a system with three classes and four drives. The size of the requests for the three classes is assumed to be 1 GB, 2 GB, and 3 GB, respectively. The paper considers various combinations of degrees of striping for the three classes. For example, the combination "112" refers to the case where the data for the first two classes is not striped; however, the data for the third class is striped over two tapes. At low arrival rates, the policy "444," representing maximal striping, is shown to have the lowest response time. At high arrival rates, the nonstriping policy ("111") has the lowest response time. However, different combinations of striping ("112" or "122" or "222") are optimal at different intermediate arrival rates. The optimal striping combination is

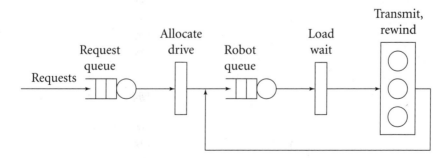

Figure 10.4   Queuing model for tape striping.

highly dependent on the workload parameter. There seems to be no simple heuristic to predict the best striping combination.

It is also shown in [23] that certain striping combinations (e.g., "333") are never optimal regardless of the arrival rates. This is due to the bandwidth fragmentation because the "333" always causes at least one drive to be idle. At low loads, "444" is the optimal policy. With increasing loads, the performance of "444" begins to degrade faster than "333". However, at the point where "333" begins to perform better than "444", the "222" policy becomes optimal. This is due to the increased contention introduced by the "333" policy as compared to the "222" policy. Determining the optimal striping combination is thus not simple.

10.5   Cost Analysis and Placement Implications

In the previous sections, we have considered storage organization techniques (strict hierarchy, staging, striping). We showed that it may be more cost-effective to store infrequently used multimedia objects on the tertiary storage and stage them onto the secondary storage. This is true even though staging multimedia data from the tertiary storage to the secondary storage requires additional bandwidth compared to the direct playback policy.

A mathematical model for determining the multimedia objects to be stored in the tertiary storage in a staging system is described in [14]. The model assumes that the multimedia data may be stored in an expanded storage,[1] disk, or tape. All three types of storage are attached to the main memory bus of the CPU, and multimedia data in the expanded storage or disk has to be retrieved into the main memory before playback. Hence, each byte of multimedia data in the expanded storage or disk is transferred twice across the system bus (once from storage to memory and then from memory to network). As a result, a stream being played from the expanded storage or disk consumes twice its bandwidth on the memory bus. In contrast, a stream being played from the tertiary storage consumes four times its bandwidth on the memory bus.

From this, it can be seen that the total load on the system bus is given by $v_{\text{mem}} + 2(v_{\text{es}} + v_{\text{disk}}) + 4v_{\text{tape}}$, where v_{mem}, v_{es}, v_{disk}, and v_{tape} are, respectively, the number of streams serviced from memory, expanded storage, disk, and tape. Clearly, $v_{\text{mem}} + 2(v_{\text{es}} + v_{\text{disk}}) + 4v_{\text{tape}} \leq v_{\text{bus}}$, where v_{bus} is the capacity of the system bus. (It is assumed that all streams have the same bandwidth). Also, $v_{\text{mem}} + 2(v_{\text{es}} + v_{\text{disk}}) + 4v_{\text{tape}} \leq v_{\text{cap}}$, where v_{cap} is the capacity of the system. The

---

[1]This is a large memory attached to the CPU, similar to a solid-state disk.

expanded storage is more expensive and faster than the secondary storage, which in turn is more expensive and faster than the tertiary storage [14]. Hence, the most popular multimedia objects can be stored in the expanded storage, less popular multimedia objects in the secondary storage, and the least popular multimedia objects in the tertiary storage. The cost of storing a multimedia object i in the expanded storage is given by $L_i c_{es}$ where L_i is the size of the ith multimedia object and c_{es} is the cost per byte of the expanded storage. Similar equations can be devised to determine the cost of storing multimedia objects on disk or tape. The cost of storing a multimedia object on disk may be determined by the expected demand for the multimedia object instead of the space required to store it. Details of the equations and their use for allocating multimedia objects to tape so as to minimize the overall system cost are given in [14].

10.6   Summary

Tertiary storage is used in multimedia systems for the storage of infrequently used multimedia data. When this data is accessed, it needs to be staged in to secondary storage. A major issue that needs to be addressed is the extra latency for servicing the user due to the time taken to stage in the multimedia data. The staging time can be reduced by ensuring that only infrequently accessed data is stored on tertiary storage and that there is a sufficient number of tertiary storage devices to stage in the requested data. Additionally, the first part of some or all files on tertiary storage can be stored on-line. This allows playback of the requested data to be started in parallel with retrieval of the entire object from tertiary storage. Finally, the time taken to retrieve the data can be reduced by striping together tertiary storage devices.

Further Reading

Placement of multimedia data on secondary or tertiary storage is discussed in [14, 28, 19]. Striping of tertiary storage devices is discussed in [22, 7].

Part 3 References

[1] D. Anderson, Y. Osawa, and R. Govindan. A file system for continuous media. *ACM Transactions on Computer Systems*, 10(4):311–337, November 1992.

[2] M. Bach. *The Design of the Unix Operating System*. Prentice Hall, Englewood Cliffs, NJ, 1990.

[3] S. Berson, S. Ghandeharizadeh, R. Muntz, and X. Ju. Staggered striping in multimedia information systems. In *Proceedings of the ACM SIGMOD International Conference on Management of Data*. ACM, 1994.

[4] S. Berson, L. Golubchik, and R. Muntz. A fault tolerant design of a multimedia server. In *Proceedings of the ACM SIGMOD International Conference on Management of Data*. ACM, May 1995.

[5] S. Chaudhuri, S. Ghandeharizadeh, and C. Shahabi. Avoiding retrieval contention for composite multimedia objects. Technical Research Report USC-CS-TR95-618. University of Southern California, San Diego, 1995.

[6] Y. Chen, R. Kashyap, and A. Ghafoor. Physical storage management for interactive multimedia information systems. In *IEEE Transactions on Systems, Man and Cybernetics Conference*. IEEE, 1993.

[7] A. Chervenak. *Tertiary Storage: An Evaluation of New Techniques*. Ph.D. thesis. University of California, Berkeley, 1994.

[8] A. Cohen. *Segmented Information Dispersal*. Ph.D. thesis. University of California, San Diego, 1996.

[9] A. Cohen and W. Burkhard. Segmented information dispersal (SID) for efficient reconstruction in fault-tolerant video servers. Technical Report CS94-390. University of California, San Diego, 1994.

[10] A. Dan, D. Dias, R. Mukherjee, D. Sitaram, and R. Tewari. Buffering and caching in large scale video servers. In *Proceedings of IEEE CompCon*. IEEE, 1995.

[11] A. Dan, S. Dulin, S. Marcotte, and D. Sitaram. The design of a storage server for continuous media. *IBM Systems Journal*, 36(2), 1997.

[12] A. Dan, M. Kienzle, and D. Sitaram. Dynamic policy of segment replication for load-balancing in video-on-demand servers. *Multimedia Systems*, 3(3):93–103, July 1995.

[13] A. Dan and D. Sitaram. An online video placement policy based on bandwidth to space ratio (BSR). In *Proceedings of the ACM SIGMOD International Conference on Management of Data*, pp. 376–385. ACM, May 1995.

[14] Y. Doganata and A. Tantawi. A cost/performance study of video servers with hierarchical storage. Technical Report RC 19119. IBM Research Division, 1993.

[15] D. Ford and S. Christodoulakis. Optimal random retrievals from CLV format optical disks. In *Proceedings of Very Large Data Bases*. ACM, September 1991.

[16] B. Furht, S. W. Smoliar, and H. Zhang. *Video and Image Processing in Multimedia Systems*. Kluwer Academic Publishers, Norwell, MA, 1995.

[17] S. Ghandeharizadeh, S. Kim, and C. Shahabi. On configuring a single disk continuous media server. In *Proceedings of the ACM SIGMETRICS Conference*. ACM, May 1995.

[18] S. Ghandeharizadeh, S. Kim, C. Shahabi, and R. Zimmerman. Placement of continuous media in multizone disks. In S. Chung, ed., *Multimedia Information Storage and Management*, Chapter 2, pp. 23–59. Kluwer Academic Press, Boston, MA, 1996.

[19] S. Ghandeharizadeh and C. Shahabi. On multimedia repositories, personal computers, and hierarchical storage systems. In *Proceedings of ACM Multimedia Conference*. ACM, 1994.

[20] S. Ghandeharizadeh, D. Wilhite, K. Lin, and X. Zhao. Object placement in parallel object-oriented database systems. In *Proceedings of the International Conference on Data Engineering*. ACM, 1994.

[21] S. Ghandeharizadeh, R. Zimmermann, W. Shi, R. Rejaie, D. Ierardi, and T. Li. Mitra: A scalable continuous media server. Technical Report USC-CS-TR96-628. University of Southern California, Los Angeles, CA, August 1996.

[22] L. Golubchik and S. Marcus. On multilevel multimedia storage systems. In *Second International Workshop on Multimedia Information Systems*, pp. 14–18. U.S. Army Research Office, 1996.

[23] L. Golubchik, R. Muntz, and R. Watson. Analysis of striping techniques in robotic storage libraries. In *Procedings of the 14th IEEE Symposium on Mass Storage Systems.* IEEE, 1995.

[24] C. Gopal and J. Buford. Delivering hypermedia sessions from a continuous media server. In S. Chung, ed., *Multimedia Information Storage and Management,* Chapter 9, pp. 209–235. Kluwer Academic Publishers, Boston, MA, 1996.

[25] D. Grossman and H. Silverman. Placement of records on a secondary storage device to minimize access time. *Journal of the ACM,* 20(3): 429–438, July 1973.

[26] R. Haskin and F. Schmuck. The Tiger Shark file system. In *Proceedings of IEEE CompCon,* pp. 226–231. IEEE Press, 1996.

[27] M. Kienzle, R. Berbec, G. Bozman, C. Eilert, and M. Eshel. Multimedia file serving with the OS/390 IBM LAN server for MVS. Technical Report RC-20432. IBM Research, Yorktown Heights, NY, April 1996.

[28] M. Kienzle, A. Dan, D. Sitaram, and W. Tetzlaff. Using tertiary storage in video-on-demand servers. In *Proceedings of IEEE CompCon.* IEEE, 1995.

[29] K. Knowlton. A fast storage allocator. *Communications of the ACM,* 8(10):623–625, October 1965.

[30] S. Leffler, M. McKusick, M. Karels, and J. Quaterman. *The Design and Implementation of the 4.3 BSD Unix Operating System.* Addison-Wesley, Reading, MA, 1989.

[31] T. Little and D. Venkatesh. Popularity-based assignment of movies to storage devices in a video-on-demand system. *Multimedia Systems,* 2(6):280–287, January 1995.

[32] C. Liu and J. Layland. Scheduling algorithms for multiprogramming in a hard real-time environment. *Journal of the ACM,* 20(1): 46–61, January 1973.

[33] M. Livny, S. Khoshafian, and H. Boral. Multi-disk management algorithms. *Performance Evaluation Review,* 15:69–77, May 1987.

[34] P. Lougher and D. Shepherd. The design of a storage server for continuous media. *The Computer Journal,* 36(1):32–42, 1993.

[35] J. Ousterhout and F. Douglis. Beating the I/O bottleneck: A case for log-structured file systems. *Operating Systems Review,* 23(1):11–28, 1989.

[36] D. Patterson, G. Gibson, and R. Katz. A case for redundant arrays of inexpensive disks (RAID). In *Proceedings of the ACM SIGMOD International Conference on Management of Data.* ACM, 1988.

[37] P. Rangan and H. Vin. Designing file systems for digital video and audio. *Operating Systems Review,* 25(5):81–94, October 1991.

[38] P. Rangan and H. Vin. Efficient storage techniques for digital continuous multimedia. *IEEE Transactions on Knowledge and Data Engineering,* 5(4):564–573, August 1993.

[39] P. Rangan, H. Vin, and S. Ramanathan. Designing an on-demand multimedia service. *IEEE Communications Magazine,* 30:56–65, July 1992.

[40] A. Reddy. Improving the interactive responsiveness in a video server. In S. Chung, ed., *Multimedia Information Storage and Management,* Chapter 12, pp. 283–301. Kluwer Academic Publishers, Boston, MA, 1996.

[41] A. Reddy and J. Wylie. Disk scheduling in a multimedia system. In *Proceedings of ACM Multimedia Conference.* ACM, August 1993.

[42] A. Reddy and J. Wylie. I/O issues in a multimedia system. *IEEE Computer,* 27(3):69–74, 1994.

[43] P. Shenoy and H. Vin. Failure recovery algorithms for multi-disk multimedia servers. Technical Report 96-06. University of Texas at Austin, 1996.

[44] T. Teory and T. Pinkerton. A comparative analysis of disk scheduling policies. *Communications of the ACM,* 15(3):177–184, March 1972.

[45] D. Terry and D. Swinehart. Managing stored voice in the Etherphone system. *ACM Transactions on Computer Systems,* 6(1):3–27, February 1988.

[46] W. Tetzlaff and R. Flynn. The block allocation problem in video servers. In *International Symposium on Multimedia Communications and Video Coding.* Polytechnic University, Brooklyn, NY, October 1995.

[47] R. Tewari, R. King, D. Kandlur, and D. Dias. Placement of multimedia blocks on zoned disks. In *Proceedings of Multimedia Computing and Networking.* SPIE, 1996.

[48] H. Vin and P. Rangan. Designing a multi-user HDTV storage server. *IEEE Journal of Selected Areas in Communication,* 11(1):153–164, January 1993.

[49] H. Vin, P. Shenoy, and S. Rao. Efficient failure recovery in multi-disk multimedia servers. In *Proceedings of the International Symposium on Fault-Tolerant Computing,* June 1995.

[50] C. K. Wong. *Algorithmic Studies in Mass Storage Systems.* Computer Science Press, New York, 1983.

[51] P. Yu, M. Chen, and D. Kandlur. Grouped sweeping scheduling for DASD-based multimedia storage management. *Multimedia Systems,* 1:99–109, 1993.

PART 4

Cache Management

11

Caching Overview

11.1   Introduction

In a multimedia system, storage and bandwidth are critical resources because any presentation requires a large volume of data to be delivered in real time. As explained earlier, these data files are large in comparison to the data requirements of most traditional applications and so demand a large space for storage and a large bandwidth for transport [15, 6, 10, 26]. Each multimedia object is streamed at its playback rate from the storage device(s) to the presentation device(s). As further explained in Part 2, to guarantee quality of service, the playback bandwidth is reserved on the entire delivery path(s), which consists of many system components. This makes proper usage of such critical resources even more challenging.

The rapid development and deployment of large-scale multimedia applications have been hindered by the lack of available server and network delivery bandwidth [11]. New networking infrastructures are being deployed, although at a slow pace, to tackle this problem, but delivery bandwidth and storage space continue to be critical resources for such applications. The caching of multimedia documents in local storage can reduce the required retrieval bandwidth (see Figure 11.1). For example, storage of frequently used documents in client nodes or in intermediate distribution server nodes can reduce the expensive network bandwidth required for retrieval of documents from remote servers. Similarly, storage of documents shared by many users in the server memory can reduce disk retrieval bandwidth. In Figure 11.1, multimedia data is cached from the remote servers to the local server node memory or disk storage.

Multimedia applications can be quite diverse in terms of the sizes of the accessed documents. In a movie-on-demand application, a single long video may be watched for a long duration (say, two hours). In contrast, in a multimedia database system, say, for previewing movie trailers, many small video clips may be

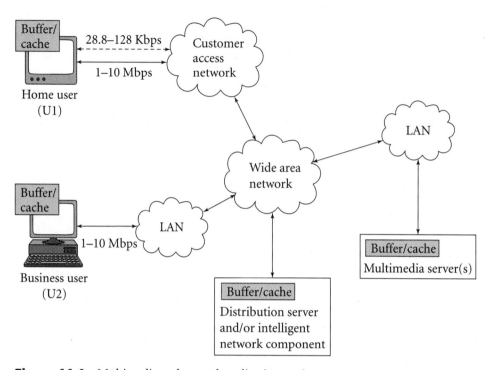

Figure 11.1   Multimedia end-to-end application environment.

retrieved in response to client commands. Many small media segments may also be combined to form interesting composite media documents, which can then be played back according to the predefined order upon receiving a single playback request. Figure 11.2 illustrates the creation of a single composite document from many small media segments (e.g., text, image, video, and audio clips) and the resulting bandwidth required to play back such a composite document [55]. Here, the composite document represents a news clip for an Olympic event, a swimming competition. The clip starts with the introduction of all participants in textual and image form, followed by an immediate video clip of the semifinal event. Near the end of the video, two more small windows pop up to provide close-up shots of the lead contenders. The same process is repeated for the final competition. Generally speaking, the quality and bandwidth requirements for each individual clip may be different. In any case, the resulting instantaneous bandwidth requirement for such a composite document fluctuates widely (see Figure 11.2). Guaranteeing jitter-free playback for such documents would necessitate reserving maximum bandwidth for the entire duration of the playback. However, the bandwidth requirement profile can be smoothed (and, hence, the amount of required maxi-

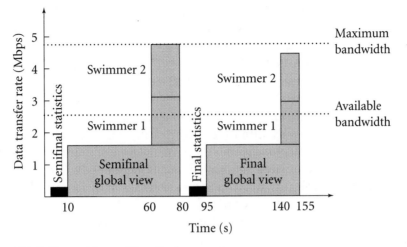

Figure 11.2 Composite multimedia document.

mum bandwidth can be reduced) by prefetching the required data blocks in advance while the reserved bandwidth is underutilized. Of course, the amount of prefetched data will depend on the available local or primary storage.

The access pattern within a single multimedia document (i.e., a single video or a composite document) may not be uniform and/or the playback sequence may not always be linear. By caching (and/or prefetching) related data blocks that are to be re-referenced either by the same client or by different clients, the number of data blocks retrieved from the secondary storage devices can be reduced. The data blocks that are retrieved continuously in a linear fashion are referred to as a *continuous object presentation unit (COPU)* [38]. Figure 11.3 illustrates the effect of

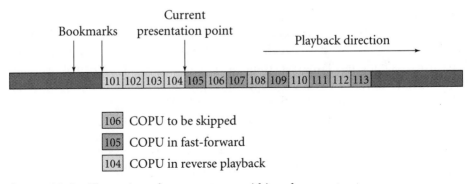
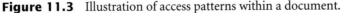

Figure 11.3 Illustration of access patterns within a document.

VCR control operations on the access patterns within a document. During regular playback, the data blocks are retrieved in a linear fashion (say, 101, 102, 103, . . .). However, upon receiving a `fast-forward` command, only the selected (say, alternate) set of data blocks may be presented. The user may also mark any data block within the document and skip to a selected data segment for resuming continuous playback.

In a general environment, the mix of applications accessing various types of documents may vary greatly with time. Additionally, for all applications, access patterns may change rapidly with time (e.g., with the time of the day or in response to the availability of new videos in the applications mentioned). The caching policies need to handle the very different characteristics of different applications. Thus, it is necessary for multimedia caching policies to perform well under all workloads containing both large as well as small video objects.

An important requirement for a multimedia caching policy is to guarantee continuous delivery even when a stream is being served from the cache [14]. Replicating data at the local site, however, can be expensive. Hence, for caching to be cost-effective, only the frequently accessed data or the data that is more likely to be reaccessed soon is cached. The mix of workload, access patterns within a document, and the popularities of the multimedia objects may change with time, making continuous delivery a difficult objective.

11.2 Data Prefetching and Its Relationships to Buffering and Caching

Both buffering and caching concern the use of primary storage to avoid delay and/or overhead in accessing secondary storage [10]. Anticipating their use, the data blocks needed by an application may already be present in the memory or prefetched from secondary storage. However, the distinction between the use of buffering or caching lies in the performance objectives, application requirements, and the usage of the primary storage. Strictly speaking, buffering is used to avoid access delay, and caching is used to avoid access overhead and/or delay. When the data blocks are prefetched on behalf of the currently consuming data stream, this is regarded as *buffering*. However, if the data blocks retrieved on behalf of a playback stream are retained in the storage for future data streams even after they are delivered to the current stream, the process is referred to as *caching*.

Data moved from one system component to another (say, from disk to client) is temporarily stored in the primary storage, termed a *buffer*. Typically, a unit of data movement consists of (1) retrieval of the unit of data from the source device to a data container (buffer), and (2) subsequent delivery of the data unit from the buffer to the destination device (see Figure 11.4). The two processes work in uni-

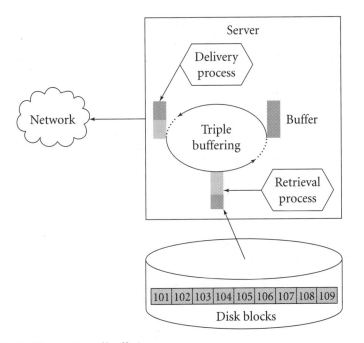

Figure 11.4   Illustration of buffering.

son: Once enough data is retrieved to fill a buffer slot, it is then passed to the delivery process. In the figure, three buffers are used in the data movement from the disk to the network. This is referred to as *triple buffering*.

Any mismatch in speed between the delivery and retrieval processes may result in either buffer overflow or buffer underflow. In the former case, the newly retrieved data is written over the previously retrieved data before it is delivered, and in the latter case, the buffer contains no data for delivery. Note that the access paths to the sources and/or the destinations may be shared across many data streams, but even in the absence of sharing, the access time to different data blocks may be different. Hence, the retrieval and/or delivery processes are not always smooth; that is, operations are not uniformly spread over time. Buffering can mask such short-term fluctuations in speeds.

Multiple buffer slots may be used to avoid jitters in the delivery process. If a single buffer slot is used, then the delivery process is bursty because the retrieval and delivery processes use the same buffer slot in turn. In double buffering (the use of two buffer slots for data movement), when a buffer slot is being filled the data can be concurrently delivered from the second buffer slot. The two buffers are exchanged by the retrieval and delivery processes at the end of a cycle. To further avoid unpredictability in the data access time and, hence, any possibility of jitters, additional buffer slots can be used. The jitters possibility becomes negligible when there are more than three buffers [10]. However, multiple buffer slots introduce large access latencies during the starting of a stream because all the buffer slots need to be filled before the delivery process can start.

Buffering can also help to smooth burstiness in the instantaneous data consumption rate or to adapt to the available bandwidth in various components in the delivery path. The instantaneous data rate can fluctuate widely even for a single variable-bit-rate (VBR) video stream [51]. Under VBR, the bit rate is allowed to vary during the creation of a compressed video; that is, different amounts of data bits are allocated to different sets of frames while maintaining a certain quality. During a very active scene (e.g., a car chase) where the background changes rapidly, a larger amount of data bits is required for capturing the image quality, while during a slow scene a small amount of data bits is required to capture the difference across picture frames. The resulting requirement for bandwidth is highly variable; the bandwidth requirement will vary even more for a composite media document, as was illustrated in Figure 11.2.

Figure 11.5 illustrates the use of prefetching to alleviate the problem of both variable data consumption rates and/or variability in bandwidth and buffer in any system component on the delivery path. The solid line illustrates the variability in the data consumption rate of a playback stream and, hence, in bandwidth requirements. As mentioned earlier, the resources available to a playback stream (i.e., the buffer and bandwidth) can vary with time in a shared system (as illustrated in the figure). If the available bandwidth is smaller than the required instantaneous bandwidth, jitters will occur. However, data can be prefetched using the currently available bandwidth to fill in the available buffers so that a future increase in data consumption rate can be met from the local buffers. The figure further illustrates that all available buffers may not always be filled, depending on the available band-

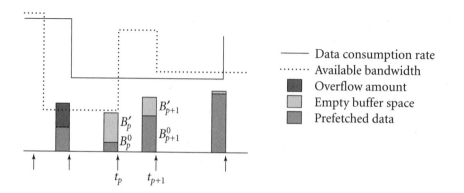

Figure 11.5 Illustration of prefetching for smoothing traffic.

width. Similarly, all available bandwidth cannot always be used because that would cause buffer overflow.

Once the prefetched data blocks are consumed by the delivery process, the buffer slots become available for reuse. However, if the data in these buffer slots is maintained for future reference, then the storage slots are referred to as the *cache blocks*. Note that new buffer slots need to be allocated to the current stream. Figure 11.6 illustrates the relationship between buffering and caching. The cache manager maintains the list of currently used slots (either buffer or cache) as well as free slots. A single server may receive data from multiple sources (e.g., remote servers or local secondary storage devices such as disks) and may deliver data to many clients. As explained earlier, buffer slots are needed for all data transfers. The cache manager employs various cache management algorithms to determine when and what data to retain and when to turn these cache blocks into free blocks. It interacts with the QoS management component (not shown in the figure) during starting or termination of a stream and/or during VCR control operations. It also employs efficient prefetching algorithms for dealing with burstiness in traffic, as explained earlier. Finally, both memory and secondary storage can be used as cache—that is, temporary data storage (see Figure 11.6). However, their different characteristics (bandwidth, space, access latency) dictate different usage and different management policies. We will address these issues in more detail in the next two chapters.

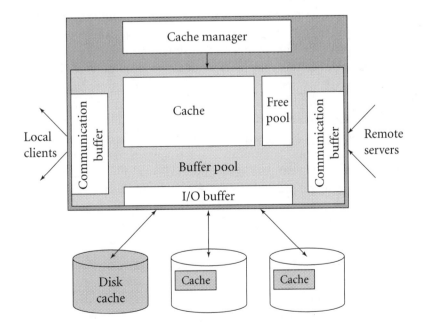

Figure 11.6 Illustration of caching in a local server.

In the next two sections, we first establish various underlying objectives of caching policies in different environments and then characterize these policies in terms of their management principles and usage of information.

11.3   Caching Objectives

Caching may be employed in many different ways in different parts of a system, and to satisfy multiple objectives. Of course, in all cases the overall objective is to improve total utilization of the system resources and to provide a higher effective throughput. The manifold objectives of caching are as follows:

- *Increasing server capacity.* The capacity of a server is the number of concurrent streams it can serve. If the CPU (i.e., the processing requirements associated with each unit of delivered data) or the network interfaces are not the bottleneck resources, the retrieval path from the storage devices (e.g., disk bandwidth, controller capacity) will be the bottleneck. By storing all or parts of frequently accessed multimedia objects in the server memory, a larger number of clients can be served by the server and, hence, its capacity is effectively increased.

- *Reducing access latency.* Access time changes with the location of the data in the storage hierarchy. For example, the data stored in memory can be delivered by the server instantly to the clients, whereas the access times for the data stored in disks may be on the order of many milliseconds. This may include seek times and queuing times for the disk bandwidth to be available. The access times for the elements further down in the hierarchy (e.g., tapes, CD-ROM, jukebox, etc.), may increase by an order of magnitude [53, 32].

    For many applications, improving interactive response times can be very important. For example, in video-on-demand applications, support of VCR control operations such as `fast-forward`, `fast-backward`, `skip` (to a scene), and so on requires quick access to different parts of the video [38]. Similarly, in virtual reality applications, the navigation of a landscape requires quick access to a different part of the media object [37]. Certainly, predicting the access pattern and prefetching the data to be accessed in the future to the cache can satisfy these response-time requirements. As we have seen in storage scheduling (Part 3), these are the same techniques employed to guarantee normal playback without jitters.

- *Reducing network bandwidth requirements.* A large-scale video server consists of a local server and remote storage servers. The local server delivers the data to its local clients, and the remote storage servers store the original copies of the data. Local or remote servers in turn can consist of a group of nodes and disks. Based on the client request patterns, the local server caches data on the local disks and memory in order to avoid the communication overhead of getting it from the remote site and to improve performance. Given the slow deployment of network infrastructure and the higher cost of network bandwidth, reducing the network bandwidth requirement can be a very important objective.

■ *Balancing load across storage devices.* Caching can be employed to cope with additional challenges in a large-scale distributed multimedia environment consisting of many heterogeneous servers and storage devices. Depending upon the initial placement of data and the current popularities of the multimedia objects, one or more sets of servers and/or storage devices can be the bottlenecks. By employing a shared cache on the common part of the delivery paths from these servers and/or devices, and by caching selectively the data from the bottleneck servers and/or devices, the load can be better balanced across all system resources. In Figure 11.6, the shared cache at the local server memory can balance the load across the local storage devices. Similarly, the shared cache (memory or disk) at the local server can be used to balance the demands across remote servers.

■ *Supporting data migration in storage organizations.* As the long-term popularities of the data change with time, the proper placement of data across various storage devices becomes difficult. An important objective of the data placement policy is to match the bandwidth and storage capacities of the devices to the requirements of the files stored on these devices [15]. As seen in Part 3, any mismatch can result in poor utilization of both of these resources. Periodic readjustment of data placement can be used to achieve proper data placement. However, to keep the system operational at all times, and to avoid the high overhead of migration of data files, caching can be used to naturally replicate the popular data files and/or balance the load across system components. By turning cached data as permanent copies and removing old copies of data that are accessed infrequently, an effective data migration policy can be devised. In [12], a dynamic segment replication policy through copyback of playback streams is used to balance the load across striping groups (i.e., storage devices containing blocks of a file). Here, the migration of data segments via caching leads to hierarchical striping of data files across heterogeneous sets of storage devices.

11.4 Characterization of Cache Management Policies

In the next two chapters, we will detail caching policies and operations in two very different environments: memory and storage caches. The caching policies in the two environments differ significantly because the characteristics of the resources (i.e., caches) also differ significantly. Here, we first characterize the caching policies in terms of their broad objectives and/or the information used during runtime operations. We also outline the common issues addressed by all caching policies.

- *Stream-dependent caching vs. block-level caching.* Multimedia applications are distinguished from traditional applications not only by their requirements for a large space for storage and a large bandwidth for transport but also by the requirement of continuous delivery [15, 6, 10, 26]. Hence, traditional caching policies employed for nonmultimedia applications are not appropriate for multimedia applications. Block-level caching policies (e.g., LRU) that cache unrelated sets of blocks instead of complete multimedia objects cannot guarantee continuous delivery of streams. In a multimedia environment, large multimedia objects (e.g., a movie) need to be cached in their entirety. Also, traditional policies such as LRU and CLOCK [19, 20, 43, 22] are based on the concept of a hot set of data, which is typically much smaller in size than the total set of data. This is also true for the database buffer management policies that exploit the semantics of queries in identifying a hot set [50, 8, 10]. Generalizing the concept of a hot set in a multimedia environment (i.e., storing the most frequently accessed videos in the cache) may not be very useful because multimedia objects are large. Additionally, detecting changes in the frequency of access to various multimedia objects is difficult; bringing newly hot objects into the cache may require a long time [14]. However, in multimedia applications the relationships across playback streams can be established to support a following stream from the cached data by a preceding stream [14, 16]. Other forms of semantic caching, such as identification of a COPU, also differ from block-level caching [38].

- *Memory vs. storage caching.* Caching policies depend on the resource constraints of the local server. The objectives of memory-caching policies are to improve the utilization of cache space—that is, to serve as many streams as possible for a given cache space. However, if a secondary storage device is treated as a cache (i.e., a container of temporary data) either to avoid accessing remote servers or to alleviate a bottleneck in another secondary storage device, the management policies are different from those of a memory cache. Even though the bandwidth of a memory cache is rarely a bottleneck, the secondary storage needs to ensure proper usage of both bandwidth and space. The storage caching policies need to account, therefore, not only for the constraint in space but also for the bandwidth required for both reading from and writing to the cache [58].

- *Caching vs. prefetching.* A related aspect of caching is the prefetching of blocks to be accessed by a single stream, rather than sharing of retrieved blocks across streams. Prefetching of blocks (also referred to as *buffering* in [10]) can mask the variance in response time (e.g., disk response time) and, hence, can avoid jitters in presentation. Prefetching is also used to smooth the burstiness introduced by data compression in a single, long data stream [51, 25] or composite multimedia documents [34, 55]. The policies in [51, 25] address optimal delivery schedules consisting of piecewise constant rates such that neither does the prefetching of data overflow the client buffer nor does the chosen delivery rate cause buffer underflow. Prefetching for smoothing burstiness in the end-to-end delivery path for retrieving composite documents is addressed in [34, 55]. Finally, prefetching can be employed to avoid jitters in retrieving composite documents stored across multiple devices [6, 56].

11.4.1 Common Issues to Be Addressed by All Caching Policies

- *Adaptive workload.* All caching policies should cope with dynamic changes in workload and heterogeneity arising from large and small multimedia files. Additionally, all caching policies need to cope with challenges in a large-scale distributed multimedia environment consisting of many heterogeneous servers. The issues include (1) routing of requests to ensure good cache hits in each server, and (2) balancing of loads across servers.

- *Support for VCR control.* Another important issue in the multimedia environment is providing support for VCR control operations (e.g., pause, resume) by clients. VCR control interrupts the sequential reading of multimedia files and, hence, the optimizations exploited by caching policies. Note that the problem of dealing with VCR control arises as well in other aspects of multimedia operations (e.g., batching, load balancing). Hence, a general policy is required in a multimedia environment for dealing with VCR control operations and the resulting unpredictable bandwidth requirements. In [13, 21, 18], a general policy of setting aside a portion of the server capacity for dealing with VCR operations is proposed. This can be integrated with the GIC policy, as shown later. The access patterns generated by VCR control operations (e.g., skip) should also be exploited by a caching policy [38].

- *Integration with other resource optimization policies.* A number of caching policies have been proposed specifically for multimedia environments [14, 42, 10, 23, 49, 31]. These policies exploit the unique access characteristics of multimedia documents: multiple clients accessing the same (popular) set of documents sequentially separated by small time intervals. Thus, the blocks retrieved by one client can be reused by other closely following clients. An alternative way to exploit closely following streams in a long video is to group or batch related requests and serve them using a single stream [18, 13, 31, 28]. In the presence of batching, the caching policy needs to be integrated with the batching policy [31]. Yet another alternative is to start the playback streams as they are requested and merge closely following streams by slowing down the preceding streams and speeding up the following streams [28]. In [33], caching is integrated with merging by serving closely following streams from cache until they are merged.

Apart from integration with other resource management policies for dealing with closely following streams, in a large-scale distributed video server environment with many heterogeneous devices, caching policies need to be integrated with other resource management policies for dealing with load balancing, data migration, and coordinated data prefetching for composite documents.

11.5   Summary

In this chapter, we reviewed the relationship of caching policies to other resource management policies, especially prefetching and buffering. To avoid jitters in presentation and to smooth burstiness in data consumption rates, data blocks are prefetched in advance from storage devices or remote servers and are temporarily kept in buffer slots until they are consumed by the corresponding presentation streams. The retrieved data can be further maintained in cache for future references. We also reviewed the objectives of various caching policies: to increase server capacity, to reduce access latency, to reduce bandwidth required to access remote servers, to balance load across storage devices and/or servers, and to support data migration. We also took a close look at the design issues of various caching policies: stream-dependent vs. block-level caching, memory vs. storage caching, adaptiveness in dealing with changing workload, support for VCR control operations, and, finally, integration with other resource optimization policies. In the next two chapters, we address in further detail the design of caching policies for two very different types of environments: memory with practically no bandwidth constraints, and storage with both bandwidth and space constraints.

12

Memory Cache

12.1   Introduction

The memory cache is characterized by a large bandwidth but a limited space. Memory is also expensive in comparison to secondary storage space. Therefore, the primary objective in memory caching policies is to serve as many requests as possible from a small size of cache. As in any cache management policy, two sets of issues need to be addressed: when to place a data element in the cache and when to replace a data element (either on demand or proactively) to make room for other data elements. Traditional caching policies identify the hot set of data items either via estimation or via direct hints from an application and then attempt to retain only this hot set of data items [19, 43, 50, 8, 22]. However, multimedia files are large, and caching other than metadata would require a significant amount of cache space. As shown in [14], caching only the entire hot set of videos is rarely cost-effective. Fortunately, there are other techniques that retain only fragments of media data to achieve the various objectives of caching: reducing access latency and increasing the cache hit ratio.

In this chapter, we will first briefly review the traditional caching policies and enumerate the disadvantages of adopting such policies. We will then focus our attention on caching policies that retain only fragments of the entire media object, particularly, on a policy that exploits knowledge of relationships across delivery streams. We will explore the use of such a caching policy in various contexts within a media server.

12.2   Overview of Memory Caching Policies

12.2.1   Traditional Caching Policies

Traditional caching policies, such as LRU [19], CLOCK [43], HOTSET [50], DBMIN [8], and others [20, 22], are widely used in various software systems—for example, operating systems, databases, etc. Such block-level caching policies retain unrelated but frequently accessed data blocks in the cache. In a multimedia server, to guarantee continuous delivery the media objects need to be cached in their entirety, and, hence, the only way to use such caching policies would be to adopt these policies to cache entire hot objects. However, the larger size of typical media objects makes such policies unsuitable for various reasons. First, all traditional caching policies rely on identifying and retaining a hot set of data blocks, which is very small compared to the entire data set. Employing this policy in a video-on-demand environment, where a typical video may be of several gigabytes, would imply a very large memory cache, even for caching the hottest videos. Second, most caching policies are adaptive; that is, as the hotness changes with time, a new hot set is identified and retained, replacing the old hot set. Again, in a media server, any such operation would be quite difficult; the server performance would be degraded during such transitions, and making the transitions would require a long time.

12.2.2   Stream-Dependent Caching

The caching policies that can exploit the sequential access patterns in long videos and the knowledge of the relationships across delivery streams can benefit from a small cache by retaining only for a short duration the relevant fragments of a media object. A number of policies [14, 16, 42, 49, 31, 33, 38] have been proposed in the context of the multimedia server to take advantage of the sequential access pattern. However, the main differences among these policies are in the way this information is used by the policies, the objectives, and the integration with other resource optimization policies.

Viewer enrollment window. In multimedia servers, continuous delivery is guaranteed by controlling the number of streams to be delivered concurrently. Also, to avoid jitters, data is prefetched for all streams into the buffer, and, hence, the buffers are refreshed in a periodic manner. Typically, a small number of buffers is allocated to each stream via double and triple buffering, as illustrated in the previous chapter. However, when multiple streams access the same video and if a large buffer is allocated to the first stream, the subsequent streams can be served from that buffer [49]. As illustrated in Figure 12.1(a), the streams v_1 through v_n are

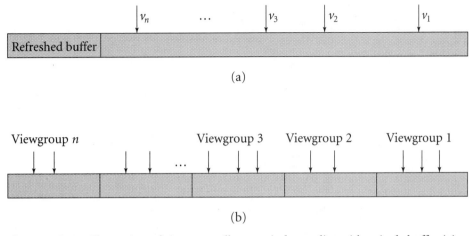

Figure 12.1 Illustration of viewer enrollment window policy with a single buffer (a) and a partitioned buffer (b).

accessing the same video, and the streams v_2 through v_n are served from the buffer without any further prefetching. The buffers are refreshed on behalf of v_1 periodically. The number of viewers is controlled such that buffer refreshment for v_1 does not overwrite any blocks to be consumed by other viewers. The viewers for the same video are accepted during an enrollment window only if further enrollment does not cause the buffer refreshment to overwrite blocks to be read by this stream.

The policy can be improved by partitioning the buffer and allocating each buffer partition to a viewgroup (see Figure 12.1(b)). This results in multiple enrollment windows, and each viewgroup creates a run of streams that are served from the same buffer partition. The policy is further improved by partitioning the buffer adaptively; that is, upon arrival of a new viewer after all enrollment windows are closed, a new viewgroup is created by reclaiming some unused buffer space and allocating this buffer partition to the new viewgroup. As can be seen later, the interval caching policy caches only the shortest intervals and thus forms viewgroups sharing a buffer partition only if the streams are very close to each other; that is, not all streams are part of a viewgroup.

BASIC. This policy is so termed due to the simplicity of its approach to buffer replacement [45]:

> *When a buffer is to be allocated, BASIC selects the buffer which contains the block that would not be accessed for the longest period of time by the existing progressing clients if each client consumed data at the specified rate from that moment on.*

Buffer locations	Time to access
106	41
106	40
1026	
1019	
104	10
105	28
130	
175	
117	7
118	8
1111	3
1112	4

Figure 12.2 Illustration of the BASIC policy.

Figure 12.2 illustrates this policy via a simple implementation, where for each block in the buffer, its time to reaccess is estimated and a list is created in this order. Clearly, the policy takes into account the access patterns and relationships across streams. However, the policy has a high implementation overhead because it reestimates this information on every service cycle and block replacement. The article [45] discusses the implementation overhead of this policy and suggests ways to improve it, one of which is to create a sorted free list on every kth service cycle. This is referred to as the BASIC/k policy.

DISTANCE. The DISTANCE policy explicitly makes use of the distance relationship across streams in its formulation of caching policy [45]. The distance, d_i, of a client, c_i, from an immediately following client, c_{i+1}, is measured by the offset in the number of blocks. For a client with no immediately following clients, the distance is assumed to be very large. Figure 12.3 illustrates the operations of this policy. The policy sorts all clients in an increasing order of their distances. In each service cycle, it first frees consumed buffer in the previous cycle, cb_i, in the increasing order of d_i.

> Since, when a buffer is to be allocated, the most recently freed buffer is selected, a buffer consumed by a client, which is followed by a consecutive client at a greater distance or which has no clients following it, will be selected [45].

Clearly, the DISTANCE policy has a lower implementation overhead than the BASIC policy because the distance calculation changes only if a client pauses or stops or a new stream arrives. As in most policies, an admission control policy is necessary for correct operation of the DISTANCE policy.

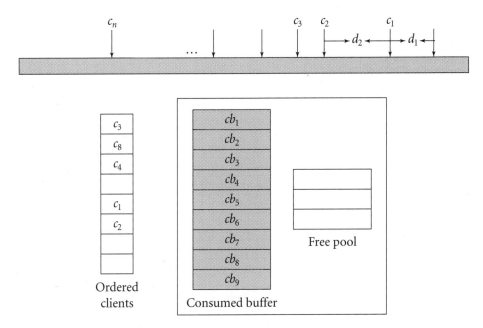

Figure 12.3   Illustration of the DISTANCE policy.

We will see shortly that the essence of the DISTANCE policy is the same as that of the interval caching policy. However, the policies differ in the details of their operations—that is, the approach to buffer allocation to client streams. Whereas the DISTANCE policy assumes a service cycle for freeing all buffers and subsequent reallocation to client streams, the interval caching policy assumes that the responsibility lies with the individual streams in deciding when to retain a buffer for the following streams.

Interval caching (IC). The main idea behind the IC policy is illustrated in Figure 12.4. The small arrow marked S_{ij} shows the playback positions of stream j on video object i. In the interval caching policy [14], the data blocks between a pair of consecutive streams S_{ij} and $S_{i(j+1)}$ accessing the same video object, i, is referred to as an *interval.* The two streams associated with an interval are referred to as the *preceding* and the *following* streams. By caching a running interval, the following stream can be served from the cache using the blocks brought in by the preceding stream. The size of an interval is estimated as the time difference between the two streams in reading the same block. The number of blocks needed to store a running interval (i.e., interval size times the compression rate) is defined to be the cache requirement of an interval. To maximize the cache hit ratio and

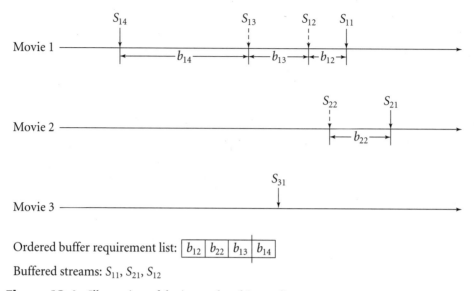

Ordered buffer requirement list: $\boxed{b_{12} \mid b_{22} \mid b_{13} \mid b_{14}}$

Buffered streams: S_{11}, S_{21}, S_{12}

Figure 12.4   Illustration of the interval caching policy.

minimize the I/O, the interval caching policy orders the intervals in terms of interval sizes (but not in terms of cache requirements) and caches only the shortest intervals. The estimated size of an interval is the time to reaccess for all the blocks in that interval. Hence, the interval caching policy that caches the shortest intervals becomes the OPTIMAL policy, where optimality is defined as the policy of retaining the data blocks to be accessed the earliest.

The ability to choose a small set of intervals from a large set of samples allows the IC policy to exploit the variation in interval size due to the variation in inter-arrival times. The IC policy also incurs low implementation overhead because changes in the interval list may occur only due to the arrival of a new stream or termination of a current stream. Therefore, algorithms for reordering the interval list and allocation and deallocation of cache to intervals are executed only at the times of arrival and ending of a playback stream. The run-time operation of this policy is straightforward. Once an interval is chosen to be cached, its preceding stream places all blocks in the cache upon consumption, in contrast to placing them in the free pool for noncached intervals. The following stream reads the blocks from the cache and places them in the free pool, unless it is also a preceding stream of another cached interval.

Generalized interval caching (GIC). Although the interval caching policy is optimal for streams accessing long videos, it is not useful for clients accessing short media objects because in the latter case no running intervals can be formed. In a

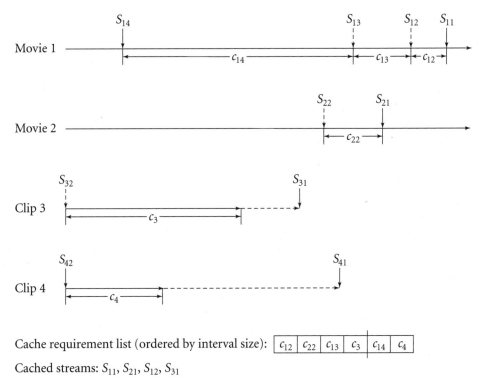

Cache requirement list (ordered by interval size):

Cached streams: $S_{11}, S_{21}, S_{12}, S_{31}$

Figure 12.5 Illustration of the GIC policy.

general-purpose media server, the workload may consist of large videos as well as many short media objects. The generalized interval caching policy [16] integrates the concept of stream-aware cache management for caching intervals in large video objects as well as temporal locality in retaining short video objects. The example in Figure 12.5 shows various streams reading large movies 1 and 2 and video clips 3 and 4.

For small video objects that are not being accessed concurrently, the definition of an interval is extended as follows. In Figure 12.5, arrow S_{32} represents a stream presently reading small video object 3, and arrow S_{31} represents the position that would have been reached by the previous stream accessing object 3 if the object had been larger. (S_{31}, S_{32}) is defined to form an interval for object 3 even though stream S_{31} has already terminated. The interval size in this case is defined to be the time interval between two successive accesses of the same object. However, the cache requirement is equal to the size of the object and is smaller than the interval size times the data rate. Therefore, if the interval is selected for caching, the entire video object will be cached. The anticipated interval size for an object can be estimated from the sizes of the previous intervals. In the GIC policy, the size of the last interval is assumed to be the anticipated interval size. The GIC policy thus caches intervals that may be either video segments or entire video objects. The policy maximizes the number of streams served from the cache by ordering all intervals (current or anticipated) in terms of increasing interval size (see Figure 12.5) and allocating cache to as many of the intervals as possible. The detailed operations of this policy as well as its performance in various contexts are explored later in this chapter.

Split and merge (SAM). The split and merge policy focuses on the temporary use of buffer to facilitate VCR control operations by integrating with the batching policy where multiple clients are served via a single stream [33]. When a client sharing a common delivery stream with other clients performs a VCR control operation (pause, fast-forward, reverse, etc.), a new stream is created splitting from the common stream. At the end of the VCR control operation, the new playback stream for this client is served from the buffer (if possible) as in the IC policy. However, SAM attempts to merge this new stream with another closest stream by speeding up/slowing down (as applicable) this stream and/or the nearest target stream [28] and in the process freeing up the buffer. Clearly, SAM can be integrated with any other cache management policy because merging of streams always saves resources and the selection of streams to serve from the cache is controlled by the cache management policy. Another way to address the VCR control operations and unpredictable surges in resource requirements is to use contingency server capacity [18, 13]. We will illustrate this later in the context of integration of VCR control operations with the GIC policy.

L/MRP. The primary focus of the L/MRP policy [38] is to address caching under nonsequential access patterns generated by VCR control operations. As discussed in Chapter 11, the L/MRP policy defines a set of continuous object presentation units, or COPUs, that contains data to be accessed by an access sequence (e.g., skip alternate blocks, reverse playback until a marked point, etc.). Clearly, the same data page may belong to multiple COPUs. The caching policy evaluates which COPU to retain or prefetch into the cache. The L/MRP policy can be easily integrated with other caching policies by fencing off a part of the cache to deal with such VCR control operations.

Hypergraph access hints. In accessing a video game or other interactive and/or composite media documents, the access pattern is not sequential but may follow a set of likely access sequences over many small media objects. The access pattern can be modeled as navigation of a hypergraph, where each node represents playback of a small media object and links determine the next set of objects to be played back [53]. By examining the access history, from any node the most likely set of follow-up nodes can be identified. This information can be used both for data clustering and placement on disks, as well as to prefetch and cache data effectively.

12.3   The Generalized Interval Caching Policy

We will now focus on the GIC policy because it deals with a wide range of workload, can be easily integrated with other resource optimization policies, and has been adapted to deal with various objectives (e.g., routing and load balancing) in distributed systems with heterogeneous components. After describing in detail the implementation of this policy, we will explore its performance in various contexts. For this purpose, we describe a general workload that captures the complexities described earlier (e.g., interactive sessions, movie-on-demand, dynamic load changes) that need to be addressed by a multimedia caching policy. Subsequently, we demonstrate the superior performance of the GIC policy under various workload scenarios.

Recall that under the GIC policy, intervals are created and destroyed only during open and close operations on files containing media objects. When an open request is received, it is necessary to decide whether or not to cache the newly formed interval. Upon a close request, an interval will be destroyed, possibly allowing caching of another interval. The interval may also be destroyed or recreated upon pause and resume (i.e., VCR control operations). The open, close and VCR control operations are detailed in the following subsections.

12.3.1 Starting of a New Client Request

Starting a new request may create a new interval with its closest previous stream on the same media object. In order to determine whether to cache this new interval, the algorithm presented in Figure 12.6 first computes the size of the new interval and its cache requirement [17]. All the blocks of frequently requested small objects may already reside in the cache, and thus this new interval can be served from cache. If the interval is not already cached, the algorithm determines if it is desirable to cache it. The GIC policy attempts to retain the blocks with the lowest interval size because these are the blocks to be accessed earliest, and so caches frequently referenced object segments. The policy computes the total replaceable cache space (i.e., from the free pool and less-desirable intervals with a larger interval size). If the cache requirement of the new interval can be satisfied—that is, it is smaller than the replaceable cache space—it can be cached by allocating blocks from the free pool and by deleting the less-desirable larger intervals (if needed). Note that deleting an existing cached interval requires the stream reading this interval to be now served from disk. The blocks of a running cached interval are

```
open:
    Form new interval with previous stream;
    Compute interval size
          and cache requirement;
    Reorder interval list;
    If not already cached
       If space available,
          Cache this new interval;
       else if this interval is smaller
               than existing cached intervals
               and sufficient cache space
               can be released
          Release cache space from
               larger intervals;
    Cache this new interval;
```

Figure 12.6 Details of open in generalized interval caching policy.

retained until they are read and discarded by the concurrent following stream. In contrast, caching blocks of a predicted interval causes the corresponding multimedia object to be retained in the cache for reuse by an anticipated following stream. An associated flag indicates whether an interval is real or predicted.

12.3.2 Ending of a Client Request

Ending a multimedia stream results in the issuing of a close request. This has an effect only if the current stream is the following stream in an interval. The associated interval no longer exists because its preceding stream has already ended, and the allocated cache can be released to the free pool. Figure 12.7 describes the subsequent steps executed by the GIC policy. The newly released space may make it possible to cache another interval. Hence, the GIC policy considers the smallest uncached interval to determine if it should be allocated cache. The allocation algorithm used is the same as that for the arrival of a new stream.

12.3.3 Switching of Streams between Disk and Cache

Switching streams from cache to disk or vice versa is a straightforward and low-overhead operation. All streams are marked with a source flag indicating from what source the stream is being served and a block_disposal state flag indicat-

```
close:
    If following stream of a real interval
        Delete the interval;
        Free allocated cache;
        If next largest interval can
                be cached
            Cache next largest interval;
```

Figure 12.7 Details of `close` in generalized interval caching policy.

ing whether the blocks read by this stream (from cache or disk) are to be discarded. The `source` state flag can take on two values—DISK or CACHE—that indicate whether the stream is being served from disk or from cache, respectively. During block retrieval, the `source` flag is consulted to see whether the next block for the stream should be retrieved from the disk or from the cache. The `block_disposal` state flag can take on two values—DELETE or RETAIN. Initially, the `block_disposal` flag is set to DELETE. This indicates that blocks retrieved for the stream should be deleted after transmission to the client. If it is determined that an interval should be cached, the `block_disposal` flag of the preceding stream of the interval is set to RETAIN. This causes the blocks retrieved for the preceding stream to be retained so that they can be used by the following stream. Switching streams between disks and cache can be accomplished by appropriately setting the values of the flags.

12.3.4 VCR Control

An interactive application may allow clients to pause and restart viewing at arbitrary times. Hence, the dependencies across streams (i.e., the preceding and following relationship) are affected as well as the caching decisions taken by the GIC policy. As discussed in Part 2, the challenges posed by the VCR control operations and the resulting unpredictable bandwidth requirements affect all aspects of resource optimization (e.g., batching, caching) and so need to be solved in a general way. If resources are released during a `pause`, they may not be available in general at the time of a `resume` request. On the other hand, not releasing resources leads to inefficient usage of resources. As proposed in [18, 13] and discussed in Part 2, VCR control operations, including `pause` and `resume` requests, can be handled by setting aside a small pool of channels (i.e., resources needed for delivering a stream) called *contingency channels*. Under the contingency channel method, upon a `pause`, resources are released immediately either to the contingency pool or to a waiting request. The resume requests are served using resources from this contingency channel pool. The method provides a *statistical guarantee* that with high probability (e.g., 99%) a resume request can be serviced within a small prespecified delay. It is shown in [13] that this method is more efficient than reserving resources for all paused streams.

The proposed contingency channel method can easily be integrated with the GIC policy. A cached interval is deleted when a sole following stream reading from the cached interval pauses. The preceding stream remains unaffected other than changing its retain status flag. However, pausing of a preceding stream results in further actions. Its following stream may need to be switched to disk. If both a paused stream and its following stream have been reading from the cache, the two intervals can be merged into a single interval; that is, the blocks previously read by the paused stream continue to be cached. If the GIC policy favors another interval over this merged interval, the total cache allocated to the merged interval will be freed and its following stream will be moved to disk. The caching algorithm then reallocates this cache to other interval(s) to be cached. Upon resume, a new stream is needed to serve this request. Sometimes, the resumed stream may lie in the middle of a cached interval, and it will immediately be served from the cache. Otherwise, the contingency capacity is used to serve it from disk, and the GIC policy is rerun as before to determine if the newly created interval should be cached.

12.4   Performance Evaluation of the GIC Policy

The performance of this policy has been studied via simulation in [14, 17]. Theoretical analysis of the interval caching policy and obtaining explicit expressions may be quite a difficult task; the problem can be related to the general problem of obtaining order statistics. The server considered in these studies are single servers with a single set of striped disks with a prespecified bandwidth. The studies modeled explicitly any change in disk load due to arrival and ending of client requests, as well as switching between cache and disks. However, individual block I/Os were not modeled—for obvious reasons: they are expensive to model and their absence does not affect the caching results. Admission control was modeled by rejecting an incoming request that caused the disk bandwidth to exceed the disk capacity. The cache was modeled as a collection of 1 MB blocks. Hence, the cache space required for cachable segments is always rounded up to the nearest megabyte. The required length of the simulation was estimated through trial runs made using the method of batch means. With a simulation duration of 8 hours, after ignoring the initial transient (1.5 hours), 99% confidence intervals of less than 10% were obtained for important quantities, such as the average number of streams reading from the cache. Thus, the simulations were run, in general, for 8 hours.

12.4.1 Workload

We now describe the workload used to study the effectiveness of the GIC policy [16, 17]. Two types of applications, interactive and long videos, were considered to model a general multimedia environment. In interactive applications, short video objects may be displayed in response to frequent client queries. Examples of such applications will be numerous in the future and include news-on-demand, shopping, and other service-oriented applications. Users may view short news clips in a news-on-demand application and in a shopping application browse short product advertisements before making a purchase. On the other hand, in a non-interactive application, such as movie-on-demand, client interactions are infrequent and the length of the displayed video objects is typically very long. A general multimedia workload was generated by combining an interactive workload (representing interactive applications) and a noninteractive workload. The arrival of new client requests was modeled as a Poisson process with a mean interarrival time of T seconds. Upon arrival, client sessions were randomly classified as interactive or noninteractive in accordance with an interactive probability.

Interactive workload. A general multimedia environment may contain various different interactive applications (e.g., catalog shopping, news-on-demand, educational training). In an interactive application, clients establish a session during which they select various short clips interactively. It is assumed that the video objects are selected according to an access distribution. The interactive workload was thus defined by the following parameters:

- *Video object access skew.* Access to small video objects is assumed to be skewed so that 80% of the accesses are to 20% of the video objects.

- *Video object length distribution.* It is assumed that the length of the short video objects is distributed uniformly between L_{min} and L_{max}.

- *Viewing time per individual clip.* In many interactive applications video banners consisting of a short clip are repeatedly displayed (e.g., a logo shown until the client makes a selection). This kind of behavior is modeled by assuming that each clip is viewed for a random viewing time, T_v. Viewing time is assumed to be independent of the length of a clip and can be smaller than the playback duration of an entire clip, with a minimum of 5 seconds.

- *Client session duration.* Client sessions are assumed to be of length T_s, with clients repeatedly selecting clips until the length of the session exceeds T_s.

Long video workload. Clients executing a movie-on-demand application are assumed to select long video objects according to a Zipf distribution with parameter 0.271, which fits empirical data on video rental frequencies well [60]. It is assumed that the server contains N_l long video objects of length L_l.

12.4.2 Workload Parameters

Table 12.1 shows the default workload parameters chosen for evaluating the GIC policy. The request interarrival time, T, was chosen so as to correspond to a server simultaneously serving, on average, 400 streams. This value is typical of the range of active clients expected for future video-on-demand servers. Various mixtures of interactive and long video workloads were modeled by varying the interactive probability. From the duration of interactive sessions and the length of videos, it can be seen that with the default value, 50% of all I/O requests are made by the interactive sessions. All videos are assumed to be MPEG-1 with a delivery rate of 192 KB/s. Hence, the total amount of storage required per movie is 1 GB. For interactive applications, the total size of the video catalog (all of the video clips) is 125 minutes. The number of video clips was varied in the simulation to study its impact on the server capacity. Experiments varying other parameters are reported in [16].

12.4.3 Admission Control

Caching increases the number of streams that can be served by a video server. The server capacity can be defined as the request rate that can be supported with no or

Table 12.1   Default workload parameters for analysis of GIC policy.

Parameter	Default value
Number of clips	500
Length of clips	1 to 30 s
Average viewing time	30 s
Interactive session length	30 min
Number of long videos	92
Length of long videos	90 min
Request interarrival time	6.25 s
Interactive probability	0.8

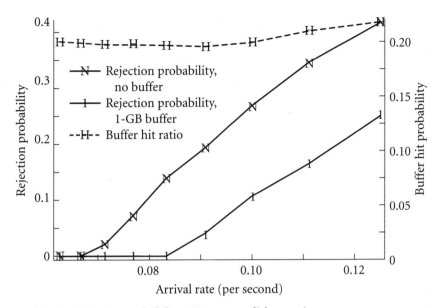

Figure 12.8 Rejection probability; 400-stream disk capacity.

a small rejection probability. Figure 12.8 shows the rejection probability as a function of the arrival rate for a system with a disk capacity of 400 streams. The curve plotted with "N" is for a system without any cache, while the curve plotted with "1" is for a system with 1 GB cache. In both cases, the rejection probability is 0 in the region where the system capacity is not exceeded. After this point, the rejection rate rises approximately linearly. It can be seen that the 1 GB cache has increased the system capacity by 25%, considering the arrival rates where the rejection probabilities become nonzero (0.067/s and 0.085/s). The curve plotted with "H" shows the corresponding overall cache hit ratios. The cache hit ratio is defined as the number of reads served from the cache as a fraction of the total number of reads. It can be seen from the graph that the hit ratio (which is approximately constant) is 0.22. Estimation of server capacity as a function of hit ratio translates to a 25% increase, which matches with the earlier estimate considering the nonzero rejection probability points. Hence, only the cache hit ratio was studied in the subsequent experiments.

12.4.4 Cache Hit Ratios

The GIC policy performs well under a wide range of workload parameters. We first consider the base mixed workload in Figures 12.9 and 12.10. Figure 12.9

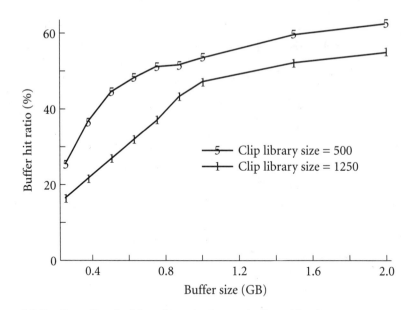

Figure 12.9 Overall cache hit ratio under base mixed workload.

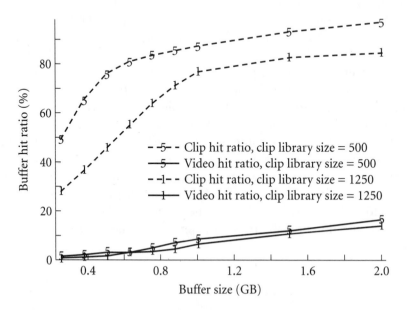

Figure 12.10 Interactive and movie cache hit ratios.

shows the variation in the overall cache hit ratio as a function of the cache size. The two curves are for interactive library sizes of 500 clips and 1250 clips. For a given cache size, as expected, the overall hit ratio with 500 clips is higher than that with 1250 clips because with a smaller number of clips, a larger fraction of the accesses falls on the clips retained in the cache. The hit ratios of the individual components of the workload are shown in Figure 12.10. The clip hit ratio shown in the figure is defined as the fraction of clip reads satisfied from the cache. Similarly, the movie hit ratio is the fraction of movie reads serviced from the cache. The clip hit ratio is higher, because access to the short videos is more likely to be found in the cache and only the shortest intervals of long videos are satisfied from the cache. However, both clip and movie hit ratios are smaller for the workload with 1250 clips.

Many other variations in workload mix and parameters—for example, interactive dominated vs. noninteractive dominated, average clip size, etc.—are studied in [17]. The GIC policy was found to perform well (i.e., to provide significant cache hit and improve server throughput) under all workloads.

12.5   Affinity Routing for Multimedia Applications

We have discussed the effectiveness of the GIC policy in dealing with heterogeneous workloads in a single-server environment. Caching policies in large-scale single-server systems exploit economies of scale arising from concurrent requests; the large number of concurrent requests makes cache reuse more likely. However, as discussed in Chapter 3, a large-scale server may actually be a distributed server built from individual smaller servers. Caching policies for such distributed architectures may need to address additional concerns. For example, caching policies may need to consider load balancing across server nodes. Figure 12.11 illustrates the architecture of a typical distributed server (see Chapter 3). It consists of front-end nodes that retrieve video data from shared disks or storage servers. There is no shared memory, so each front-end node and storage server node will have its own cache. In effect, the total amount of cache in the system is partitioned across the server nodes. If requests are routed without considering the data being accessed (e.g., at random), it is likely that related requests for the same file will be directed to different nodes. Therefore, the cache hit ratio will be low. Routing of related requests for the same file to the same node (with the objective of producing a high cache hit ratio) is referred to as *affinity routing* [17].

The following section describes caching policies for a distributed multimedia server. For this, two new concepts are needed: path-based routing and asset groups

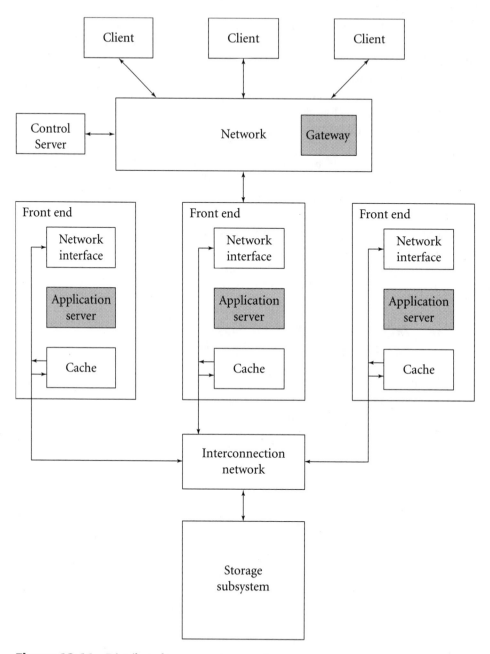

Figure 12.11   Distributed server environment.

[17]. As discussed in Chapter 4, a logical channel (or path) is the set of resources necessary to deliver multimedia data. In a distributed server, this includes the path from the storage nodes to the front-end nodes, including cache. Path-based routing refers to routing policies that consider resource availability in the complete path. Asset groups are a logical grouping of the related files that may be accessed together. For example, in a catalog shopping application, the data for a particular section of the catalog could be considered to be an asset group.

12.5.1 Distributed Server Environment

As discussed earlier in Chapter 3, the resource manager is responsible for setting up a logical channel to service the client request (see Figure 12.11). Therefore, the resource manager is responsible for monitoring the load on the various devices and admission control. It is also therefore logical for the resource manager to route requests based on its knowledge of the load on various devices and the characteristics (specified later) of the incoming request. The application server is responsible for handling application requests (e.g., listing available video clips). Once an application session has been established (by selecting an available application server, for example), the client interacts directly with the selected server. However, in an interactive session, it may be necessary to switch a client to a different node if the current node runs out of capacity. This situation may arise, for example, due to load fluctuations that result in a sudden rise in the load at a particular node. This is similar to handling VCR controls such as pause and resume in video playback, so the techniques described in Chapter 4 may be used to minimize the occurrence of such an eventuality. However, if switching is still required, it is logical for the switching to be performed in coordination with the resource manager.

Path-Based Routing

In a distributed system consisting of many components (e.g., network nodes, storage servers), bottlenecks can occur in any component. Caching at the network nodes can reduce the retrieval bandwidth needed from the storage servers, thereby eliminating bottlenecks in the system. However, as explained earlier, network caching may not be effective if the resource manager routes requests independently of the data being accessed by the request. Therefore, it is necessary to take the access affinity of the network nodes into account when routing.

Affinity routing in multimedia servers differs from affinity routing in other distributed server environments such as file systems [54] or database access [67]. The difference arises due to the necessity, in a multimedia server, of reserving bandwidth on all the components on the delivery path to the client. Traditional affinity routing policies consider mainly the access affinity of the data being accessed and the load balancing on the front-end nodes. In contrast, the resource manager in multimedia servers has to also consider the load on all the other components in the logical channel [17]. A policy that considers bottlenecks on the entire logical channel needed to deliver data to the user is called a *path-based* affinity routing policy.

Asset Groups

Affinity routing for multimedia servers may be based purely on the identity of the data being accessed. However, this may be disadvantageous for interactive multimedia applications. Consider an application that accesses many different short video clips. If routing is based purely on the identity of the clip, successive requests for different clips may be directed to different network nodes. This may not be desirable because setting up a logical channel across a network results in a long latency in addition to processor overhead. Furthermore, if the application server has built up a state, this state would need to be distributed across the multiple network nodes. This switching can be reduced if applications group related clips into asset groups that are known to the resource manager [17]. If requests specify the asset group(s) they are likely to access, the resource manager can then route requests for clips in the same asset group to the same node. This will eliminate switching when different clips in the same asset group are requested.

Details of Path-Based Routing

We next describe the details of the path-based routing policy [17].

1. *Asset group–based routing.* Let F_{aff} be the set of nodes that have one or more applications accessing the same asset group(s) as the request. For each node $F_{aff,i}$ in F_{aff}, define the affinity α_i to be the number of application sessions accessing the same asset group(s). Consider the nodes $F_{aff,i}$ in decreasing order of α_i, and select a node $F_{aff,i}$ that has enough free resources to satisfy the request.

2. *Data-based routing.* If none of the nodes in F_{aff} can satisfy the request, consider the set of nodes F_{data} that caches some of the data to be accessed by the request. Select any node from F_{data} that has sufficient resources to service the request.

3. *Random.* If none of the nodes F_{data} is suitable, pick a random node, F_{rand}, with sufficient resources to serve the request.

4. *Reject.* If no such node F_{rand} can be found, reject the request.

This node selection policy is used when setting up a logical channel. However, interactive applications make many requests during a single session. Due to the fluctuating load on the server nodes, as well as the unpredictable demands of the application (the application may, for example, suddenly request a high-bandwidth stream), it may not be possible to satisfy the request from the current node. Contingency capacity can be reserved on the current node to minimize the likelihood of this happening (see Chapter 4). Otherwise, the node selection policy can be reexecuted to select another node.

12.5.2 Workload Parameters

We next describe simulation experiments to evaluate the effectiveness of the affinity routing policy [17]. The simulation modeled a distributed server storing 560 video clips with length varying from 1 to 60 seconds (see Table 12.2). The clips were assumed to be distributed evenly over eight asset groups, with the access to the clips being skewed within the asset groups. To evaluate system performance, the cache hit ratio as well as the maximum achievable server throughput was used. These measures are compared against the corresponding measures for an idealized large single server. The idealized large single server is assumed to have hardware resources equal to the aggregate of the resources possessed by the distributed server. For example, if the total cache size of the idealized single server is 288 MB (sufficient to store a 30-minute 1.2 Mbps video), the distributed server is assumed to have a total cache size of 288 MB distributed among its nodes. Other capacities of the idealized single server are shown in Table 12.3.

Table 12.2 Simulation parameters for analysis of affinity routing.

Workload parameter	Default value
Number of clips	560
Length of clips	1 to 60 s
Interactive session length	30 min
Number of asset groups	8
Number of long videos	100
Length of long videos	30 min
Request interarrival time	1.4 s

Table 12.3 Idealized large single server configuration.

Resource	Total capacity
Disk bandwidth	1024 streams
Cache size	288 MB
Network capacity	1280 streams

12.5.3 Distributed Server Configurations

The experiments studied two different types of server configurations that are likely to occur in practice. The symmetric configuration modeled a distributed server built out of identical nodes. However, in practice, distributed servers may also consist of heterogeneous nodes. This situation was studied using many asymmetric configurations. Even in symmetric configurations, due to variations in the cache hit ratio at various nodes, distributing the hardware resources among the various nodes does not result in equal or balanced utilizations of all resources. Therefore, the experiments assumed that only the network capacity of the server was evenly distributed over all the nodes. The other hardware resources were varied to study the sensitivity of the affinity routing policy. Among the asymmetric configurations, only a specific type of asymmetric configuration was studied: one built from two types of server nodes—a base node and a larger node with a capacity three times that of the base node.

12.5.4 Study of Performance of Affinity Routing Policy

We first study how the performance of the affinity routing policy varies with the number of nodes in the server. Three different workloads, generated by varying the mix of interactive and long video applications, were used. The number of simultaneous sessions that could be supported was measured (see Figure 12.12). It can be seen from Figure 12.12 that affinity routing is effective for all three workloads, since the server capacity does not decline very significantly. This is due to the fact that even with a large number of nodes, the cache hit ratio is fairly high [17]. Figure 12.13 compares the affinity routing policy with a random routing policy. As can be seen, for a small number of nodes, the system capacity with affinity routing can be as large as 14%.

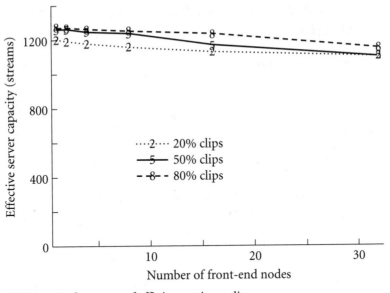

Figure 12.12 Performance of affinity routing policy.

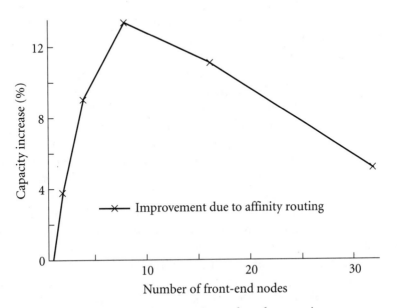

Figure 12.13 Comparison of affinity routing and random routing.

12.5.5 Impact of Number of Asset Groups on Affinity Routing

The performance of an affinity routing policy can be expected to vary with the number of asset groups. If there is only one asset group, requests for any clip may be directed to any node. This will result in a poor cache hit ratio. Conversely, if the number of asset groups is large, the requests for similar files can be directed to a small number of server nodes. These results are confirmed experimentally in [17] using experiments that vary the number of asset groups.

12.6 Caching for Load Balancing Across Servers

The previous section pointed out that the disk bandwidth required from the storage servers depended upon the cache hit ratio. This observation leads to the idea that caching can be used to correct load imbalances among storage devices. We describe policies that exploit caching for load balancing next.

12.6.1 Overview of the CLB Policy

As discussed in Chapter 9, it is likely that a multimedia server will contain multiple logical storage devices. First, because the physical storage devices may be heterogeneous, it is difficult to aggregate all physical storage devices into a single logical storage device. Second, the use of multiple storage devices may be advantageous in terms of failure characteristics (see Chapter 9). Due to varying access rates to the different files stored on the devices, load imbalance may arise among them. Load balancing by dynamically replicating (or caching) multimedia objects in disk [12] is described in Chapter 13. The following section describes a complementary policy of caching in memory called the *caching for load balancing* (CLB) policy. Later, we describe simulation results that show the CLB policy effectively increases the throughput of the overall system by reducing the load imbalance across servers.

As described earlier, the GIC policy retains the smallest intervals in the cache, which results in maximizing the number of streams served from the cache. In a single storage server environment, this results in maximizing the total server capacity (since this is equal to the total number of streams served from the storage devices and the cache). However, in a distributed server, caching lightly loaded devices may be wasteful of cache space. We will describe how the GIC policy can be modified to take the load on the storage devices into account.

The CLB policy is a bimodal policy. Under normal conditions, it attempts to balance the load among the various storage devices. It does this by caching only streams from heavily loaded disks—that is, disks whose load is greater than the average load. However, when the system is overloaded, rejection of requests due to insufficient system capacity may be unavoidable. Under this environment, the CLB policy no longer attempts to balance the load; instead, it attempts to minimize the rejection rate. It does this by only caching streams from overloaded devices. Because the GIC policy maximizes the number of cached streams, caching only overloaded devices will result in minimizing the rejection rate.

12.6.2 Performance of the CLB Policy

The performance of the proposed caching load-balancing policy was studied via simulation. The workload used is similar to that described in the previous section and models a server containing a mixture of long video and small video objects [17]. To assess the effectiveness of the CLB policy, the load imbalance between the disks with and without the CLB policy was compared. The load imbalance was defined as $100(v_S - v_s)/v_s$ where v_S and v_s are the average number of viewers of the most heavily loaded and least heavily loaded storage device, respectively. A distributed storage subsystem with a capacity of 512 viewers and 288 MB of total cache space was assumed. The number of storage devices was varied from two to six.

We first study how well the CLB policy performs with varying values of load imbalance. Figure 12.14 shows the load on a server with two logical storage devices as the load imbalance is varied. Both the load with and without caching are

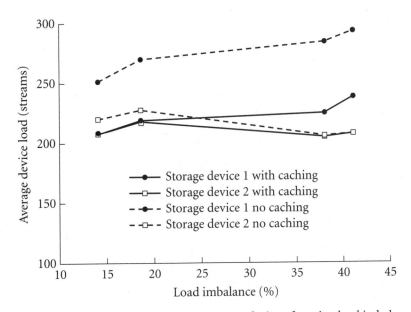

Figure 12.14 Impact on average load on storage device of varying load imbalance.

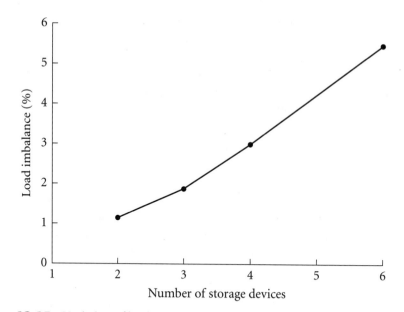

Figure 12.15   Variation of load imbalance vs. number of storage devices.

plotted. In all cases, there is a substantial reduction in load imbalance under the CLB policy; for lower values of load imbalance, the load imbalance is completely eliminated. Figure 12.15 shows the load imbalance with caching as the number of storage devices is varied. In all cases, the load imbalance without caching is 18%. It can be seen that the CLB policy reduces the load imbalance to 6%. Additional results in [17] show that this translates to an increase in system capacity of 20%.

12.7   Summary

Caching in memory can increase the capacity of a media server in terms of the number of streams it can handle. Traditional caching policies that identify and retain a small hot set are not suitable for multimedia due to the larger sizes of media objects. However, caching policies that exploit the knowledge of streams following one another can be quite effective in caching media data.

Multimedia applications can be quite diverse; in a movie-on-demand application, long videos are played back with little user interaction, whereas in multimedia database applications, relatively short clips are displayed in response to frequent user requests. In general media server environments, the workload can differ greatly in terms of file sizes, number of videos, and other parameters. The requirements of applications may also vary with time. Caching policies need to take into account all of these requirements as well as access patterns within a media document. VCR control operations (e.g., pause and resume) that alter sequential accesses to media objects pose further challenges to a caching policy.

The generalized interval caching policy that caches small intervals in large videos as well as entire small media objects can be quite effective for diverse multimedia workloads. It automatically adapts to changes in workload, and it can also be integrated with various other resource optimization policies—for example, the policy of setting aside contingency capacity for supporting VCR control operations. The simulation study shows that the GIC policy can be very effective in an environment with a diverse workload.

In a large-scale complex distributed server environment containing many front-end nodes and storage devices, the available cache spreads over multiple nodes. The GIC policy can be used to manage a cache within each node. However, intelligent routing of related requests by exploiting affinity of accesses to the same server is required to achieve an effective cache hit ratio. The affinity routing policy must take into account further requirements of a multimedia server—continuous delivery. The affinity routing policy reviewed in this chapter embraces the concept of path-based routing by taking into account the availability of bandwidth on each server component and the concept of grouping related small files (e.g., clips needed by an application) into asset groups. The effectiveness of such affinity routing policies has been demonstrated in simulation studies.

A further requirement of a caching policy in a distributed server is balancing load across multiple storage devices or servers, where, depending on the placement of multimedia objects across the storage devices and nonuniform access to them, load imbalances may occur. An extension of the GIC policy, called the *caching for load balancing* policy, preferentially caches the videos on the heavily loaded disks and can effectively balance the loads across disks. Again via simulation study, the CLB policy was shown to be effective over a wide range of workloads.

13

Disk Cache

13.1   Introduction

Disk and other storage caching differs from memory caching in two important respects. First, unlike memory, disk caches cannot be assumed to have a very large bandwidth. As described in detail later, the process of inserting objects into the disk cache may use up bandwidth that could be used to service client requests. Therefore, disk caching policies have to optimize usage of both the bandwidth and storage space of disks, unlike memory caching policies, where the primary constraint is the amount of memory available. Second, memory caches generally operate within the limits of a single system; that is, multimedia data stored on disks is cached within memory in the same system. In contrast, disk caches may operate in a distributed environment; that is, multimedia data stored in the disk of one system may be cached on the disk of another system. As discussed later in the chapter, the issues addressed in the copying of multimedia data between disks of the same system (generally termed *replication*) and disk caching in distributed systems are somewhat different.

In spite of the differences between disk and memory caching policies, there are also a number of similarities. Disks can also be used to store prefetched multimedia data, reducing access latency. Disk caching policies also need to consider issues common to all caching policies, such as when to insert a block into the cache and which block to replace. In the following sections, we first discuss disk caching among the disks of a single system. Next, we discuss distributed disk caching. We will briefly review the distributed system issues in disk caching and then discuss disk caching and prefetching policies. In our discussion, we consider modifications of traditional policies before discussing in detail a policy specifically for multimedia objects.

13.2 Caching Among Disks in a Single System

Disk caching in a single system is mainly motivated by the need to reduce load imbalances among the different disks. Before discussing policies for single-system disk caching, we first summarize (from Part 3) some relevant features of the storage subsystem in a multimedia server and discuss how the load imbalance may arise. Subsequently, we discuss policies for load balancing.

As discussed in Part 3, the storage subsystem of a video server may contain many physical storage devices. To evenly distribute the load, multiple physical devices may be combined into a single logical storage device. This can be accomplished by striping multimedia files over the physical devices in a logical device. However, it is not desirable that all the physical devices in the server be combined into a single logical device. First, it is simpler to organize devices with different physical characteristics into different logical devices. Next, reconfiguration of the system (e.g., adding a disk) and recovery from failure are also simplified if there are multiple logical devices. This is because only the affected logical device has to be taken off-line during reconfiguration or recovery. Finally, by making additional replicas of frequently accessed multimedia data on different logical disks, the availability of the system can be increased.

Each logical storage device has a finite playback capacity and controls admission of new requests. Due to nonuniform access to multimedia data and the fact that different logical devices will store different data, there will be load imbalance among the different logical devices. As a result, requests for access to multimedia data on heavily loaded devices can be rejected even though unused bandwidth may be available on lightly loaded devices. This inefficiency can be eliminated by caching data from heavily loaded devices onto lightly loaded devices [12]. This reduces the future load on the heavily loaded device because future requests for the cached data can be directed either to the heavily loaded disk or the copy on the lightly loaded device.

As noted in Chapter 9, dynamic replication policies among logical storage devices of a single system are complementary to static data-placement policies. Without dynamic replication policies, there will always be load imbalances among the different logical storage devices in the system (as noted above). Without good data-placement policies, dynamic replication policies may create a lot of overhead in the process of trying to balance the load as well as be unable to achieve good load balance.

13.2.1 Overview of Dynamic Replication Policies

Multimedia objects are large; hence, dynamic replication of entire objects may be wasteful of storage space. Replicating arbitrary fragments of objects may be com-

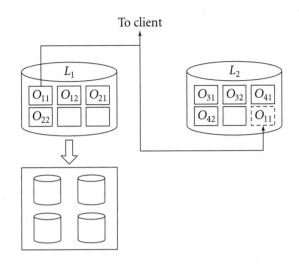

Figure 13.1   Illustration of DPSR policy.

plex due to the necessity of handling allocation and release of variable-sized disk segments. One possible solution is to divide multimedia objects into a small number of fixed-size segments [12]. For example, a movie may be divided into 10 segments. Division into segments also has the advantage of making the system more responsive to load changes. This is because it takes less time to copy a segment.

We provide an overview of the dynamic policy of segment replication (DPSR) [12], a dynamic replication policy that segments multimedia objects and replicates selected segments. The operation of the policy is illustrated in Figure 13.1. A key feature of the policy is the use of copyback streams, explained below. The figure shows two logical devices, L_1 and L_2, each with a number of segments of various multimedia objects. For example, L_1 contains segment O_{12}, the second segment of multimedia object O_1. As indicated by the solid lines, segments O_{11}, O_{12}, O_{21}, O_{22}, O_{31}, O_{32}, O_{41}, and O_{42} were placed on their respective disks by a placement policy that attempted to balance the load among the various storage devices. The DPSR policy requires that some segments be left empty for use as a cache for load balancing. Later we will show that the total empty space required is small, on the order of 5%. During operation, if a logical device is overloaded, the DPSR policy replicates one or more segments that are already in the process of being played back. This is illustrated in Figure 13.1 where a stream requested by a client from segment O_{22} is simultaneously being used to replicate the segment to empty space on logical disk L_2. Such streams are referred to as *copyback* streams. The use of copyback streams in the DPSR policy avoids further overloading disks that are already overloaded. Because different segments of different objects may be replicated on different logical devices, the DPSR policy may be considered to perform hierarchical striping of data.

The DPSR policy can be used for migration of objects as follows. Segments that are placed on logical devices during initial placement can be marked as *permanent* segments, while segments created by replication can be marked as *temporary* segments. During operation, most of the references to a segment may be directed to a temporary segment rather than to the permanent segment. In this case, the temporary segment can be converted into a permanent segment, and the original permanent segment can be freed for replication. This effectively results in the migration of a segment from one logical disk to another.

13.2.2   Details of DPSR Policy

Four decisions need to be made by the DPSR policy. These decisions are (1) when to replicate, (2) the selection of a segment to replicate, (3) selection of a target logical device, and (4) which segment to replace (if there is no free segment). We discuss each of these decisions in turn.

When to replicate. Replication of segments is required when a logical device becomes overloaded. However, if replication is initiated too early, the system may perform unnecessary replication among various disks. Late replication may result in the system not being able to quickly respond to changing load. Additionally, if replication has already been initiated from a heavily loaded logical device, the future load on the logical device may be lower than the current load. As a result, further replication may be unnecessary. Therefore, the DPSR policy compares both the current as well as projected future load on a device against a prespecified threshold. Replication is initiated if both the current and future loads are greater than the threshold.

Selection of segment to replicate. The reason for replicating a segment is to shift future load from a highly loaded logical device. This implies that a segment selected for replication should be currently heavily loaded; otherwise, it will not be possible to reduce future load greatly by replicating the segment. Additionally, if the segment already has replicas on devices that are currently lightly loaded, it may not be beneficial to replicate the segment because it may be possible to shift future load to the currently existing replicas. Hence, the DPSR policy selects a segment for replication from a highly loaded disk as follows. For a heavily loaded disk, the DPSR policy maintains the payoff from replicating each of the segments on the disk. The payoff is an estimate of the future load that can be shifted from the disk. It takes into account the current load on the segment as well as the existence of other replicas of the segment. Because the DPSR policy uses copyback streams, it can start replication of a segment only when a user starts playback of that segment. When a user starts playing a segment, the DPSR policy checks if the segment is the segment with the highest payoff on the logical device. If so, the policy decides to try to replicate the segment.

Selection of target logical device and segment. When selecting a target logical device for replication, the DPSR policy attempts to find a lightly loaded device. However, it does not use the current load, an approach that has two disadvantages. First, if a segment is being replicated onto the logical device, its future load may be greater than the current load. Second, use of the current load could lead to the hot-spot problem where multiple highly loaded logical devices select the same lightly loaded logical device as a target. Hence, the DPSR policy selects the logical device with the lowest future load as a target. Additional checks (e.g., that the future load of the target logical device is less than the source device) are also performed [12]. The DPSR policy then needs to select a target segment on the device to replace. If there is no empty segment, the DPSR policy selects an inactive segment.

13.2.3 Experimental Results

The performance of the DPSR policy has been studied using simulation [12]. The results show that as load imbalance arises among logical devices, copyback streams start replicating segments from highly loaded devices to lightly loaded devices. This results in the heavily loaded disks never becoming overloaded. With even a small amount of cache, the DPSR policy is able to provide very good load balancing.

13.3 Issues in Distributed Disk Caching

Figure 13.2 illustrates the typical distributed disk caching environment under discussion. Multimedia data is stored on one or more servers connected to a computer network. A number of clients may also be directly connected to the network. More commonly, the clients will be on a distinct subnetwork and access the multimedia data through a caching server or proxy cache. The term *proxy cache* is used because a caching server acts as a proxy for the actual server. Use of the proxy cache has a number of advantages [35, 2]. From the performance point of view, the access time latency is reduced because frequently accessed multimedia data is fetched from the proxy cache instead of from the remote server. Furthermore, the proxy cache is likely to be more reliable than a geographically dispersed link. Hence, the proxy cache also improves the availability of server multimedia data. The proxy cache enhances the security of the clients as well by isolating the client subnetwork from the external network. Finally, the proxy cache can also

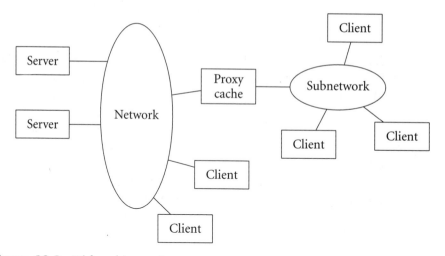

Figure 13.2 Disk caching environment.

implement policies on the type of multimedia data or sites that the clients can access by denying requests that violate these policies. More details on the security use of proxy caches as firewalls can be found in [7].

A number of issues arise in such systems. Should proxy caches be allowed to retrieve data from each other in addition to retrieving data from servers? If so, how can proxy caches discover the existence of other proxy caches and communicate with each other? How can security and access control be guaranteed in such systems? The answer to these and other questions will clearly depend upon the workloads in such systems. We discuss these and other issues in the rest of this section.

13.3.1 Workload Characterization

A great deal of work has been done in studying workloads on the Internet for evaluating the effectiveness of proxy caches [46, 66]. As in the single-server workloads considered in earlier chapters, the frequency of access to multimedia objects follows a Zipf distribution [27, 9]. The frequency of access to various servers in the network also follows a Zipf distribution [64]. In fact, the distribution is extremely skewed: 50% of the accesses are to only 1% of the sites, and 80% of the accesses are to 26% of the sites. Additionally, 90% of the data comes from 25% of the accessed sites [1]. All of these facts indicate that there is good locality of reference and, hence, that proxy caching should be effective. Interestingly, the distribution of multimedia object sizes appears to be heavy tailed; that is, extremely large object sizes may appear with nonnegligible probability. Details can be found in [9].

There are a number of factors that can limit the effectiveness of proxy caching. Generally, if the server maintains information about the state of the client, caching may not be possible. This is because the response to the client may then depend on the state. A common reason for state maintenance is security; servers may want to know whether a client has authenticated to the server or not. In Web protocols, there are a number of methods by which the server can maintain client state information. First, the server may use server procedures (e.g., CGI scripts) for dynamically generating a Web page. The state information, as well as other parameter information, can be encoded in the URL passed to the server. Early studies showed that such scripts form a small fraction of the workload (less than 2%) [36]; however, more recent studies seem to show that their use is increasing [1]. Another method is the use of cookies, which encode state information and are invisibly embedded in Web pages. A current study indicates that as much as 30% of all requests have embedded cookies [24].

13.3.2 Single-Level vs. Hierarchical Caches

Traditional file system caches have been single level; that is, if the cache does not have the data requested by the client, it attempts to retrieve the data directly from the server [29, 40, 52]. An alternative is a hierarchical cache, where proxy caches can retrieve needed multimedia data from other close proxy caches. See Figure 13.3 (for simplicity, the clients are not shown in the figure). If clients on subnetwork B3 want to access multimedia data from the server on subnetwork A, they would first contact the proxy cache on subnetwork B3. If this proxy cache does not have the requested multimedia data, it may relay the request to its siblings on subnetworks B1 and B2, as well as up one level to the proxy cache on subnetwork B and the server on subnetwork A. The requested data would be retrieved from the closest server.

From this description, it can be seen that in a hierarchical cache the caches closest to the client are preferred for data retrieval. Therefore, the most frequently accessed multimedia data would tend to be cached closest to the client. Less frequently accessed multimedia data is cached at higher levels. However, if the hit rate to caches higher in the hierarchy is low, hierarchical caching may not be worthwhile.

Studies of multilevel caching in distributed file systems have shown that the hit rate for the proxy caches at higher levels is low (around 20%) [3, 39]. However, the hit rates for multilevel proxy caches on the Internet is higher [5, 4, 2, 27]. This is due to two factors [5]: The first factor is the hierarchical organization of the

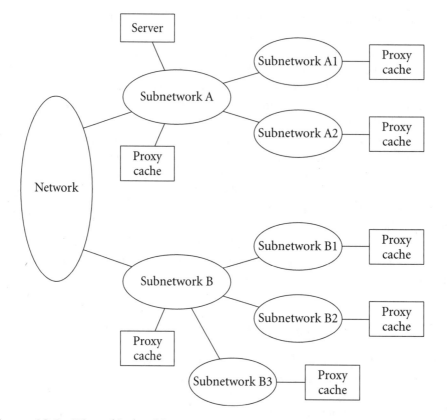

Figure 13.3 Hierarchical caching.

Internet; the second factor is the fact that the shared data is actually changing slowly (for example, the image of the lead story on the home page of a news site). If the shared multimedia data was completely static, the hit rate of proxy caches higher in the hierarchy would be low because the frequently accessed data would be found in proxy caches closest to the client. This point is supported by results in [2], where the hit ratio to proxy caches with unchanging data showed a declining trend with time.

13.3.3 Caching Protocol

In a hierarchical caching system, it is necessary for the proxy caches to communicate with each other. Interproxy cache communication is required so that the caches can retrieve data from one another. Additionally, control operations, such as checking that the cached data has not become outdated, are necessary. Caching protocols have been developed to allow proxy caches to communicate with each other. Note that this same functionality can also be achieved with the protocols used by the clients to retrieve multimedia data (e.g., RTSP). In other words, the proxy caches can also use client retrieval protocols (such as RTSP) to communicate with each other. However, the caching protocols are more lightweight and also provide functions specially tailored for caching.

The most commonly used caching protocol today is the Internet Cache Protocol (ICP) [63], which has a number of implementations [41, 44] and is based on the work done in [5]. Figure 13.4 illustrates how proxy caches that support the RTSP multimedia protocol (described in Chapter 2) can use ICP. Initially, the client establishes a TCP connection with proxy cache PC_1 and then sets up an RTSP connection through the `Setup` command. After this, the client sends a `Describe` command requesting a description of the video file to be played. If the requested data is not in the cache, PC_1 sends an `ICP_OP_QUERY` command to PC_2.[1] If PC_2 has the data in its cache, it will reply with a `ICP_OP_HIT` command. PC_2 could also have responded with `ICP_OP_MISS` if it did not have the object or with `ICP_OP_HIT_OBJ` and enclosed the object in the response. Subsequently, PC_1 relays the client requests to PC_2 and relays the response back to the client. In particular, the `Play` command is relayed to PC_2. In response, PC_2 sends multimedia data which is relayed to the client and possibly cached by PC_1.

ICP is not specialized for any particular data-access protocol. As a result, it can be used to support caching of any data-access protocol (e.g., FTP). However, the disadvantage is that it does not support data protocol-specific queries. For example, when requesting an image, the HTTP protocol allows clients to specify the image types they can display in the HTTP header. This information cannot be passed between proxy caches using ICP. Therefore, it may be desirable to develop specialized caching protocols for popular data-access protocols. An example is the Hyper Text Caching Protocol (HTCP) [61], a protocol specialized for the caching of Web objects. In addition to allowing querying of cache state between caches (as in ICP), HTCP also allows caches to pass HTTP headers received from the client.

13.3.4 Content Discovery

In a system with multiple caches, the process by which one cache can discover the contents of neighboring caches is an important issue. In the ICP protocol, this process is entirely dynamic; each cache interrogates neighboring caches with every

---

[1]If there are multiple other proxy caches, PC_1 could simultaneously send the query to the other caches as well.

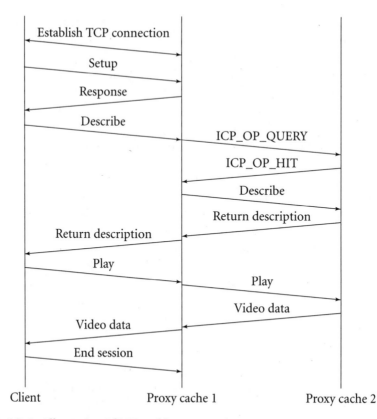

Figure 13.4   Illustration of ICP caching protocol.

request for the data it needs. It may be more efficient, instead, for caches to store information about data available in other caches. We discuss two approaches. The first approach prepartitions the URL space among the various caches, while the second approach defines a protocol that allows caches to maintain a distributed directory of the objects available in each cache.

The Cache Array Routing Protocol (CARP) divides a set of URLs among a set of loosely coupled proxy caches [59]. The set of proxy caches is stored in the proxy array membership table, which is maintained in a consistent state by the set of caches. A hashing function is used to determine the proxy cache that should be requested for any particular URL. Therefore, CARP partitions the URL space among the proxy caches.

In contrast, the CRISP Web cache [47] maintains a partially replicated directory of cached content. Each proxy cache maintains a graph of the network connecting it to other proxy caches in its neighborhood, including the communication overhead. This information is used by the proxy cache to decide which other caches to retrieve the data from as well as to decide which caches to notify of changes in content. The result is that each node will contain information only about the data of other caches in its neighborhood. Storage space is saved by not storing information about data in far-away caches. Details can be found in [47].

13.3.5 Partial Fetching of Data

The protocols we have described implicitly assume that on a cache miss the entire multimedia object is fetched from a remote location. However, multimedia data, particularly visual data, is heavily redundant. Thus, network bandwidth can be conserved by retrieving only part of the multimedia data. In [48], the multimedia stream is split (virtually) into a number of substreams. The substreams are arranged into a hierarchy, with the lowest level containing the most important data. If network bandwidth to the source is limited, the proxy fetches and plays back to the client only the lowest layers. Higher layers are fetched and played back, if cache space and network bandwidth are available, on subsequent requests. Thus, the cache converges to a state where the most popular multimedia data has the highest resolution and less popular multimedia data has lower resolution.

13.3.6 Security and Access Control

Multimedia data on the Internet may be subject in general to two types of access restrictions. Confidentiality restrictions are those that allow only certain users to view or use the data. These restrictions are similar to access controls in traditional computer systems. Data may also be subject to commercial restrictions that, for example, allow it to be viewed only a limited number of times or only on payment of a fee. Supporting access restrictions in a distributed system is difficult for two reasons. First, there may be no universal method of identifying clients. This makes it difficult to specify the restrictions desired on the data. Second, as seen in the commercial restrictions, the type of access restrictions desired may be very diverse. This diversity may be difficult to enforce in a distributed system of proxy caches. We describe the methods by which these restrictions can be enforced next.

Security and access control can be easily enforced in the important special case where the network is the internal network belonging to a single organization such as a company or a university. This is because the two difficulties we have described do not apply. Because the network belongs to a single organization, it can be assumed that there will be some method of uniquely identifying users. The second difficulty is also not important because most commercially available proxy caches provide facilities by which the access control to cached objects can be enhanced.

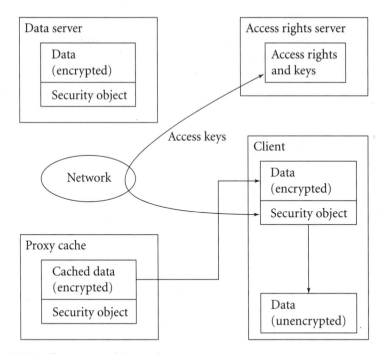

Figure 13.5   Illustration of Cryptolope.

Because all the proxy caches belong to the same organization, they can be enhanced to provide whatever access restrictions are desired.

If the network is a heterogeneous network like the Internet, there are two basic methods for security and access control. The first method is to disallow caching of controlled objects so that clients are always forced to retrieve such objects from the server. This is supported in ICP via the ICP_OP_DENIED response. If a proxy cache receives an ICP_OP_DENIED response from a server in response to a query, it knows that it is not allowed to cache the object. In the Harvest proxy cache [5], this response is sent back to the client in a manner that forces it to rerequest the object together with authentication information (e.g., user ID and password). The new request is then forwarded to the server. If the server then returns the data, this data is relayed to the client by the proxy cache.

If caching is desirable, encryption can be used to ensure that the data is not useful unless the access restrictions are verified. In the Cryptolope [30], the multimedia data is packaged together with a security object (see Figure 13.5). The encrypted data can be decrypted only by the security object when it is supplied an appropriate key. To view or display the data (which can be from a proxy cache), the user invokes the security object. The security object first enforces the access restrictions and may contact other servers on the network for authorization. For example, if every view of the data is to be charged for, the security object may notify a billing server. After receiving authorization, the security object obtains a key that allows it to decrypt the data. A similar idea is used in the MagicGate system [57], which implements the security object in hardware. The MagicGate system is designed for digital music and contains a special player that contains an embedded microchip. When a user desires to play a selection, the microchip contacts an authorization server. If the user is authorized to play the selection, the player decrypts the music stream. As in current noncomputer systems, these methods do not make unauthorized access impossible; they merely make it very difficult.

13.4   Disk Caching Policies

To see the distinction between disk caching and memory caching policies, consider the relative performance of two memory caching policies, the GIC policy and the frequency-based caching policy, when they are used for disk caching. Recall that the GIC policy is based on the observation that if two consecutive multimedia streams are reading the same multimedia file, the second stream can be served from cache by caching the moving window of blocks between the two streams (see Chapter 11 for details). The GIC policy optimally chooses pairs of streams so as to maximize the hit ratio. On the other hand, the frequency-based caching policy attempts to keep the most frequently used multimedia files in cache.

First, consider the relative performance of the two policies when used to cache multimedia data on a disk with a very low bandwidth and large space. Because the GIC policy caches a moving window of blocks, it will use some of the disk bandwidth for writing blocks. On the other hand, the frequency-based caching policy would be able to use the entire bandwidth for reading blocks. Hence, its hit ratio would be better than that of the GIC policy. This is in direct contradiction to the results obtained with memory caching, where the GIC policy outperforms frequency-based policies. Next, consider a disk with a small storage space and very high bandwidth. Because the bandwidth of the disk is very high, the fact that the GIC policy uses some of it for writes does not matter. As in caching in memory, the GIC policy would be able to optimally use the disk memory so as to provide a hit ratio substantially higher than frequency-based policies. This is in contradiction to the first case considered.

This discussion shows that the relative performance of caching policies (when used for disk caching) depends upon how well the policies utilize the disk bandwidth as well as disk space. Therefore, unlike memory caching policies, disk caching policies have to optimize bandwidth usage as well as space usage. In memory caching, the memory bandwidth can be assumed to be virtually infinite. As a result, memory caching policies can focus on optimizing space usage. As discussed in Chapter 11, disk caching policies for multimedia can be based on adaptations of traditional caching policies or they can be specifically designed for multimedia. Such policies are used, for example, in [5, 62]. Traditional caching policies have been described in Chapter 11, so we do not repeat the discussion here. Instead, we consider policies specifically designed for multimedia servers.

13.4.1 Resource-Based Caching

We now describe the resource-based caching (RBC) policy [58], a disk caching policy specifically for multimedia servers. As we have mentioned, for disk caching, both cache space and bandwidth have to be taken into consideration. Therefore, the RBC policy considers both the bandwidth as well as space of cachable entities when deciding which entities to cache. Note that as in the GIC policy, the cachable entities can be a fragment of an object rather than a whole object. The caching problem is modeled as one of selecting the entities to cache so as to maximize the gain, subject to the constraints that the total space and bandwidth requirements of the selected entities must be less than the bandwidth and space of the disk (otherwise, the caching is not feasible). This is a two-constraint knapsack problem, which is solved by the RBC policy using heuristics. For simplicity, in our discussion of the RBC policy we consider only caching of real-time streams such as video and audio. Details of how the RBC policy can be used for non-real-time data such as text files and images are given in [58].

Cachable entities in RBC policy. The cachable entities that could be cached by the RBC policy may be entire objects or fragments of objects. As in the GIC policy, the motivation for caching fragments of objects is to optimize usage of space. Recall from Chapter 11 that object fragments cached by the GIC policy consist of moving intervals of blocks between pairs of consecutive streams. A disk caching policy that caches intervals will incur a write overhead for every read from the cache because every block read from the cache by the second stream has to be first inserted into the cache by the first stream. This overhead can be reduced by combining adjacent intervals into runs, where the first stream writes data into the cache and the succeeding streams read data from the cache (see Figure 13.6). Therefore, the RBC policy may attempt to cache runs or entire objects.

Each cachable entity in the RBC policy has associated with it a resource requirement consisting of a bandwidth requirement as well as a space requirement. The space requirement of the entity is simply the space occupied by the entity— the object size in the case of an entire object and the number of blocks in the case of a run. The bandwidth requirement of a run is the total bandwidth of the streams

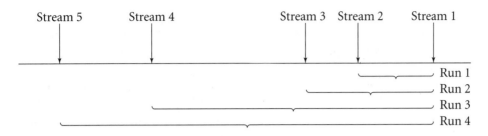

Figure 13.6 Illustration of runs in RBC policy.

reading or writing the run. For example, in Figure 13.6 the bandwidth of stream 1 is required to write run 3 into the cache, and the bandwidth of streams 2, 3, and 4 is needed to read the run. Therefore, the requirements of run 3 is four times the bandwidth of a single stream. The bandwidth requirement for an object is simply the number of streams reading the object, unless the object is being written. In the latter case, it is equal to the sum of the bandwidths of the streams reading and writing the object.

Optimization metric. As stated earlier, the RBC policy associates a gain with each cachable entity and selects the cachable entries so as to maximize the gain. Different aspects of cache performance can be maximized by selecting different definitions for the gain. In a multimedia caching policy, it is reasonable to maximize the total bandwidth served from the cache. This would produce the greatest reduction in the total bandwidth of data that has to be fetched from the network, an important objective because (as seen in Chapter 2) network bandwidth is a major bottleneck. We will show how to define the gain for cachable entities to achieve this objective. The detailed definition of gain incorporates the playback rate, the frequency of access, and the size of the object. Interestingly, these are the factors used to derive a heuristic measure for a greedy policy that minimizes the user response time [65]. Therefore, we conjecture that the RBC policy produces low user response times as well. With other definitions of gain, other cache performance metrics can be optimized [58].

The objective is to maximize the bandwidth served from the cache, so the gain associated with a cachable entity is the bandwidth that would be served from the cache if the entity is inserted into the cache. For a run i, this is the total bandwidth of the readers of the run; that is, $gain_i = V_{r,i}P_i$, where $V_{r,i}$ is the number of readers of the run and P_i is the bandwidth or playback rate of each reader. For an object j, the gain is computed as the average number of readers, v_j, of the object times the bandwidth of the object, P_j. v_j can be computed as the time taken to play the object

$T_{\text{tot},j}$ divided by the average interarrival time of requests $t_{\text{inter},j}$ to the object. For example, if it takes 10 seconds to play an object and requests to play the object arrive every 20 seconds, the average number of readers is 0.5.[2] Therefore, $\text{gain}_j = T_{\text{tot},j}/t_{\text{inter},j}P_j$.

The computation of $t_{\text{inter},j}$ can be carried as $t_{\text{inter},j} = T_{\text{acc},j}/V_{\text{tot},j}$, where $V_{\text{tot},j}$ is the total number of viewers of the object and $T_{\text{acc},j}$ is the time between the first and last access to the object. This would require having two counters. However, if the access rate to the object changes over time, the average interaccess time will also vary, and this method does not capture these variations. An alternative method is to compute the aged interaccess time; this is computed as $t_{\text{inter},j,k} = (1 - \alpha) T_k + \alpha t_{\text{inter},j,k-1}$. Here, α is an aging factor, T_k is the time interval between the kth and $k - 1$th accesses, and $t_{\text{inter},j,k}$ is the value of $t_{\text{inter},j}$ after the kth access. α is generally chosen to be between 0 and 1; values of α close to 0 produce average values that are biased towards the average of recent interarrival times, whereas values close to 1 produce average values that are long term.

Choice of entity to cache. As with any caching policy, the decisions made by the RBC policy can be accomplished in two stages. First, the RBC policy tentatively selects a cachable entity. Next, it selects one or more cachable entities to remove from the cache. The policy then checks if the cachable entity selected in the first step can be inserted into the cache following removal of the entities selected in the second step. If so, the new cachable entity is inserted after removal of the old cachable entities. We first describe the process of selection of the cachable entity and then the process of deciding which cachable entities to remove.

When deciding which entity to cache, the RBC policy attempts to effectively use cache bandwidth as well as space. Selection is driven by consideration of what is currently more scarce—cache bandwidth or space, as illustrated graphically in Figure 13.7. The RBC policy represents the current selection state of the cache by $(\rho_{\text{bw}}, \rho_{\text{sp}})$, where ρ_{bw} is the current bandwidth utilization of the cache and ρ_{sp} is the current space utilization. The possible cache selection states can be divided into three regions: the space priority region, where ρ_{sp} is significantly greater than ρ_{bw}; the bandwidth priority region, where ρ_{bw} is significantly greater than ρ_{sp}; and the equal priority region, where ρ_{sp} and ρ_{bw} are approximately equal. In the space priority region, the RBC policy selects the cachable entity with the lowest space requirement. In the bandwidth priority region, for reducing bandwidth wastage for writes, the RBC policy selects the cachable entity with the lowest write overhead. This is defined as the entity with the lowest ratio of write bandwidth requirement to total bandwidth requirement. In the equal priority region, the policy selects the

---

[2]This can be formally justified using Little's law for queuing systems.

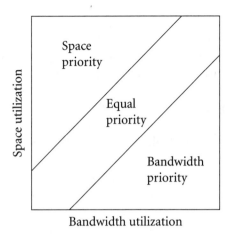

Figure 13.7 Selection of entity to cache.

entity that reduces both space as well as bandwidth wastage. Details of the heuristic measure used can be found in [58].

Selection of entities to remove. After selection of a cachable entity, the RBC policy has to decide which, if any, entities to remove. As before, the state of the cache needs to be considered. There may or may not be sufficient space to insert the new cachable entity; also, sufficient cache bandwidth may or may not be available to

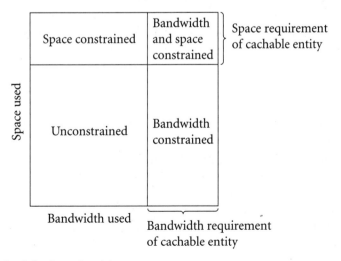

Figure 13.8 Selection of entities to remove.

satisfy the cachable entity's bandwidth requirement. The RBC policy represents the replacement state of the cache by (sp, bw) where sp is the cache space currently in use and bw is the current cache bandwidth in use. The set of cache replacement states can be divided into four regions (see Figure 13.8). In the unconstrained region, sufficient space and bandwidth are available to insert the new element; in the bandwidth- and space-constrained region, neither is available. In the space-constrained and bandwidth-constrained regions, neither sufficient space nor bandwidth, respectively, is available. In the unconstrained region, the selected entity can be inserted into the cache. In the other regions, however, it is necessary to select some entities to remove. The RBC policy defines a goodness measure for each region and attempts to remove cachable entities in the cache with goodness measures lower than the new cachable entity. The efficiency of the process can be improved by maintaining sorted lists in order of goodness measure. Details can be found in [58].

Performance of the RBC policy. The performance of the RBC policy is studied in [60] using simulation. The simulation used synthesized workloads similar to those found in measurements of various Web proxy caches. We summarize some of the important points.

A series of experiments was run where the cache bandwidth was fixed and the cache size was varied. The results showed that when the cache size was small, the RBC policy cached intervals, as in the GIC policy. As discussed at the start of this section, this is because the GIC policy optimizes usage of cache space without regard to cache bandwidth. However, as the cache size becomes large, the RBC policy starts caching entire objects. This is because frequency caching of entire objects conserves cache bandwidths. A second series of experiments was run comparing the RBC policy to other well-known policies, such as the frequency-based policy. It was shown that for the workload studied, the hit ratio of the RBC policy is at least 29% higher than the other policies.

13.5   Summary

There are two major differences between disk caching and memory caching. Unlike memory, a disk has a limited bandwidth. Therefore, disk caching policies have to consider constraints imposed by disk bandwidth as well as disk space. Additionally, disk caching may operate in a distributed system environment or from disks in a system to other disks in the same system.

Caching among disks in a single system is generally performed for the purpose of load balancing. Load imbalance may arise from the uneven access rates to different multimedia data in a system. The DPSR policy divides multimedia files into fixed-size segments and replicates segments from highly loaded disks to lightly loaded disks [12]. The use of segments instead of whole files reduces the amount of cache storage required as well as improves the responsiveness of the system (due to the shorter copying time). For copying from the highly loaded disks, the DPSR policy does not require an additional stream but uses a stream that is already playing. The DPSR policy typically requires only 5% additional disk cache space to achieve very good load balancing.

On the Internet, disk caching is performed by proxy caches. Proxy caches reduce both the network bandwidth needed to retrieve multimedia data and the response time. Access patterns to multimedia data on the Internet have been studied in order to evaluate the effectiveness of caching. The access rates to both individual files as well as servers have been found to be skewed, indicating that caching should be effective. Proxy cache hit rates have been found to be fairly high in spite of the presence of lower-level client caches, probably due to the fact that proxy caches act as a distribution infrastructure for the Internet. Caching protocols have been developed to allow proxy caches to cooperate over the Internet. The ICP protocol allows proxy caches to broadcast requests for data not in the cache and retrieve data from the nearest cache. In contrast, the CARP protocol partitions the data among a collection of proxy caches, and the CRISP policy maintains a directory of data in nearby caches. Access control issues in caching can be solved in one of two ways. First, the client can be forced to retrieve the data from the original server. Alternatively, an encrypted form of the data can be cached, and the client may obtain from the server a key to decrypt the data.

The RBC policy is a disk caching policy specifically for multimedia. It considers constraints due to both bandwidth and space. The policy can cache whole objects or fragments of objects. The caching policy associates a net gain for each object or fragment and selects entities for caching so as to maximize the gain.

Further Reading

The DPSR policy for caching among disks of a single system is found in [12]. A comprehensive survey of access patterns to multimedia data over the Internet is found in [46]. The performance of proxy caches has been studied in [35, 2]. The design decisions involved in building proxy caches have been well described in [5]. Multimedia disk caching policies that take disk bandwidth as well as space into consideration have been described in [58].

Part 4 References

---

[1]   G. Abdulla, E. Fox, and M. Abrams. Shared user behaviour in the World Wide Web. In *Proceedings of WebNet*. Association for the Advancement of Computing in Education, Charlottesville, VA, 1997.

[2]   M. Abrams, C. Standridge, G. Abdulla, S. Williams, and E. Fox. Caching proxies: Limitations and potentials. *World Wide Web Journal*, 1(1):119–133, 1995.

[3]   R. Alonso and M. Blaze. Dynamic hierarchical caching for large-scale distributed file systems. In *Proceedings of the International Conference on Distributed Systems*. IEEE, 1992.

[4]   H. Braun and K. Claffy. Web traffic characterization: An assessment of the impact of caching documents from NCSA's web server. In *Proceedings of the International World Wide Web Conference*, October 1994.

[5]   A. Chankhunthod, P. Danzig, C. Neerdaels, M. Schwartz, and K. Worrell. A hierarchical Internet object cache. In *Proceedings of the Usenix Conference*. International World Wide Web Conference Committee, 1996.

[6]   S. Chaudhuri, S. Ghandeharizadeh, and C. Shahabi. Avoiding retrieval contention for composite multimedia objects. Technical Research Report 95-618. University of Southern California, 1995.

[7]   W. Cheswick and S. Bellovin. *Firewalls and Internet Security : Repelling the Wily Hacker*. Addison-Wesley, Reading, MA, 1994.

[8]   H. T. Chou and D. J. Dewitt. An evaluation of buffer management strategies for relational database systems. In *Proceedings of Very Large Data Bases*. The Very Large Data Bases Endowment, Inc., Stockholm, Sweden, 1985.

[9]   C. Cunha, A. Bestavros, and M. Crovella. Characteristics of WWW client traces. Technical Report 95-010. Boston University, 1995.

[10] A. Dan, D. Dias, R. Mukherjee, D. Sitaram, and R. Tewari. Buffering and caching in large scale video servers. In *Proceedings of IEEE CompCon*. IEEE, 1995.

[11] A. Dan, S. Feldman, and D. Serpanos. Evolution and challenges in multimedia. *IBM Journal of Research and Development*, 42(2):177–184, 1998.

[12] A. Dan, M. Kienzle, and D. Sitaram. A dynamic policy of segment replication for load-balancing in video-on-demand servers. *Multimedia Systems*, 3(3):93–103, July 1995.

[13] A. Dan, P. Shahabuddin, D. Sitaram, and D. Towsley. Channel allocation under batching and VCR control in video-on-demand servers. 30(2):168–179, November 1995.

[14] A. Dan and D. Sitaram. Buffer management policy for an on-demand video server. Technical Report RC 19347. IBM Research Report, 1994.

[15] A. Dan and D. Sitaram. An online video placement policy based on bandwidth to space ratio (BSR). In *Proceedings of the ACM SIGMOD International Conference on Management of Data*. ACM, May 1995.

[16] A. Dan and D. Sitaram. A generalized interval caching policy for mixed interactive and long video environments. In *Proceedings of Multimedia Computing and Networking*. SPIE, 1996.

[17] A. Dan and D. Sitaram. Multimedia caching strategies for heterogeneous application and server environments. *Multimedia Tools and Applications*, 4(3):279–312, May 1997.

[18] A. Dan, D. Sitaram, and P. Shahabuddin. Dynamic batching policies for an on-demand video server. *Multimedia Systems*, 4(3):112–121, June 1996.

[19] A. Dan and D. Towsley. An approximate analysis of the IRU and FIFO buffer replacement schemes. In *Proceedings of the ACM SIGMETRICS Conference*. ACM, January 1990.

[20] A. Dan, P. S. Yu, and J. Y. Chung. Characterization of database access pattern for analytic prediction of buffer hit probability. *The VLDB Journal*, 4(1), January 1995.

[21] J. Dey, J. Salehi, J. Kurose, and D. Towsley. Providing VCR capabilities in large-scale video servers. In *Proceedings of ACM Multimedia Conference*, pp. 25–32. ACM, 1994.

[22] W. Effelsberg and T. Haerder. Principles of database buffer management. *ACM Transactions on Database Systems*, 9(4), December 1984.

[23] M. L. Escobar-Molano, S. Ghandeharizadeh, and D. Ierardi. An optimal memory management algorithm for continuous display of structured video objects. Technical Research Report 95-602. University of Southern California, 1995.

[24] A. Feldmann, R. Caceres, F. Douglis, G. Glass, and M. Rabinovich. Performance of web proxy caching in heterogeneous bandwidth environments. To appear in *The Proceedings of IEEE Infocomm.* IEEE, 1999.

[25] W. Feng, F. Jahanian, and S. Sechrest. An optimal bandwidth allocation for the delivery of compressed prerecorded video. Technical Report CSE-TR-260-95. University of Michigan, August 1995.

[26] E. A. Fox. The coming revolution in interactive digital video. *Communications of the ACM,* 7(32):794–801, July 1989.

[27] S. Glassman. A caching relay for the World Wide Web. *Computer Networks and ISDN Systems,* 27(2), 1994.

[28] L. Golubchik, J. Lui, and R. Muntz. Reducing I/O demand in video-on-demand storage servers. In *Proceedings of the ACM SIGMETRICS Conference,* pp. 25–36. ACM, 1995.

[29] J. Howard, M. Kazar, S. Menees, D. Nichols, M. Satyanarayan, R. Sidebotham, and M. West. Scale and performance in a distributed file system. *ACM Transactions on Computer Systems,* 6(1):51–81, February 1988.

[30] IBM Corporation. Cryptolopes: Overview. In *http://www.software.ibm.com/ security/cryptolope/about.html.*

[31] M. Kamath, K. Ramamritham, and D. Towsley. Continuous media sharing in multimedia database systems. In *Fourth Intl. Conf. on Database Systems for Advanced Applications,* Singapore. IEEE, April 10–13, 1995.

[32] M. Kienzle, A. Dan, D. Sitaram, and W. Tetzlaff. Using tertiary storage in video-on-demand servers. In *Proceedings of IEEE CompCon,* pp. 225–233. IEEE, 1995.

[33] W. Liao and V. O. K. Li. The split and merge protocol for interactive video-on-demand. *IEEE Multimedia,* 4(4), 1997.

[34] T. D. C. Little and A. Ghafoor. Multimedia synchronization protocols for broadband integrated services. *IEEE Journal on Selected Areas in Communication,* 9(9):1368–1382, December 1991.

[35] A. Luotonen and K. Artis. World Wide Web proxies. *Computer Networks and ISDN Systems,* 27(2), 1994.

[36] S. Manley and M. Seltzer. Web facts and fantasy. In *Proceedings of the Usenix Symposium on Internet Technologies and Systems.* Usenix, December 1997.

[37] E. Mesrobian, R. R. Muntz, E. Shek, S. Nittel, M. LaRouche, and M. Krieger. Oasis: An open architecture scientific information system. In *Sixth International Workshop on Research Issues in Data Engineering: Interoperability of Nontraditional Database Systems,* New Orleans, LA. IEEE, February 1996.

[38] F. Moser, A. Krais, and W. Klas. A buffer management strategy for inter-active continuous data flows in a multimedia DBMs. In *Proceedings of Very Large Data Bases*. The Very Large Data Bases Endowment Inc., Zurich, Switzerland, 1995.

[39] D. Muntz and P. Honeyman. Multi-level caching in distributed file systems. In *Proceedings of the Usenix Winter Conference*. Usenix, January 1992.

[40] M. Nelson, B. Welch, and J. Ousterhout. Caching in the sprite network file system. *ACM Transactions on Computer Systems*, 6(1):134–154, 1988.

[41] Netscape Corporation. Netscape Proxy Server. In *http://www.netscape.com/comprod/proxy_server.html*.

[42] R. Ng and J. Yang. Maximizing buffer and disk utilizations for news-on-demand. In *Proceedings of Very Large Data Bases*. The Very Large Data Bases Endowment Inc., 1994.

[43] V. F. Nicola, A. Dan, and D. M. Dias. Analysis of the generalized clock buffer replacement scheme for database transaction processing. In *Proceedings of the ACM SIGMETRICS Conference*, pp. 35–46. ACM, 1992.

[44] Novell Corporation. Novell BorderManager FastCache. In *http://www.novell.com/bordermanager/fastcache*.

[45] B. Ozden, R. Rastogi, and A. Silberschatz. Buffer replacement algorithms for multimedia databases. In S. Chung, ed., *Multimedia Information Storage and Management*, pp. 163–180. Kluwer Academic Publishers, Boston, MA, 1996.

[46] J. Pitkow. Summary of WWW characterizations. In *Proceedings of the International World Wide Web Conference*. The International World Wide Web Conference Committee, April 1998.

[47] M. Rabinovich, J. Chase, and S. Gadde. Not all hits are created equal: Cooperative proxy caching over a wide-area network. In *Third International WWW Caching Workshop, http://wwwcache.ja.net/events/workshop/*, Manchester, England. Trans-European Research and Education Networking Association, June 1998.

[48] R. Rejaie, M. Handley, H. Yu, and D. Estrin. Proxy caching mechanism for multimedia playback streams in the Internet. Technical Report 99-709. University of Southern California, 1999.

[49] D. Rotem and J. Zhao. Buffer management for video database systems. In *Proceedings of the International Conference on Data Engineering*. IEEE, 1995.

[50] G. Sacco and M. Schkolnick. Buffer management in relational database systems. *ACM Transactions on Database Systems*, 11(4):473–498, December 1986.

[51] J. Salehi, J. Kurose, Z. Zhang, and D. Towsley. Supporting stored video: Reducing rate variability and end-to-end resource reservation through optimal smoothing. Technical Report Umass-TR-95-98. University of Massachusetts, Amherst, November 1995.

[52] M. Satyanarayan, J. Kistler, M. Okasaki, E. Siegel, and D. Steere. Coda: A highly available file system for a distributed workstation environment. *IEEE Transactions on Computers,* 39(4):447–459, April 1990.

[53] V. Shastri, V. Rajaraman, H. Jamadagni, P. Rangan, and S. Kumar. Design issues and caching strategies for CD-ROM based multimedia storage. Technical Report. IISc, 1997.

[54] D. Sitaram, A. Dan, and P. Yu. Issues in the design of multi-server file systems to cope with load skew. In *IEEE Parallel and Distributed Information Systems.* IEEE, 1993.

[55] J. Song, A. Dan, and D. Sitaram. Efficient retrieval of composite multimedia objects in the JINSIL distributed system. In *Proceedings of the ACM SIGMETRICS Conference.* ACM, June 1997.

[56] J. Song, A. Dan, and D. Sitaram. Jinsil: A middleware for presentation of composite multimedia objects in a distributed environment. Technical Report RC 21381. IBM Research, January 1999.

[57] Sony Corporation. Sony develops copyright protection solutions for digital music content. In *http://www.sony.com/SCA/press/feb_25_99.html.*

[58] R. Tewari, H. Vin, A. Dan, and D. Sitaram. Resource based caching for web servers. In *Proceedings of Multimedia Computing and Networking,* San Jose, CA. SPIE, 1998.

[59] V. Valloppillil and K. Ross. Cache array routing protocol. Internet draft. In *http://www.ircache.net/Cache/ICP/carp.txt.*

[60] *Video Store Magazine.* Advanstar Communications, Inc., December 1992 (published weekly).

[61] P. Vixie and D. Wessels. Hyper text caching protocol (HTCP/0.0). Internet draft. In *http://www.ircache.net/Cache/ICP/htcp.txt.*

[62] D. Wessels. Squid internet object cache. In *http://squid.nlanr.net/Squid,* 1996.

[63] D. Wessels and K. Claffy. Internet cache protocol (ICP) version 2. Internet draft. In *http://www.ietf.org/rfc/rfc2186.txt.*

[64] S. Williams, M. Abrams, C. Standridge, G. Abdulla, and E. Fox. Removal policies in network caches for World Wide Web documents. In *Proceedings of the ACM SIGCOMM Conference,* 1996.

[65] R. Wooster and M. Abrams. Proxy caching that estimates page load delays. In *Proceedings of the International World Wide Web Conference.* The International World Wide Web Conference Committee, 1997.

[66] W3C. Web characterization activity—status report. In J. Pitkow, J. Hjelm, and H. Nielsen, eds., *http://www.w3.org/TR/NOTE-WCA.*

[67] P. Yu and A. Dan. Performance analysis of affinity clustering on transaction processing coupling architecture. *IEEE Transactions on Knowledge and Data Engineering,* 6, 1994.

About the Authors

Dinkar Sitaram is currently Director of the Technology Group at Novell Corporation, Bangalore. His research group investigates the areas of network security, multimedia, directory systems, and distributed computing. Previously, he was a Research Staff Member at the IBM T. J. Watson Research Center, Yorktown Heights, NY. At IBM, he played a leading role in the design and development of video servers on various IBM platforms and published extensively on multimedia servers. He holds several top-rated patents and has received an IBM Outstanding Innovation Award and several IBM Invention Achievement Awards for this work. He received his Ph.D. from the University of Wisconsin–Madison and his B.Tech. from IIT Kharagpur.

Asit Dan has been with the IBM T. J. Watson Research Center since 1990 and has been at the forefront in the research and development of video servers on various IBM platforms. He has published extensively on the design and analysis of video servers and transaction processing architectures. He holds several top-rated patents and has received two IBM Outstanding Innovation Awards, six IBM Invention Achievement Awards, and the honor of Master Inventor for his work in these areas. Currently, he is leading a group on the development of infrastructure for supporting business-to-business e-commerce applications. He received a Ph.D. from the University of Massachusetts–Amherst. His doctoral dissertation on "Performance Analysis of Data Sharing Environments" received an Honorable Mention in the 1991 ACM Doctoral Dissertation Competition and was subsequently published by the MIT Press.

Index